World Libraries on the Information Superhighway: Preparing for the Challenges of the New Millennium

Patricia Diamond Fletcher
University of Maryland Baltimore County

John Carlo Bertot
University at Albany, State University of New York

IDEA GROUP PUBLISHING
Hershey USA • London UK

Senior Editor: Mehdi Khosrowpour
Managing Editor: Jan Travers
Copy Editor: Maria M. Boyer
Typesetter: Tamara Gillis
Cover Design: Connie Peltz
Printed at: BookCrafters

Published in the United States of America by
        Idea Group Publishing
        1331 E. Chocolate Avenue
        Hershey PA 17033-1117
        Tel: 717-533-8845
        Fax: 717-533-8661
        E-mail: jtravers@idea-group.com
        Website: http://www.idea-group.com

and in the United Kingdom by
        Idea Group Publishing
        3 Henrietta Street
        Covent Garden
        London WC2E 8LU
        Tel: 171-240 0856
        Fax: 171-379 0609
        http://www.eurospan.co.uk

Library of Congress Cataloging-in-Publication Data

Fletcher, Patricia Diamond, 1948-
    World libraries on the information superhighway : preparing for the challenges of the new millennium / Patricia Diamond Fletcher, John Carlo Bertot.
        p. cm.
    Includes bibliographical references (p.) and index.
    ISBN 1-878289-66-7 (paper)
        1. Internet (Computer network) 2. Library information networks. 3. Libraries--Special collections--Computer network resources. I. Bertot, John Carlo. II. Title.

Z674.75.I58 F54 2000
021.6'5--dc21   99-048437

British Cataloguing in Publication Data
A Cataloguing in Publication record for this book is available from the British Library.

NEW from Idea Group Publishing

Excellent additions to your library!

**Receive the Idea Group Publishing catalog with descriptions of these books by
calling, toll free 1/800-345-4332
or visit the IGP web site at: http://www.idea-group.com!**

World Libraries on the Information Superhighway: Preparing for the Challenges of the New Millennium

Table of Contents

Chapter I

Libraries and the Internet: Policy and Practice in the 21st Century

Patricia Diamond Fletcher
University of Maryland Baltimore County, USA

INTRODUCTION

This is an exciting time for world libraries. It is also a time of great challenge, uncertainty, change and risk. The introduction of the Internet and the World Wide Web, and the Global Information Infrastructure is creating enormous tension in the library community. The potential for a global networked community of libraries is only beginning to be understood. The challenges posed by such an entity are many and unique. According to Wedgeworth (1998) there are four main concerns to be addressed in the context of a global library community:

- Education of librarians worldwide in use of the new information and communications technologies;
- Attention to emerging technologies and trends in information use which will affect the role of libraries;
- Awareness of the importance of librarians in this increasingly complex networked milieu; and
- Understanding of the cultural similarities and differences which directly affect the service mission of libraries.

These concerns are global in nature. Today, it is all but impossible to find a library that has not been affected by the revolution in information and communications technologies. Libraries are by their very nature information intensive, and information and communications technologies, thus, have become a basic work tool. In a recent study by Bertot and McClure (1998), the authors' found that 83.6% of public libraries in the United States have some form of Internet connection. Of this number, 87.7% provide public access to the Internet to their patrons. Numbers such as these are impressive, but may obscure the reality of Internet access to library patrons. The United States has heavily invested in its information infrastructure. Efforts led by the Federal government, such as the National Partnership for Reinventing Government, the President's Information Technology Advisory Committee, and the National Information Infrastructure initiative, have encouraged scientists and the private sector to explore and adopt new information technologies. Other countries are not as sophisticated. A recent cover story in *CIO Enterprise* magazine (Abramson, 1998) highlights the differences among countries. Level of connectivity, cost of service, quality of service and access to vendor support vary greatly from country to country. For example, in Russia, the telecommunications support is good in Moscow, but not beyond the city limits. In Mexico, the skill level of those working in the information industry is below standard. The hardware and software found in Brazil is excessively expensive. China suffers from a serious lack of support from information technology vendors. These technology barriers and others (e.g., nationalism, culture, legislation, urban vs rural) make the library's road a rocky one.

These concerns, however, must be addressed in a context that has been enriched by the more traditional library practices and roles. Libraries are replete with experience and skills which enable the institution to respond and meet the challenges of global connectivity. This book, *World Libraries on the Information Superhighway: Preparing for the Challenges of the Next Millennium*, represents the thoughts and experience of librarians and academics on the changing role of libraries in a global networked community. Diverse and important topics are addressed here which acknowledge the strengths of traditional library practices and the challenges of reconfiguring these practices in a digital world. It is apparent, upon reading these chapters, that the library is alive and well in our world. Librarians have become adept at anticipating and capitalizing on the changes wrought by information and communications technologies.

The chapters set forth here are indicative of the universal role which libraries continue to play in our lives. They demonstrate a variety of library contexts and practices. The first section of the book looks at the agendas for national libraries in a digital world. Within this section, the authors address content and delivery, national policy and practice and strategies for success in a national arena. The main role of a national library is the capture and preservation of information that is relevant to the nation and its people. The transition to electronic information poses new challenges for national libraries in finding valid and reliable information before it "disappears," making it accessible to the public and preserving it for history. How national libraries do this, in a manner that is timely, useful, and legal, is of concern. The roles of the respective governments in relation to national collections of an electronic nature are many and evolving.

The second section of this book addresses the academic library environment. Great strides have been made in this arena in utilizing the Internet to transform service delivery and scope. Academic libraries serve a special population where the focus is on research. How these libraries access and make available electronic information to their patrons raises many issues. The increasing networked nature of academic libraries also calls into question more complex issues such as government involvement, ownership of electronic materials, cost sharing and serving a virtual population.

In the third section the focus is special projects undertaken by libraries to address specific issues across a variety of domains – the public library, library consortiums and virtual libraries. Within these domains, the authors explore development of electronic community networks, multilingual electronic delivery mechanisms and expert systems in a military digital library environment. Again, the political context is called into play here, with the impact of national information agendas being felt. Issues relevant to successful implementation of these special projects are delineated. Following some of the milestones of these projects can be useful in library settings other than the three discussed in this section.

The final section of this book raises some policy and practice challenges, which if not being addressed currently, certainly need our thought and attention. The concerns of archivists, the role of scientific and technical information dissemination, subject access to Web documents, and the special needs of both libraries and their users in developing nations are considered. A design for digitizing and using archival materials is presented as a template for use. The organization of materials on the Web is analyzed, and suggestions for a subject access approach for information retrieval are offered to bring some sense to the plethora of data out there. Information dissemination to a population that is becoming more diverse as users sign on to the Internet requires a new approach for diffusion of scientific materials. And what about the populations that do not have Internet access? The development of an equitable and global information infrastructure is called for which enables a society of information literate people, not a society of information "have-nots."

Taken as a whole, it is hoped that this collection will stimulate creativity and attention to an institution that has been with us over the centuries. The move to an electronic library environment, one that is becoming more global in nature, is exciting. Common themes emerge in this book. First is the assertion that the Internet is here to stay and libraries must avail themselves of its potential for information retrieval. Second is the lack of any reliable or valid metrics for assessing the quality of data on the Internet. Within this is a need for access tools which would mimic the centuries of experience in subject cataloguing and indexing resident in the library community. Third are the national and international agendas, laws, cultures, languages and the like that libraries are trying to anticipate. Finally, what we read here is a concern for universal access to information, a concern greatly exacerbated by the growth of electronic information. The library as a social institution is called into play here. How to make sure that as a society, as a global community, we enhance information access is, to libraries, a fundamental question. As Peter R. Young (1996) asserts, postmodern librarians will continue to confront all of the age-old difficult questions they always have, regardless of whether the media is print or electronic. The fundamental issues of librarianship remain.

REFERENCES

Abramson, Gary. (1998) The global enterprise: Emerging challenges. *CIO Enterprise*. June 15, 1998. http://www.cio.com/archive/enterprise/061598_emerge_content.html

Bertot, John Carlo, and McClure, Charles R. (1998). *The 1998 National*

Survey of U.S. Public Library Outlet Internet Connectivity: Final Report. Washington, DC: The U.S. National Commission on Libraries and Information Science.

Wedgeworth, Robert. (1998). A global perspective on the library and information agenda. *American Libraries*, 29 (6): 60–68.

Young, Peter R. (1996). Librarianship: A changing profession. *Daedalus*, 125 (4): 103-126.

Chapter II

Building National Collections of Internet Publications

Jasmine Cameron and Margaret E. Phillips
National Library of Australia

Fundamental to the idea of national libraries is the notion that they should take responsibility for collecting, recording, providing access to and preserving their own national imprint. The extension of publishing beyond the realm of print into a variety of media forms, including online publications, adds complexity to, but does not change the fundamental role and responsibilities of national libraries. This chapter explores the issues that must be resolved in order to ensure that today's Internet publications will still be available to researchers in the centuries to come. The transient nature of Internet publications, the huge volume of them and the difficulty of identifying what exists are challenges for national libraries. Collection building, description of resources, efficient resource discovery, technical infrastructure, permanent naming and preservation are areas that need focussed attention and development. A number of national libraries have active programs to find solutions and the progress being made is described.

A prime responsibility of national libraries around the world is the collection, description, preservation and provision of long-term access to their national imprint. The use by publishers of electronic media, including the Internet, for the dissemination of works adds a new dimension of complexity to the task of national and other deposit libraries. It does not, however, relieve them of the responsibility for the care of information published in this way. This role for national libraries has been endorsed by the International Federation of Library Associations (IFLA), which supports the treatment of online publications as part of the national imprint incorporated into the national bibliography (International Federation of Library Associations [IFLA], 1998).

The challenge for national libraries is threefold: capture online publications before they disappear forever; find the ways and means to preserve them in an ever-changing technical environment; and achieve this in a situation where there are as yet few standards, a multiplicity of formats, a dearth of technical solutions and infrastructure for accomplishing the task and a variety of views on what should be preserved.

There are two broad categories of Internet publications. Firstly, there are the traditional commercial titles whose publishers are exploiting the new medium to make their titles available electronically.

Secondly, there is the non-commercial sector comprising what is sometimes referred to as "grey literature." These publications are mostly available without charge and are published by individuals and organizations whose prime business is usually something other than publishing. Grey literature is often a spin-off from the main interest or activity — an annual report, for instance, a newsletter or a promotional site.

Some types of publications traverse both groups. E-journals and other publications made freely available by universities are part of an institution's core academic activity but, in other respects, they do fall into the grey literature category. Government publications may be commercial or non-commercial, depending upon the characteristics of a particular title.

The non-commercial sector is much more prolific online than it has been in print, and many publishers of online material have not previously published in print. Individuals and organizations that lack the resources to achieve publication in print (perhaps because the quality was too low or the market not broad enough for their work to be taken on by a commercial publisher) are easily able to disseminate information and ideas on the Internet. This gives rise to a large volume of publishing which receives little or no quality control. It is difficult to identify and appears in a wide variety of formats.

These two sectors are publishing at different rates in different countries, and each national library needs to frame its response to online publishing according to the particular situation in its country. In the Netherlands, for example, companies publishing academic journals in print moved quickly to provide electronic versions as well. This has meant that there has been a strong focus at the National Library of the Netherlands on transferring large amounts of digital information from relatively few sources, dealing with proprietary software built into titles, and providing restricted access to commercial material.

In contrast, in Australia, there is as yet comparatively little commercial publishing on the Internet. While the National Library of Australia, through its PANDORA Project, has considered in its policy and planning the need to accommodate commercial online publications, to date its practical experience has been almost entirely with grey literature (National Library of Australia, *PANDORA Project*, 1998). This type of publishing presents the need to deal individually with a large number of publishers, a wide range of file formats and varying degrees of skill in setting up sites. Being able to provide unrestricted access to titles in the PANDORA Archive, however, has been one of the advantages of dealing with this type of material.

In the digital environment, there is the difficulty of defining what is a "publication." Are all Web sites publications? Are databases available on the Web publications? Who has responsibility for ensuring the preservation of their information content? The clear responsibility defined for national collecting agencies in the analogue world is blurring. It is harder to distinguish between an organizational record (the responsibility of national archives) and a publication (the responsibility of national libraries). New alliances are being forged between once quite separate institutions: national libraries, university libraries, archives, museums and galleries. There are great opportunities to provide better and more integrated access to heritage materials regardless of location.

It should be noted here that, as well as collecting and preserving Internet publications, national libraries are using the Information Superhighway to provide access to analogue collections, including manuscripts, printed books, sound recordings and pictures, which they are digitizing and mounting on the Web. The Library of Congress, the British Library and the Bibliothìque Nationale de la France are prominent examples of libraries that are using the Internet in this way. Significant though this work is in providing a much greater degree of access to important national collections to the constituents who own them and to the rest of the world, it is not the focus of this chapter. This chapter deals with what national libraries are doing to ensure long-term access to publications originally created and distributed in online form. (Sometimes there is a simultaneous print version.) This chapter explores the issues that must be resolved in order to ensure that today's online publications will still be available to researchers in the centuries to come.

LEGAL DEPOSIT AND BUILDING A COLLECTION OF THE NATIONAL IMPRINT

The Role of Legal Deposit

Most (though not all) national libraries depend heavily on legal deposit to assist them to build their collection of the national imprint. Legal deposit legislation has traditionally not been worded to include electronic media in the notion of a "book" or "library material." Unless definitions of library material are extended to include electronic publications, there is the risk that much documentary heritage in these formats will be lost. There is an urgent need for national libraries to lobby their governments for amendments to existing legislation, and a number have been doing so.

In Australia, legal deposit provisions at the national level are encompassed by the Commonwealth *Copyright Act 1968*, which is under review. In a joint submission to the Copyright Law Review Committee by the National Library of Australia and the National Film and Sound Archive, it was recommended:

> ...[t]hat the scope of publications to be covered by the legal deposit provisions of the revised Copyright Act be extended to include microforms, audio-visual materials of all kinds and electronic publications, both networked and artifactual (e.g., CD-ROM), and all formats yet to be developed, in addition to the print-based publications currently included. (National Film and Sound Archive and National Library of Australia, 1995, paragraph 6.3.1).

The International Conference on National Bibliographic Services held in Copenhagen in November 1998 reaffirmed the value of legal deposit and recommended that "states should, as a matter of urgency, examine existing deposit legislation and consider its provisions in relation to present and future requirements; and, where necessary, existing legislation should be revised…" (IFLA, 1998, clause 1).

While not all countries employ formal legal deposit provisions, all need some arrangements to ensure collection of the national imprint. The National Library of the Netherlands, for example does not have legal deposit legislation but, since 1974, has successfully built its collections through voluntary agreements with publishers. Through its Dutch Deposit of Electronic Publications (DDEP) program, the National Library of the Netherlands has been exploring with publishers of electronic titles the means for archiving and providing access for the indefinite future, well beyond the commercial life of the titles concerned (Noordermeer, 1997).

Whatever arrangements national libraries rely on for building their collections, they need to extend them into the electronic environment, to document the national imprint, to enable long-term access to electronic publications and to serve the public interest in allowing fair access to and use of them.

Comprehensive versus selective collecting

Libraries, including national libraries, have well-developed procedures for acquiring traditional library materials, and these have been fairly readily extended to electronic publications in physical format, such as CD-ROMs and floppy disks (though licensing arrangements are often a problem). Online publications, however, require an entirely new approach.

Depending on the type of publication in question, a library may negotiate with a publisher to send titles to it online by File Transfer Protocol (FTP) or on a physical carrier such as a compact disk or zip disk. Alternatively, a gathering robot may be sent out to the Internet address of a title, to "capture" it and copy it to the electronic archive. This latter approach is commonly used with the freely available grey literature.

Different national libraries have adopted varying policies in relation to collecting grey literature on the Internet. Some national libraries, the National Libraries of Sweden and Finland, for example, are attempting to take snapshots of their country's whole domain, while others, like Australia and Canada, are being more selective. The National Diet Library of Japan also intends to collect Internet publications selectively (Y. Saito, personal communication, February 25, 1999).

There are advantages and disadvantages in each approach. Those national libraries taking regular snapshots of the entire domain argue that their collections will be much more comprehensive and more illustrative of Web publishing in their countries than the selective approach will achieve. Neither approach is, in fact, comprehensive, as there are many publications whose structures resist the efforts of any robot currently available to download them. (Publications based on programs that create pages "on-the-fly" are one instance of this.) There is also some concern that copyright issues are likely to remain a major obstacle to providing access to snapshots well into the future. In addition, there is the problem of knowing what has been gathered and whether each title has been gathered successfully and is therefore readable.

Those national libraries taking the selective approach argue that much of the material available on the Internet has no current or long-term research value. The National Library of Australia, for example, stresses the advantages of archives of high quality publications, fully described in the National Bibliographic Database, with titles available for immediate access because of agreements negotiated with publishers and quality control processes that ensure that each archived title is accessible and functional.

NATIONAL BIBLIOGRAPHY AND THE DESCRIPTION OF INTERNET PUBLICATIONS

Online publications require two different types of description: title level full cataloguing for the purposes of inclusion in the national bibliography and for the integration of electronic with print and other library resources; as well as description of parts of the title for the purpose of resource discovery.

Title Level Cataloguing

As well as collecting the national imprint, national libraries are responsible for cataloguing it and producing the national bibliography. Because of the volume of online material involved, it is tempting to rely on lower levels of description such as that provided by automatically generated metadata, or on that provided by the publisher. However, the final recommendations of the IFLA International Conference on National Bibliographic Services emphasized the need to strengthen national bibliographic control (IFLA, 1998).

Electronic publications, including online publications, should be fully catalogued and included in national bibliographies, providing a clear statement of a national library's intention to preserve the item as part of the national imprint. In practice, the National Library of Australia has found cataloguing online publications the least problematical aspect of dealing with this type of material (National Library of Australia, 1998, *Developing national collections...*, paragraph 14).

A very interesting project in the area of description of electronic publications is the BIBLINK Project (Linking Publishers and National Bibliographic Services) which commenced in May 1996. The aim of the BIBLINK consortium, led by the British Library, is to produce a prototype system for the exchange of metadata between publishers of electronic documents and national bibliographic agencies. The system will enable a publisher to transmit bibliographic data to a national bibliographic agency (NBA), the NBA to adapt the data to its own requirements and then to return the enhanced record to the publisher. The NBA will receive timely and authoritative bibliographic information in advance of publication. The publishers' publications will be recorded in the national bibliography as soon as possible after publication, and any metadata appearing in the publication will have been verified by the NBA (Bourne, 1998).

Describing Parts of a Publication

In addition to description at the title level, there is also a need for description of parts of the whole for more reliable resource discovery than is currently available from commercial search engines. In the print world, traditional indexing and abstracting services have undertaken this kind of description. In Australia, indexing services such as ACER (Australian Council of Educational Research), APAIS (Australian Public Affairs Information Service) and the Australian Institute of Family Studies are already indexing e-journals. The problem of broken links to cited Internet addresses is already being encountered. To ensure the longevity of links to cited materials, the National Library will archive any Australian online publication that is being indexed by a service anywhere in the world. It is negotiating with these services to include the permanent name of the archived version in the citation.

The Internet enables another means of description of parts of the whole for enhanced resource discovery — national metadata repositories and associated search engines. The Nordic countries lead the way in this area, and a suite of tools has been developed by the Nordic Metadata Project, which enables the creation of metadata and Uniform Resource Names for Internet documents (Nordic Metadata Project, n.d.). Metadata generated through the Dublin Core generator (Nordic Metadata Project, 1998, *Dublin Core Metadata Template*) is gathered into the Nordic Web Index (Nordic Metadata Project, 1997) and is searchable. The Nordic Metadata Project has also created a test Dublin Core to MARC converter (Nordic Metadata Project, 1998, *d2m: Dublin Core to MARC converter*) which facilitates description and control of Internet documents by enabling conversion from one standard to another. The Nordic tools have been effective in demonstrating a model for the description, unique identification and location of Internet publications.

Permanent Naming

Unique identifiers were developed by the print publishing industry to enable the precise identification of a title or an edition of a title for distribution and inventory control. They have also had an important role in national bibliography, where the ability to distinguish between versions of a title is essential. In the print world, ISBNs and ISSNs have been used by publishers to identify titles. These numbering systems, however, cannot be applied to all types of Internet publications and, in any case, lack the ability to provide a link directly from a unique identifier to the online resource itself.

A permanent naming system for digital objects is essential to the business of national libraries. Uniform Resource Locators (URLs) which are the current means of locating documents on the Internet are not persistent and do not uniquely identify a work for national bibliographic or resource discovery purposes. Some permanent naming schemes, including Uniform Resource Names (URNs) and Digital Object Identifiers (DOIs), are able to incorporate ISBNs and ISSNs.

The Conference of Directors of National Libraries has taken up this issue and, in Amsterdam in August 1998, formed a working party under the leadership of the Library of Congress to determine appropriate measures for the implementation of a permanent naming system.

MANAGING A NATIONAL COLLECTION OF INTERNET PUBLICATIONS

Library systems designed for the acquisition and management of traditional library materials such as printed books, films, CD-ROMs and microform are not suitable for the management of Internet publications. The collection, storage, management of, provision of access to and long-term preservation of online publications require sophisticated technical infrastructures which are not yet available. There are many facets of the management of Internet publications, which are yet to be fully resolved and standardized. Much work is taking place within the global library community and other research organizations to establish the standards as well as the technical and organizational infrastructure necessary for the sure management of these materials.

Different models for managing national collections of digital publications are emerging. A number of national libraries have established projects to address the issues and to develop policy, procedures and technical capability. Each has similar concerns: developing selection criteria for Internet publications, establishing mechanisms for acquiring them, description, management of collections, authenticity and preservation.

Current Projects

The Kulturarw3 Heritage Project at the Royal Library, National Library of Sweden, is one such project. Its aim is to "test methods of collecting, preserving and providing access to Swedish electronic documents which are accessible online in such a way that they can be regarded as published." (National Library of Sweden, 1998, paragraph 1). One of the interesting aspects of this project is its investigation of the logistics of regularly collecting the entire Swedish domain.

EVA is a Finnish project coordinated by the Helsinki University (The National Library of Finland) involving libraries, publishers and expert organizations. Its central aim is "to create methods and tools to collect, register and archive electronic publications distributed on the Internet and to investigate conditions for long-term preservation of them in libraries." (Helsinki University Library, 1997, paragraph 1). It is closely related to the Nordic Metadata Project. Like the National Library of Sweden, the National Library of Finland is endeavouring to create a series of snapshots of the freely available Finnish domain (Lounamaa & Salonharju, 1998).

Through the PANDORA Project (Preserving and Accessing Networked Documentary Resources of Australia), the National Library of Australia is addressing similar issues (National Library of Australia, 1998, *PANDORA Project*). It has established a proof-of-concept archive (National Library of Australia, 1999, *PANDORA Archive*) to gain experience at a practical level and has concurrently worked at the theoretical level to define the requirement for an archive management facility to support a large and robust archive of Internet publications. The National Library of Australia takes a selective approach to archiving Internet publications (National Library of Australia, 1999, *Guidelines for selection…*).

The National Library of Canada was the first national library to become involved in electronic archiving, starting its Electronic Publications Pilot Project (EPPP) in 1994 (National Library of Canada, 1996, paragraph 9) which soon after resulted in an archive of Canadian electronic publications (National Library of Canada, 1998). Like Australia, it has taken a selective approach to archiving. Both of these countries have archives that are already available to the public.

In the Netherlands, the creation of a national deposit collection of digital publications is one of the foci of the IWI program (Innovation in the Provision of Scientific Information), and the National Library and the State Archives are cooperating to guarantee the long-term availability and accessibility of electronic government information.

From April 1996 to February 1998, the library research department of the KB [Royal Library] carried out a project funded by IWI…. The KB workflow model for electronic publications was defined and the changes affecting the library as a result of the move towards electronic publishing were researched. All workflow aspects: production, selection, acquisition, registration, installation, bibliographic description, de-installation, technical description, migration, storage-handling, indexing, retrieval and access, were scrutinized and a small-scale model was implemented with 100 test publications (Noordermeer, Steenbakkers, & Van Der Werf-Davelaff, 1998, pp.60-61).

Selection criteria for electronic publications are the same as for the print collection, and required publications can be ordered from the publisher after which they are transferred to the Library by FTP or harvested from the publisher's site using gathering software.

The National Library of the Netherlands has established contacts with IT vendors such as AT&T and IBM for joint research and development work on electronic storage management systems. Experiments with large numbers of electronic journals are being carried out within the deposit model. Three major publishers of scientific journals and government publications, Elsevier Science, Kluwer Academic and SDU Uitgevers, deposit their publications with the Library. Approximately 400 titles are stored and handled using the IBM Digital Library system, which became operational at the National Library in January 1998 (Noordermeer, Steenbakkers, & Van Der Werf-Davelaaf, 1998, p.68).

The NEDLIB Project (Networked European Deposit Library), which is led by the National Library of the Netherlands, is exploring the possibility of a networked European deposit library (National Library of the Netherlands, 1999).

The main goal of NEDLIB, in which a number of national libraries, archives, publishers and ICT-developers cooperate, is to find ways to ensure that present day electronic publications and documents can be used now and in the future. The participants will develop a model for a generic architecture capable of processing electronic publications regardless of origin or medium, for access either by end-users or by archiving organizations (Noordermeer, Steenbakkers, & Van Der Werf-Davelaaf, 1998, p.67). Evidence of their work is the final version of the functional requirements for NEDLIB (Borbinha & Cardoso, 1998).

An effective technical architecture is crucial to the long-term management of online publications, and libraries involved in this work are in the process of developing suitable infrastructure.

The acquisition of an effective system for managing online publications is one of the primary objectives of the National Library of Australia's Digital Services Project. The Library plans to build and provide access to a distributed national collection of Australian electronic publications in cooperation with Australian creators, publishers, libraries and other collecting agencies. The Project's Information Paper articulated the National Library's vision for the integrated management of digital collections and the delivery of digital services (National Library of Australia, 1998, *Digital Services Project information paper*). After considering feedback received from industry and national and state libraries, the Library issued a request for tender in July 1999 for a Digital Collection Management Facility (National Library of Australia, 1999, *Request for tender for the provision of a digital collection management facility*).

Administrative and Management Metadata

The description of online publications for inclusion in the national bibliography and to assist with resource discovery has already been discussed. The management of an archive of online publications and the task of ensuring long-term accessibility require the collection of additional metadata. For instance, it is necessary to record, among other things, details of negotiations with publishers and capture schedules (administrative metadata); information about file formats and sizes, and preservation strategies to which the item has been subjected (preservation metadata); and information about copyright and charges for access (rights management and access control metadata).

Much of this metadata has yet to be defined. The Research Libraries Group (RLG) has led the way in formulating a set of preservation metadata elements for digital materials (Research Libraries Group, 1998). However, while these elements are suitable for the description of materials that have been converted from analogue to digital formats, they need to be expanded to accommodate items that were originally created in digital form. The National Library of Australia is working with RLG to achieve a more comprehensive set of elements.

In the course of specifying the functional requirements for archive management systems, both the PANDORA and NEDLIB projects have worked on data models (National Library of Australia, 1999; Van Der Werf, 1999). The purpose is to define the metadata that needs to be recorded to document each activity involved in archiving, preserving and providing access to online publications. The CEDARS (CURL Exemplars in Digital Archives) Project has also recognized the importance of metadata issues and has formed a working group to consider metadata needed for emulation and migration, authentication, resource discovery, rights management and evaluation, and to consider how the metadata should be managed (Day, 1998). Metadata plays a key role in any project related to the management of digital information, and there is an important task here to align the various models in order to render systems interoperable.

PRESERVATION OF NATIONAL COLLECTIONS OF INTERNET PUBLICATIONS

Collecting and storing an Internet publication are only the first steps in the process of ensuring its long-term preservation. Additional strategies must be implemented to see it through multiple changes to Web browsers, technology platforms, software and file formats.

There is as yet no accepted, proven method for the preservation of digital objects. Strategies such as migration, emulation and other models such as Digital Tablets (Kranch, 1998) and the Digital Rosetta Stone (Heminger & Robertson, 1998) are being researched, and each has its advocates and detractors. Museums of redundant hardware and software have also been proposed but this approach has serious drawbacks. All of the strategies are expensive. It is likely that preservation plans involving a mix of these methods, carefully tailoring the solution to the particular situation in hand, will be the most suitable response from libraries responsible for an archive of heritage material.

While solutions to the preservation of digital objects are critical to the national library sector in their endeavors to ensure long-term access to Internet publications, they are also critical to the research libraries that have invested significant resources in digitizing collections of analogue materials. They, too, have a strong interest in extending access to electronic files into the indefinite future. Fortunately, solutions identified for one application are often useful to the other and a number of research projects that will benefit both are under way.

In the United Kingdom, CEDARS is a three-year project by a consortium of university libraries, the British Library and others. It has a number of objectives, including to "investigate, document and promote methods appropriate to the long-term preservation of different classes of digital resources typically included in library collections, and to develop costed and scalable models." (Day, 1998, paragraph 1.2).

Also in the United Kingdom, the Arts and Humanities Data Service is a national service funded by the Joint Information Systems Committee of the Higher Education Funding Councils to collect, describe, and preserve the electronic resources which result from research and teaching in the humanities. Its study (Beagrie & Greenstein, 1998) provides 13 recommendations relating to long-term digital preservation, standards, policy framework and future research.

In the United States, research initiatives by organizations such as the Research Libraries Group (RLG), the Council on Library and Information Resources and the Preservation Department at the Cornell University Library are also of interest. The RLG, for instance, is an international consortium of universities and colleges, national libraries, archives, historical societies, museums, independent research collections and public libraries. In early 1998 it funded a study (Hedstrom & Montgomery, 1998) "to assess where guidance, education and training, storage and digital preservation services are required, in order to develop the kind of training, mechanisms for resource sharing and services that meet members' needs."

The National Library of Australia is contributing to the dissemination of information about preservation of documents in electronic formats by its coordination of the PADI (Preserving Access to Digital Information) Web site, a subject gateway to Web resources on a range of topics related to preserving access to digital information (National Library of Australia, 1999, *PADI*). The National Library is also coordinating a national research agenda on digital preservation, identifying, locating and, if necessary, developing tools and information to support decisionmaking.

ORGANIZATION AND COOPERATION

A comparatively small number of national libraries have started to address the need to ensure long-term access to Internet publications through the projects already described. The large research libraries such as the British Library and the Library of Congress, while not actually yet engaged in the work, have begun to consider the issues. The British Library, for instance, commissioned a series of studies on the acquisition and management of electronic publications, the first of which, among other things, drew some sobering conclusions about the costs involved (Hendley, 1996).

By the middle of 1998, from reports of progress on the various projects, which were emerging at workshops, conferences and on Web sites, it became apparent that sharing information, expertise and experience could provide significant benefits. The complexity of the task and the resource-intensive nature of the activities provide strong incentive to share information and cooperate in problem solving. Australia, feeling at a disadvantage because of physical distance from the rest of the world, was motivated to suggest the establishment of formal collaborative relationships. All eight libraries that were approached agreed – the national libraries of Canada, Finland, Germany, the Netherlands, Norway, Sweden, the United Kingdom and the United States.

One area in which it is expected that collaborative activity could be particularly valuable is in providing comment on each other's specifications for technical infrastructure. While each national library is dealing with a situation that is individual to the legal, commercial, social and political environment of the nation in which it operates, the technical requirements have much in common. There is value in expressing these requirements using similar concepts and language to communicate to suppliers, with some degree of uniformity, our needs for hardware and software. Suppliers may see more benefit in developing software for a community of needs rather than for one application.

The new digital environment in which national libraries are operating is forcing a reassessment of the way we do business and with whom. While it is presenting many challenges, digital technology is also providing exciting opportunities for enhancing existing services and developing new ones. These opportunities include the possibility of building mutually beneficial alliances between national libraries, between national libraries and other libraries, and between libraries and other collecting institutions such as archives, museums and art galleries.

The ability to operate effectively in this way is just one reason why the development of and adherence to standards is so important. Collecting agencies in different sectors and in different nations need to be able to exchange, transfer and share data.

Cooperation in Australia

In Australia, where the National and State libraries have a joint and overlapping mandate to collect and preserve Australia's documentary heritage, there are opportunities for cooperation. There are similar opportunities in countries like Britain, where legal deposit responsibilities and privileges are distributed among a number of libraries charged with the preservation of the nation's publishing output. In Australia, the concept of the Distributed National Collection emerged in the analogue world to enable National, State, university and other research libraries to share resources and maximize purchasing power. In the digital world, joint initiatives are even more important, because of the large volume of material to be dealt with, the high costs of acquisition, storage and preservation, and to realize the benefits that networking offers.

The National and State libraries are developing a distributed model for the selection, cataloguing, archiving and preservation of online publications. The National Collection of Australian Electronic Publications will be a cooperative enterprise that builds on the model of the proof-of-concept PANDORA Archive. In the longer term, each participating institution will collect, store, preserve and provide access to titles on its own server. In the shorter term, while technical and resource obstacles are being surmounted, the National Library will host other libraries' collections, if requested. Unified access to the distributed national collection will be provided by catalogue records for each title in the National Bibliographic Database. The need for a national metadata repository or linked distributed repositories is still being discussed and may well be an outcome of a national permanent naming service. A unified approach at the policy level will be necessary, with general agreement among participants on principles such as developing selection guidelines, cataloguing onto the National Bibliographic Database, committing to preservation strategies and negotiating arrangements with publishers for ultimate networked, open and gratis access to Australian electronic publications (Cameron, 1999).

CONCLUSION

All libraries have felt the impact of online publishing, especially its proliferation during the 1990s on the World Wide Web. There are both opportunities and threats for libraries in this new phenomenon, and national libraries have a major role to play in establishing the infrastructure and standards that will enhance access, now and in the future, to information published on the Internet. Some pundits have prophesied the demise of libraries, claiming that they will no longer be needed with all human knowledge readily available on the Internet. Online publishing has forced libraries to reassess their roles in the communities they serve, and to reexamine their business and how they provide information to their clients. There is an urgent need for new procedures and techniques for collection development, organization, management and preservation of publications in the new electronic formats.

Opportunity lies in the powerful facility provided by the Internet to disseminate information to geographically remote users. This has caused some libraries to redefine their client groups and is particularly pertinent to national libraries endeavouring to serve a nationwide clientele from a single physical location. There is also the opportunity to enter into sophisticated relationships with other libraries and collecting agencies to enable searching across multiple collections in order to supply clients with relevant information in an integrated way, wherever it might reside.

Libraries, especially national libraries, have a pivotal role to play in this new environment. The traditional skills of librarians, including collecting, describing, indexing, preserving and providing access to sources of information are as relevant to the online situation as they have been to print, microform, film, manuscript, pictorial, sound and other documentary formats. Brewster Kahle of the Internet Archive (Internet Archive, 1998) has recognized the role of libraries by depositing a copy of his archive with the Library of Congress, although whether this will be a useful gift remains unclear.

National libraries, with their responsibilities for preservation of the national imprint, are in an ideal position to provide strong leadership in the coordination of efforts to ensure that the content of the Information Superhighway today is available to the researchers of tomorrow.

REFERENCES

Beagrie, N., & Greenstein, D. (1998). *A strategic policy framework for creating and preserving digital collections* (Version 4.0). London: Arts and Humanities Data Service. [Online]. Available: http://ahds.ac.uk/manage/framework.htm

Borbinha, J., & Cardoso, F. (1998). *Functional specification for DSEP, final version* (NEDLIB – LB 5648 D1.2.1). [O-line]. Available: http://www.konbib.nl/coop/nedlib/func-spec/d121.pdf

Bourne, R. (1998). *The European BIBLINK Project.* [On-line]. Available:

http://archiv.ub.uni-bielefeld.de/veranstaltungen/1998/
bielefeld.kolloquium.4/0014.htm

Cameron, J. (1999). *National Collection of Australian Electronic Publica-*
tions. Canberra: National Library of Australia. [Online]. Available:
http://www.nla.gov.au/nla/staffpaper/cameron1.html

Day, M. (1998). *CEDARS: Digital preservation and metadata.* Bath: U.K.
Office for Library and Information Networking. [Online]. Avail-
able: http://www.ercim.org/publication/ws-proceedings/
DELOS6/cedars.pdf

Hedstrom, M., & Montgomery, S. (1998). *Digital preservation needs and*
requirements in RLG member institutions: A study commissioned by the
Research Libraries Group. Mountain View, CA: Research Libraries
Group. [Online]. Available: http://www.rlg.org/preserv/
digpres.html

Helsinki University Library. (1997). *Eva: The acquisition and archiving of*
electronic networked publications. [Online]. Available: http://
renki.lib.helsinki.fi//eva/english.html

Heminger, A. R., & Robertson, S. B. (1998). *Digital Rosetta Stone: A*
conceptual model for maintaining long-term access to digital documents.
[On-line]. Available: http://www.ercim.org/publication/ws-pro-
ceedings/DELOS6/rosetta.pdf

Hendley, T. (1996). *The preservation of digital material.* London: British
Library Research and Development Department.

International Federation of Library Associations [IFLA]. (1998). *The*
final recommendations of the International Conference on National Biblio-
graphic Services. [Online]. Available: http://www.ifla.org/VI/3/
icnbs/fina.htm

Internet Archive. (1998). *Building a digital library for the future.* [On-
line]. Available: http://www.archive.org/home.html

Kranch, D. A. (1998). Beyond migration: Preserving electronic documents with digital tablets. *Information Technology and Libraries, 17,*
138-148.

Lounamaa, K., & Salonharju, I. (1998). *EVA: The acquisition and archiving*
of electronic network publications in Finland. [Online]. Available: http:/
/www.ercim.org/publication/ws-proceedings/DELOS6/eva.rtf

National Film and Sound Archive, & National Library of Australia.
(1995). *Submission to the Copyright Law Review Committee on Legal*
Deposit. [Online]. Available: http://www.nla.gov.au/policy/

clrcld.html

National Library of Australia. (1998). *Developing national collection of electronic publications: Issues to be considered and recommendations for future collaborative actions.* [Online]. Available: http://www.nla.gov.au/nla/staffpaper/int_issu.html

National Library of Australia. (1999). *Digital collection management facility logical data model.* [Online]. Available: http://www.nla.gov.au/dsp/rft/model.html

National Library of Australia. (1998). *Digital Services Project information paper.* [Online]. Available: http://www.nla.gov.au/dsp/

National Library of Australia. (1999). *Guidelines for the selection of online Australian publications intended for preservation by the National Library of Australia.* [On-line]. Available: http://www.nla.gov.au/scoap/guidelines.html

National Library of Australia. (1999). *PADI: Preserving access to digital information.* [On-line]. Available: http://www.nla.gov.au/padi/

National Library of Australia. (1999). *PANDORA Archive: Preserving and accessing networked documentary resources of Australia.* [On-line]. Available: http://www.nla.gov.au/pandora/archive.html

National Library of Australia. (1998). *PANDORA Project: Preserving and accessing documentary resources of Australia.* [Online]. Available: http://www.nla.gov.au/pandora/

National Library of Australia. (1999). *Request for tender for the provision of a digital collection management facility.* [Online]. Available: http://www.nla.gov.au/dsp/rft/

National Library of Canada. (1998). *Electronic collection.* [Online]. Available: http://collection.nlc-bnc.ca/e-coll-e/index-e.htm

National Library of Canada. (1996). *Electronic Publications Pilot Project (EPPP): Summary of the final report.* [On-line]. Available: http://collection.nlc-bnc.ca/e-coll-e/ereport.htm

National Library of Sweden. (1998). *The Kulturarw3 Heritage Project.* [Online]. Available: http://kulturarw3.kb.se/html/projectdescription.html

National Library of the Netherlands. (1999). *NEDLIB: Networked European Deposit Library.* [Online]. Available: http://www.konbib.nl/nedlib/

Noordermeer, T., Steenbakkers, J., & Van Der Werf-Davelaaf, T. (1998). Electronic library developments in the Netherlands. *Liber quarterly, 8,* 57-80.

Noordermeer, T. (1997). Deposit for Dutch electronic publications: Research and practice in the Netherlands. *Lecture notes in computer science, Vol. 1324.*

Nordic Metadata Project. (1998). *d2m: Dublin Core to MARC converter.* [On-line]. Available: http://www.bibsys.no/meta/d2m/

Nordic Metadata Project. (1998). *Dublin Core Metadata Template.* [On-line]. Available: http://www.lub.lu.se/cgi-bin/nmdc.pl

Nordic Metadata Project. (n.d.). *Nordic countries URN-generator.* [On-line]. Available: http://www.lub.lu.se/dc/urntest.pl

Nordic Metadata Project. (1997). *Nordiskt Web Index.* [Online]. Available: http://nwi.ub2.lu.se/

Nordic Metadata Projects. (1999). [Online]. Available: http://linnea.helsinki.fi/meta/nmfinal.htm

Research Libraries Group. (1998). *RLG Working Group on preservation issues of metadata final report.* [Online]. Available: http://www.rlg.org/preserv/presmeta.html

Van Der Werf, T. (1999). *Data model for a deposit system for electronic publications.* (NEDLIB technical meeting paper). [Online]. Available: http://www.konbib.nl/nedlib/meetings/frankfurt/datamod.doc

Chapter III

Connectivity, Content and Collaboration: The Canadian Digital Library Experience

Susan Haigh
National Library of Canada

This chapter provides a brief overview of issues libraries are confronting as they attempt both to embrace the opportunities of global networked information and to balance these with traditional resources and demands. The context in which Canadian libraries operate and uniquely Canadian approaches to digital library activities are reviewed. The federal government's Connecting Canadians agenda has focussed on connectivity, but attention is shifting also to support of the creation of content. The federal department Industry Canada has been funding, within a job creation and skills development strategy, the creation of digital content by Canadian youth. The National Library is building an electronic collection of Canadiana and various other digital products and services. Substantial digital collections such as the collaborative project Early Canadiana Online are emerging. Canada's activities, which are not currently on scale with the United States or some other countries, remain largely a result of local initiative. It is hoped that increased provincial or national coordination, collaboration and funding will strengthen our libraries' role in the delivery of networked information services.

The advent of the Internet, and in particular the World Wide Web, has changed the nature of research and information seeking. In more and more disciplines, networked electronic resources outstrip print resources in currency, availability, low cost and plenitude. Increasingly, people seek—and find—the information they need instantly from their office or home desktop.

While libraries in some sectors are being used more than ever, there is clearly potential for libraries to be circumvented or ignored. While surfing has not supplanted the leisure reading of books, the Web is clearly becoming a first stop for many when information is sought. A recent Canadian public library study found that many Canadians with home Internet access are relying on it as a primary source for finding information on various topics, and that they had found such information in the past week (Ekos, 1998). A 1997 national survey of household computer use found that "search for information" was the highest cited purpose of use, at 84.4% (Statistics Canada, 1997). The main business of libraries—organizing and storing information and helping clients to use it—is being challenged.

Information professionals can list many reasons for concern about the new electronic information age. Much of the information on the Internet is not timely, nor reliable, nor, in many cases, easily found. It can be difficult to separate the "wheat from the chaff." All the search engines, while powerful, have idiosyncrasies and inherent limitations, determine relevance with limited success and produce result sets that are often too large to be useful. So, on the one hand, much good information is not easily discovered—a problem that is being compounded by the continuing explosive rate of growth in the amount of information available. On the other hand, many library professionals and researchers see a need for *more* high quality information to be made freely accessible and optimized for use in the Web environment. The need for better organization of Web resources, for more rigorous description of resources and for more substantial content is well recognized. Libraries are also concerned about the increasing gulf between those who have access to technology and the skills to use it and those who do not, a gap becoming known as the "digital divide."

INFORMATION ISSUES IN THE DIGITAL AGE

The issues that libraries as information organizations—not just in Canada, but everywhere—face in confronting the digital age have been widely documented and discussed over the past few years. Some of the more enduring and confounding include:

- *Evolution toward the hybrid library:* To most librarians, a "digital library" is likely to mean traditional functions—acquiring, organizing, describing, preserving and supporting use of information—applied to electronic resources. Because most libraries must at the same time continue these traditional functions with traditional media, a balancing act that has become known as the "hybrid library" (Rusbridge, 1998) is typically the challenge. For electronic resources, library functions must be redefined, but to what extent? How feasible or necessary is it to "acquire" digital resources in the traditional sense? What electronic services, products or collections go beyond the traditional, and might assure libraries' continued relevance? How can libraries best contribute towards the organization of such a vast array of essentially unstable and widely distributed information resources? What new criteria are needed to clarify our access, organization or preservation choices?
- *Knowledge and skills*: Many librarians are excited by the possibilities of digital libraries. But few can keep abreast of the broad issues and rapid developments in the digital information field. Gaining the necessary skills for library personnel is a transformative process, requiring time, money and reconsideration of traditional hiring criteria.
- *Standards*: Standards based on a strong international consensus and market acceptance increase the interoperability of applications, support the development of cost-effective technical solutions and promote quality of service. But constant and unpredictable technological change, coupled with a staggering number of new and proposed standards emerging from a variety of communities, have created a confusing and complicated standards environment. A recent glossary of digital library-related standards, protocols and formats produced by the National Library of Canada listed over 90 relevant standards, and the list was not comprehensive (Haigh, 1998). For descriptive metadata, for example, should we use Dublin Core, MARC or something more tailored to local needs? Given the plethora of standards to choose from, the wide range of applications and interpretation many support and the sometimes prohibitive cost of standards-based approaches, libraries can be uncertain which standards to embrace.

- *Costs:* There can be no doubt that digital library activities—whether resource digitization, data migration, Web site management, providing Web-based services, licensing electronic resources, maintaining a sound technical infrastructure or staff skills development—carry a high price tag. Cost recovery through charging is in most cases not an option, while measuring and defending a nonmonetary return on investment, such as usage and benefit to users, is difficult. Some libraries are able to shift a few resources from traditional to electronic functions, but, so far, many have found no reduction in user demand for traditional materials or in the rate of print publishing.
- *Ownership issues*: Intellectual property rights can impede or even nullify libraries' ability to transform print resources to electronic. Licensing access to electronic resources transforms libraries' traditional custodial role from owning materials to owning only equipment to access the materials and leasing the right to provide that access. Libraries are not necessarily prepared to undertake costly digital preservation activities such as conversion and migration if they only, in effect, rent the resource.
- *Preservation:* How much information loss owing to technical obsolescence and resource obscurity is inevitable, how much is acceptable, and how much is preventable by libraries and archives? Rapid technological obsolescence means that even libraries that are undertaking ambitious digitization projects are worried—with good reason—about the long-term viability of their choices of hardware, operating platforms, software applications, mark-up languages and document formats.
- *User needs and capabilities*: Many digital library projects to date have aimed to increase user access to resources that the *library* viewed of likely value to users—basically, a "build it and they will come" approach. Research is needed to better establish what Internet users most need and want from digital libraries, and to augment what is already known in terms of Canadians' connectivity, technical configurations and Web usage patterns and preferences. Particular ongoing attention needs to be paid to the special needs and adaptive technologies for persons with disabilities.
- *Leadership and coordination*: Libraries tend to look for ways to share information or costs, which is one of the reasons why there are

numerous Canadian library associations and consortia. However, as other countries have been setting up centralized, structured digital library programs, in Canada there is a continuing need for overarching coordination to sharpen the focus and thrust of our digital library efforts.

THE CANADIAN CONTEXT

The Canadian context is not an easy one in which to sharpen diverse energies into a cohesive, nationwide effort. As is the case in much of the world, Canadian libraries have been eager to establish an Internet presence. Many have developed their own Web sites and services, and an increasing number are now ready, or have already begun, to mount a small selection of their local resources for the benefit of their connected clientele and the broader Canadian and international Internet public.

Geographic factors such as vast distance between population centres point to the important ongoing role telecommunications plays in Canadians' lives. Ninety-eight percent of Canadian homes have telephone service, and 96 percent have access to cable services (73.7 percent actually subscribe) (Statistics Canada, 1997). Canada tops the Group of Eight (G8) industrialized nations in home computer, telephone and cable penetration, and telephone and Internet access charges are among the lowest in the world (Manley, 1998).

Culturally, Canadians are a language and ethnically diverse people. In our latest census (1996), 16.9 million cited English as a mother tongue; French accounted for 6.6 million, and the remaining 5 million or so cited a plethora of other languages. Officially a bilingual country, all federal government services and publications must be available in both English and French. One provincial government (New Brunswick) is also bilingual, and the rest are officially English, except Quebec whose government functions in French.

Politically, Canada is a federation of provinces and territories, and governance is split between federal and provincial parliaments. Culture and heritage responsibilities—libraries, archives, museums, parks—are to some extent borne at all levels of government; no single, central body oversees or funds Canadian libraries as a whole. Public, school and academic libraries are largely administered under municipal and provincial jurisdiction, but there is wide variance among the 10 provinces and three territories that make up Canada as to how and under what ministries library administration is undertaken.

In part owing to environmental factors, Canadian libraries welcomed the advent of the Internet as a vehicle both for strengthening local access to a wealth of world information resources, and for providing better direct service to their clients. But achieving a coordinated effort in order to most benefit from the wide-ranging opportunities afforded by the Internet remains an ongoing challenge that Canada has only begun to address.

CANADIAN APPROACHES AND PROGRESS

Networks, Connectivity, and Equipment

The Government of Canada is investing heavily in the development of an information infrastructure for the 21st Century, with the explicit goal of making Canada the most connected nation in the world by the year 2000. The Government's "Connecting Canadians" six-point agenda aims to:

- provide all Canadians with opportunity of access to a world-leading highway infrastructure,
- develop some communities into highly wired "Smart Communities,"
- further develop Canadian online content,
- develop a regulatory and legal framework conducive to making Canada a world leader in the provision of electronic commerce products and services,
- put governments and their information online so that they can be readily accessed by a connected citizenry, and
- promote Canada as a wired, high tech country to the world to attract international investment. (Government of Canada, 1998)

As in many other countries, the private sector is largely responsible for the development and deployment of the infrastructure for the information highway in Canada. The *Canadian Network for the Advancement of Industry and Education* (CANARIE)[1] was created in 1993 to speed the emergence of Canada's information revolution. CANARIE is an industry-led, not-for-profit consortium with significant support from the federal department Industry Canada and some 140 member companies, universities and organizations in the public and private sectors. CANARIE's main program components support the upgrade of Canada's commercial Internet backbone and the development of advanced technology and applications to exploit the advanced network.

Having launched CA*Net II, Canada's next-generation network, in June 1997, CANARIE is now engaged with its industry partners (Canada's telecommunications companies Bell Canada, CISCO Systems, JDS Fitel, Newbridge Networks and Northern Telecom, Inc.) in building a national optical network, CA*Net 3. This research network promises to be the world's first national Internet built directly around Dense Wave Division Multiplexing, a new Canadian-developed technology that multiplies the bandwidth of a fiber by driving data simultaneously on eight of the 32 different colors of laser light. This coast-to-coast research network will deliver up to 40 Gigabit per second capability, which is one million times the capacity of Canada's research network in 1993. It will provide Canadian universities, research centers and industry—and in many cases the libraries and information centers that support their work—with network capacity that is unmatched anywhere in the world, supporting collaborative research, cutting-edge learning and multimedia applications and developing advanced applications in tele-learning, tele-medicine and electronic commerce.

The Canadian government has also recognized that access to the Information Highway will help create opportunities for growth and jobs by providing communities with the ability to communicate with each other, conduct business, enhance job skills and exchange information and ideas. Industry Canada's *Community Access Program* (CAP)[2] helps communities obtain affordable public access to the Internet and the skills to use it effectively. By the year 2000, the program will have helped create 5,000 sites in remote and rural areas and up to 5,000 Internet access sites in urban neighborhoods across Canada.

Another Industry Canada program, *SchoolNet*[3], is working with the provinces, learning institutions and the private sector to connect all 16,500 Canadian public schools to the Internet by the middle of 1999 and extend connectivity into every appropriate classroom by the end of the year 2000. It also supports classroom learning projects by providing on-line learning products and services that help students to acquire new skills, and teachers and courseware producers to develop new media materials.

One of SchoolNet's component programs, *Computers for Schools*[4], has challenged Canadian businesses and governments to provide 250,000 used or refurbished computers for use in classrooms across the country and enable every young Canadian to experience the full benefit of information technologies for learning.

LibraryNet[5], another SchoolNet program, will have assisted over 90% of Canada's public libraries to connect to the Information Highway by the middle of 1999, and provides a number of other central services such as current awareness and a nationally licensed online Internet training module. The *Gates Library Foundation*[6], established by Bill and Melinda Gates in 1997, also has a five-year goal to provide grants to 13,000 North American libraries, including 3,000 in Canada, to fund the purchase of computers and hardware to bring Internet access to their patrons.

Content

The innovative *Canada's Digital Collections Program*[7] marries the goals of youth employment and digital content creation. The program awards contracts to Canadian businesses, cultural institutions and other organizations to hire young people (ages 15 to 30) to create original Web sites based on significant Canadian material. There have now been some 230 digital projects completed in all provinces and territories across the country. The collections they have produced range from digital versions of Attestation Papers (enlistment papers) of Canadian Expeditionary Force recruits in the First World War, to Canadian Arctic Profiles, a Web site that demonstrates how to minimize environmental damage while navigating Arctic waters.

The *National Library of Canada* (NLC)[8], as befits its mandate, is striving to become one of the richest resources for Canadian information in electronic form in the world. The Library's large and ever-growing Web site showcases three forms of digital content: a collection of Canadian-published electronic resources; a set of resources that the Library itself has digitized; and a number of products that organize access to external Canadian information resources.

Since the summer of 1994, the NLC has been acquiring, cataloguing, archiving and making available on its Web site a selection of Canadian digital publications. The *electronic collection*[9] now consists of over 2,300 titles—1,577 electronic monographs and 763 electronic serials as of May 31, 1999—that are published in Canada or by Canadians. In developing this permanent national digital collection, the National Library has wrestled with many of the fundamental digital library policy and practice issues in the areas of selection, management, preservation and access.

The NLC has also created more than 30 *digital resources* of various types since the inception of its Web service in 1994. Early on, a policy was established of creating a virtual exhibit to parallel all physical exhibitions mounted at the Library. There are now online exhibitions on topics ranging from Gardening to Science Fiction to Children's Literature Illustration[10]. There are also rich resources for learning about Canada[11], such as a site featuring the Canadian North and another about Canadian Confederation, and a number of in-depth multimedia resources focusing on famous Canadians, such as the Glenn Gould Archive. A new product entitled the Virtual Gramophone, showcasing the earliest Canadian 78 RPM recordings, brings the amount of audio on the site (using RealAudio streaming protocol) to over 30 hours. Research tools, such as searchable indexes, lists of Canadian newspapers and subject-specific research guides are also provided. Many of these projects were done in partnership with the federal Canada's Digital Collections program described earlier in this chapter or through private sector funding partnerships, and it is expected that this trend will continue.

The NLC also provides an online inventory of Canadian digital initiatives, a directory of Canadian libraries and their catalogues, a site dedicated to federal government information, and the *Canadian Information by Subject*[12] directory service. As one way of imposing order on the vast array of Web resources that any country now has, this service lists substantive Canadian Web sites by a Dewey Decimal Classification subject arrangement. Now with over 3,500 links, the site has proven to be very popular as people seek alternative ways of finding Web resources to the major Internet search engines.

The *AMICUS on the Web* service[13], a Canadian union catalogue of over 11 million bibliographic records, provides a free search service of the NLC's own catalogue and a broader fee-based union catalogue search service whose sophisticated features facilitate copy cataloguing, interlibrary loan and reference service in Canadian libraries.

In 1997, the National Library addressed a survey on digital activities to some 100 major Canadian libraries. Overall findings indicated that 66% of respondents had engaged in digitization projects involving their print collections; 46% were collecting and storing locally digital resources produced by external bodies; and 80% were undertaking to organize links to external Web resources for the benefit of their clients (Haigh, 1997). A wide range of technologies were being used to support these activities, and most libraries had not resolved the management and funding issues surrounding digital library resource development.

In fact, much of the activity to that time had been exploratory—discussing issues, planning and obtaining approvals and funding, and undertaking and evaluating pilot projects. The body of materials, especially of major Canadian research resources, in online digital form had not yet achieved "critical mass." However there was clearly momentum and a high level of interest and commitment to continuing to build digital library resource collections.

In general, the study also documented that the efforts of different types of libraries reflected their mandate, user community and collection strengths with relatively little overlap, broadly speaking:

- *Public libraries* tended to be digitizing material of local history or interest. One was creating digital audio children's stories.
- *University libraries'* digitization projects tended to be based on special collections or within broad disciplines such as architecture, music, law, education, economics or history.
- *Legislative libraries* had begun to digitize their province's legislation and sessional documents.
- A couple of *provincial libraries* were digitizing their provincial and municipal government documents.
- *Special libraries'* efforts reflect their specialized audiences: for example, the library at the Atlantic Forest Service is digitizing in their areas of forestry, entomology, soil science and related subjects.

The following gives an idea of the types of material that are starting to be digitized, although it is by no means exhaustive. Perhaps from such projects, model methodologies will emerge to encourage and rationalize Canadian libraries' efforts into more cohesive provincial or national content creation programs.

- *Early Canadiana:* The Canadian Institute for Historical Microre-production, in partnership with Université Laval, la Bibliothèque Nationale du Québec, University of Toronto, and the National Library of Canada, and with sponsorship from the Andrew W. Mellon Foundation and other organizations, has recently launched a site of digitized early Canadian texts. Early Canadiana Online[14] includes more than 3,000 books and pamphlets documenting Canadian history from the first European contact to the late 19th Century, and is particularly strong in literature, women's history, native studies, travel and exploration and the history of French Canada. Toronto Reference Library is digitizing York Minutes, Upper Canada, and Lists of Inhabitants, 1797-1823, and the York/Toronto City Directories, 1833-1900. Providing a total of 38,000+ digitized pages, this project will increase the accessibility of these high-use reference sources that document the development and population of Canada's largest metropolitan area[15].
- *Electronic texts:* Electronic Text Centers for the standards-based production of commercial and public domain texts are now operational within several Canadian university libraries including the University of New Brunswick and the University of Waterloo[16].
- *Archival Finding Aids:* University of New Brunswick is leading a project involving several Canadian university libraries and the National Library to encode literary finding aids according to the Standard Generalized Mark-Up Language (SGML) Encoded Archival Description (EAD)[17].
- *Legal and Government Information:* Various efforts are underway at provincial legislative libraries and in research libraries and archives to digitize historical statutes, journals and other legislative and government material.
- *Newspapers and Newspaper Finding Aids:* The University of Saskatchewan has developed a Web-accessible integrated Saskatchewan Newspaper Index[18]. The University of New Brunswick Electronic Text Centre publishes the full text of one of that province's newspapers, the *Telegraph-Journal*[19]. The National Library has produced a major searchable Web listing of its almost comprehensive collection of Canadian newspapers on microform[20] and is considering selective digitization of other newspaper holdings.

While digital information resources are emerging from different disciplines and corresponding to a variety of different types of print publications, Canada has a long way to go before it will have a significant corpus of digital information to constitute a "national digital collection" of depth and coherence.

Many libraries are also using the network for innovative service delivery. For example, public libraries in Canada have used their Web sites to provide a wealth of community information, tell stories of local interest, interact with their clients, conduct innovative fundraising campaigns, promote reading through online book clubs and reading games and create niche directories to Web resources.

A particularly fine example of a niche directory service is provided by Toronto Public Library (TPL), Canada's largest public library system, with 98 branches and serving a population of 2.3 million people. Their *Science Net*[21] service makes it easy for teachers and students to find the best general and Kindergarten to Grade 12 science Web sites on the Internet. Like the National Library's Canadian Information By Subject, ScienceNet uses Dewey Decimal Classification to provide a subject arrangement for its links.

Collaboration

The issues relating to digital libraries, together with Canada's unique geographic and political makeup noted earlier in this chapter, furnish the context in which, in 1997, an alliance of Canadian libraries of all types founded the *Canadian Initiative on Digital Libraries* (CIDL)[22]. This nonprofit organization aims to support communication and collaboration among Canadian libraries to meet the new challenges of the digital information age. The Initiative was founded on the premise that the significant challenges of digital libraries could better be met by libraries sharing useful knowledge and experience as they become engaged in the field. By being a vehicle for increased communication, CIDL encourages its members to adopt approaches that have proven viability or are gaining momentum and support. Now with a membership of more than 50 Canadian libraries, including many of the large research libraries, the Initiative is concentrating on education and information sharing activities that will benefit both its members and the library community as a whole. By fostering a cost-efficient growth in digital activity in Canadian libraries, the Initiative will ensure that all Canadians are ultimately better served.

Electronic publishing by libraries is a specific issue where groups have been forming to discuss and begin to resolve issues. The recently formed *Electronic Publishing Interest Group of the Canadian Library Association*[23] is working to educate libraries about document encoding standards such as the SGML Text Encoding Initiative (TEI) and metadata standards such as Dublin Core. A number of nonprofit publishers including libraries have formed the *Virtuoso Group* to engage in mutually supportive research and development work, exploiting the potential and meeting the challenges of on-line scholarly publishing. The central purpose of this group is to develop a sustainable, scholar-centered model of scholarly publishing for the next millennium.

The concept of the *Virtual Canadian Union Catalogue* (vCuc)[24] involves a decentralized, electronically accessible catalogue created by linking the databases of several institutions. A recently completed pilot project, which was a partnership among 21 Canadian libraries and eight library system vendors coordinated by the National Library, successfully demonstrated the viability of a distributed virtual catalogue using the Z39.50 protocol within a relatively cohesive group of targets. However, as the number and diversity of targets increased, a number of technical and semantic interoperability issues arose. Work is proceeding to resolve these issues, and soon Canadian librarians and end-users will be able to explore the world's information resources through a virtual union catalogue representing Canadian libraries' resources.

Canadian libraries have also been joining together in an increasing number and variety of *consortia*. Primarily, these arrangements aim to reduce costs and extend access through collective licensing to costly full-text information resources. Several provinces have province-wide sectoral or multi-type consortia, of which some of the more established examples include British Columbia's Electronic Library Network (ELN), Nova Scotia's NovaNet, and the Council of Prairie and Pacific University Libraries (COPPUL).

Some have launched a new form of regional or provincial "virtual library" with a wide range of shared resources and services available. As one example, the *Alberta Library*[25], incorporated as a nonprofit organization in January 1997, is a province-wide consortium of university, college, public and special libraries and library organizations that enables resource sharing, actively initiates and facilitates cooperative activity, coordinates communication and advocates on behalf of its members. In what may be a model for future developments in other provinces, the "Alberta Library's vision is barrier-free access for all Albertans to information and ideas, delivered in a dynamic model of cooperation extending beyond walls and current levels of performance. The Alberta Library's long-term goal is for every publicly-funded library to be an entry point to the total information resources owned by our member institutions." One of the first steps in this initiative is the establishment of a robust public library network. A project taking place over four years (completing in 2000/01) will see: 1) the implementation of a telecommunications backbone for 10 urban centers and seven system headquarters that will become the network nodes for all other public libraries; 2) acquisition of common interlibrary loan messaging and management software to expedite province-wide resource sharing; 3) enhanced public library access to electronic information resources, including access to library catalogues in remote locations, electronic mail, public access to the Internet, community access points for government information; and 4) training and education for library staff.

The promising possibility of *national licensing* of full-text information resources for Canadian libraries is also being pursued. The Canadian Foundation for Innovation[26] recently granted CAN$20M over three years to the Canadian National Site Licensing Project. This project, which is spearheaded by the Canadian Association of Research Libraries (CARL), will create a national consortium of 64 universities to negotiate with journal publishers and vendors to obtain pan-Canadian site licenses for electronic versions of scholarly journals in primarily scientific disciplines.

Toronto Public Library's *Virtual Reference Library*[27] is another example of how the Internet has allowed a library to extend its services beyond its traditional geographic boundaries. The Virtual Reference Library is designed to deliver reference and information services through the use of advanced information and telecommunications technologies, and to permit all Ontarians to take advantage of the collections and staff expertise of Toronto Public Library (TPL), that province's largest public library. Such efforts tend to be funded through sponsorship and partnership with the private sector and municipal, provincial and/or federal government.

Canada has also been active in digital library discussions and standards development internationally. The National Library participates in international standards efforts including Z39.50, the ILL protocol and metadata standards development. The NLC also hosts the Universal Dataflow and Telecommunications (UDT) Core Programme of the International Federation of Library Associations and Institutions (IFLA), as well as IFLANET, the organization's extensive Web service[28].

CONCLUSION

There is not one single "right" definition of what a digital library is, and likewise there is not one single "right" approach to building either a local or a national-level digital library. Canada will not have a single, monolithic digital library or collection. In a typical, loosely federated Canadian fashion, a range of activities on several fronts have been underway. Taken together, these provide impetus, coordination, content and infrastructure support to a national—or more accurately, nationwide—digital library effort.

Canada is at this point well advanced in terms of connectivity; we can be proud of our progress in ensuring that the information wealth of the Internet is accessible to all Canadians. The federal government's Connecting Canadians agenda is now shifting some attention to supporting the creation of digital content. While many libraries, including the National Library, have been actively engaged in digitization and other forms of Web-based services, and substantial digital collections such as Early Canadiana Online are emerging, Canada's activities are not currently of the scale and scope as those within the United States or some other countries. Our libraries' progress remains largely the result of local initiative. But the Internet allows services to traverse traditional geographic bounds, and in a vast and lightly populated country like Canada, that opens exciting opportunities to strengthen the reach and service offerings of its libraries. More regional, provincial and national coordination, collaboration and funding will strengthen our libraries' effectiveness in the areas of digital content creation, preservation and accessibility. And, as is the case with all countries, this work will continue well into the 21st Century.

ENDNOTES

[1] The CANARIE Web site is found at: http://www.canarie.ca/

[2] The Community Access Program Web site is found at: http://cap.unb.ca/

[3] The SchoolNet Web site is found at: http://www.schoolnet.ca/

[4] http://www.schoolnet.ca/cfs-ope/welcome_e.html

[5] http://www.schoolnet.ca/ln-rb/

[6] http://www.gatesfoundation.org/

[7] http://www.schoolnet.ca/collections/E/

[8] http://www.nlc-bnc.ca/ehome.htm

[9] http://collection.nlc-bnc.ca/e-coll-e/index-e.htm

[10] http://www.nlc-bnc.ca/events/exhibits.htm

[11] http://www.nlc-bnc.ca/digiproj/edigiact.htm

[12] http://www.nlc-bnc.ca/caninfo/ecaninfo.htm

[13] http://www.amicus.nlc-bnc.ca/

[14] http://www.canadiana.org/

[15] http://digit.mtrl.toronto.on.ca:8080/

[16] http://www.lib.unb.ca/Texts/ *and http://library.uwaterloo.ca/etc/*

[17] http://www.hil.unb.ca/Texts/finding_aids/Finding_aids.htm

[18] http://library.usask.ca/sni/

[19] http://www.lib.unb.ca/Texts/TJ/

[20] http://www.nlc-bnc.ca/services/news/cnie.htm

[21] http://sciencenet.tpl.toronto.on.ca/

[22] http://www.nlc-bnc.ca/cidl/

[23] http://www.lib.unb.ca/Texts/EPIG.htm

[24] http://www.nlc-bnc.ca/resource/vcuc/index.htm

[25] http://www.library.ualberta.ca/altalib/

[26] http://www.innovation.ca/

[27] http://vrl.tpl.toronto.on.ca/

[28] http://www.ifla.org/

REFERENCES

Ekos Research Associates Inc. (1998). Canadians, Public Libraries and the Information Highway: Final Report. Ekos Research Associates Inc., Ottawa. Available: http://www.schoolnet.ca/ln-rb/e/ekos/toc.html

Government of Canada. (1998). Connecting Canadians. Available: http://www.connect.gc.ca/

Haigh, S. (1998). "A Glossary of Digital Library Standards, Protocols and Formats. *Network Notes*, No. 54. Available: http://www.nlc-bnc.ca/pubs/netnotes/notes54.htm

Haigh, S. (1997). "Digital Resources in Canadian Libraries: Analysis of a National Library Survey". *National Library News*,27(6), 1-7. Available: http://www.nlc-bnc.ca/pubs/nl-news/1997/2906-e.pdf

Information Highway Advisory Council (Canada). (1995). Connection, Community, Content: the Challenge of the Information Highway. Final Report of the Information Highway Advisory Council. The Council, Ottawa, 5.

Manley, J. (1998). "Connecting Canadians." Speaking Notes for the Honorable John Manley, Minister of Industry, to the Canadian Library Association, Victoria, British Columbia, June 20, 1998.

Rusbridge, C. (1998). "Towards the Hybrid Library," *D-Lib Magazine*, July/August 1998. Available: http://www.dlib.org/dlib/july98/rusbridge/07rusbridge.html.

Statistics Canada (1997). *Household Facilities and Equipment 1997*. Ottawa.

Chapter IV

Deposit Collections of Digital Publications: A Pragmatic Strategy for an Analysis

José Luis Borbinha, Fernanda Campos and Fernando Cardoso
National Library of Portugal

This chapter presents an analysis and a recommended strategy to address the problem of the management of digital publications in deposit institutions. The perspective here assumed is of the national libraries, but part of the problem can be shared with archives and other similar institutions. In this chapter we will try to demonstrate that the problem raises new technical and formal issues to these institutions, with impact in multiple and not always clear dimensions, thus requiring a deep knowledge of the new emerging objects and also new and adjustable postures for management. To deal with the problem, we propose an approach based in a strategy taking in account three components: analysis of the structure of the problem, the concept of publication genre and the concept of scenarios. The work presented in this chapter is based on the results of the first phase of the project NEDLIB - Networked European Deposit Library, an international project promoted by a European consortium.

THE PROBLEM

National libraries and other similar institutions are usually mandated to maintain deposit collections of published documents for the purpose of preservation of cultural heritage. Through this mission, those institutions guarantee the long-term availability of those materials, especially for cultural and scientific purposes.

In some cases, the same system is also used for the registration of the copyright of the deposited materials. In those scenarios, the deposit institutions will register and preserve those works also as a proof, to guarantee to the authors the recognition of their intellectual ownership.

More recently, our society has been registering the affirmation of a new paradigm in the production and dissemination of publications. That new reality is digital publishing, and it has been forcing the deposit institutions to rethink their entire position. We have been assisting to an increasing growing in the publication of digital documents, and their preservation is a mission for deposit institutions. That raises new challenges to those institutions, requiring a thorough understanding of the new paradigm in order to deal with it in a proper way.

This chapter will proceed with an in-depth presentation of the problem and an introduction to the project NEDLIB, a project to address this problem and which context we will use to discuss it. In the next point we will focus our attention in an analysis of the problem, which will be followed by some reflections for a possible strategy to approach it in practice. After that we will refer a few examples of application that are going to be tested by the National Library of Portugal, and then we will finish with some considerations about open issues.

Deposit collections

To build their collections, the deposit institutions act usually in one or more of the following scenarios:

- *Legal deposit:* which corresponds to a system legally enforced, whereby authors, publishers or other agents must deliver one or more copies of every publication to the deposit institution (this is the usual scenario if the purpose of the deposit is not only preservation but also the copyright registration).
- *Voluntary deposit:* which corresponds to a system usually based on agreements between the deposit institution and the publishers or authors, under which those agents deliver one or more copies of each publication for preservation.
- *Proactive acquisitions*: which correspond to a system where the deposit institutions have to take the initiative to identify, select and acquire the publications relevant for deposit, according to

their defined mission and strategy.

Each country defines usually one of these scenarios as its main framework, but the coexistence of the three models is common. The exceptions are those countries, such as in the Netherlands and Switzerland, where the models of legal deposit simply do not exist. Nevertheless, and independently of the deposit framework, usually each deposit institution has also an internal rule (sometimes defined by law) to specify the so-called "deposit policy." Those policies try to make it clear what kind of works have or must be deposited, and they are fundamental to regulate the practical activities of those institutions.

In the traditional print paradigm, the selection criteria specified by the deposit policies are based on the identification of common types of publications, produced by recognised sources (usually, from registered publishers). In special cases, those criteria include also the selection of publications or documents of less common types, or produced by informal sources, but which have relevant contents as specified in the deposit policy. In this paradigm, the main problems for the deposit institution are the identification and acquisition of the proper works, assuring that the producers and the institution itself complies with the law. Once deposited, the requirements for the institution to deal with these traditional publications are quite homogeneous, comprising usually:

- The registration of the bibliographic data of the publications, most likely in catalogues supported by computing systems with data structures compatible with the family of MARC standards.
- The storage of the publications, in adequate conditions with controlled light, humidity and temperature, in order to assure a correct physical preservation (usually, specific copies of each work are also stored in special depots for long-term preservation).
- The observance of defined access and reproduction policies, comprising usually free public access inside the facilities of the institution for the majority of the publications, specific access rules for special materials (such as for example rare books, collections with socially sensitive contents, etc.), rules for private copying, etc.

This reality represents quite a very well-established scenario, with which most of the deposit institutions feel comfortable. Most of these publications are produced by large publishers, the standards and rules for cataloguing them are generally accepted, and there is an experimented market of computerized systems to help managing the processes for acquisition, cataloguing, deposit, registration, storage, search, loan, circulation, etc.

Digital deposit collections

In the traditional print paradigm, the deposit institutions concentrate their attention essentially in the type of the publication, the factor that determinates almost all the decisions to be taken. Another relevant dimension to take in account is the support of the publication (such as the type of the paper, for example), but this is important usually only because of its requirements for long-term preservation, without affecting the deposit policies in the short term.

However, in the new digital paradigm, we will see that not only the relevance of these dimensions needs to be revisited, but also other dimensions need to be identified and addressed since the very beginning. Those new dimensions may be relevant if they have a relationship with possible limitations of the deposit institution, thus imposing actual or short-term practical constraints to the mission of the deposit institution.

Those limitations can be technical, if related for example to the ability to store, access or preserve the publications, or formal, if related to new economic models and copyright threats inherent to the new paradigm.

The questions

The main questions that we need to answer to address the problem of the deposit of digital publications are:

- In a specific sense, what are the new relevant dimensions that deposit institutions have to take into account, and how will they affect their generic deposit policies?
- In a broad sense, what should be the main strategies for the deposit institutions to deal with this new problem?

These are the global questions that we will discuss and for which we will try to find some answers in this chapter.

Project NEDLIB

The reflections presented in this chapter are based in the results of the first phase of the project NEDLIB (Networked European Deposit Library). Those results were presented in the project reports (Borbinha and Cardoso, 1998; Borbinha, 1998), as also in the discussion document (Borbinha and Cardoso, 1999), which are all public documents[2]. The project was planned for 36 months, starting in January 1998, with a grant of the Program "Telematics" of the European Commission. The first phase of the project run during 1998, and it was dedicated to the analysis of the problem and the identification of the main functional requirements. The objectives of the project were defined as:

"(...) to find ways to make sure that electronic publications and documents of the present can be used now and in the future. (...) The results of NEDLIB can be used to build (cost) models for the management of networked deposit libraries and for the long-term technical infrastructures" (NEDLIB, 1997).

The project partners include, as target partners, nine European national libraries and one national archive[3].

ANALYSIS OF THE PROBLEM

A high level analysis of the problem of the deposit of digital publications produced an understanding of its structure and the identification of the main functional requirements, as explained in the following points.

Structure of the problem

First of all, we need to define the structure of the problem from the point of view of the deposit institution, in order to make possible the identification of the main states of the processes and the key blocks of the necessary architectures to support them. The structure of the problem, as identified in NEDLIB, is represented in Figure 1.

The problem of the acquisition is to determine what should be selected or accepted by a deposit institution to be integrated in its collections, and how that can or has to be done. That implies selection criteria, which are defined usually in the context of a deposit framework

Figure 1: Main blocks in the structure of the problem for the management of deposit of digital collections.

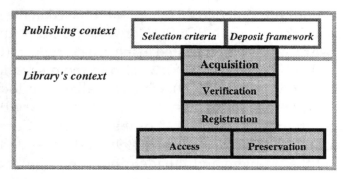

regulated by a national law for legal deposit and, in a more generic perspective, by a publishing context defined outside the library.

After the acquisition, a verification is required to confirm the shape of the deposited works, assuring their technical and logical quality. The registration of a publication in a deposit institution is related with the registration of metadata for its content and bibliographic description. It comprises the traditional tasks of indexing and cataloguing, but it can also include other new tasks now in the digital paradigm, such as those related to the registration of new metadata structures for new requirements for technical management and handling.

The potential offered by the digital paradigm opens attractive perspectives for easier access and the development of new services to be provided by the deposit institutions. However, that reality also raises new potential threats to the copyright and economic interests of the publishers, implying new cares and responsibilities to the deposit institution.

Finally, the problem of the preservation of digital publications represents a completely new world of new and unforeseen issues. In generic terms, this problem needs to be addressed from three perspectives: physical preservation, logical preservation and intellectual preservation.

Actors

The modelling of the structure of the problem is represented in Figure 2 as a UML use case diagram (Erikson & Penker, 1998). In that modelling we identify the main actors of the problem as being: the manager, the agent and the user.

The manager represents the staff of the deposit institution (librarian, archivist, etc.), with a direct intervention and responsibility in all the phases of the process. The agent represents the publisher, the author or other similar actor involved in the acquisition stage, and thus playing a potentially fundamental role in the deposit of the publication (in the digital paradigm, and especially in the on-line case, the distinction between the author and the publisher is sometimes complex to distinguish and sometimes even irrelevant).

Users are relevant in the access, where their actions can depend on the librarian (for example to assist in the searching, to provide support for specific requests, to grant access to special collections or publications, etc.). The identification of the user can be also very important in the case of remote access to the deposit institution (a new feature in the digital paradigm).

Functional requirements

The main functional requirements related with these blocks and processes are resumed in Table 1 and shortly described in the following points.

Acquisition

For countries or institutions with a legal deposit framework for printed publications, a tendency has been to extend such framework also to include digital off-line publications. That has been done by adapting the law or just by negotiating with the publishers. However, this approach cannot be directly transposed for on-line publications, where the traditional concepts of "document," "publication", and in sometimes even of "publisher" and "author" may have no direct relation with the printing of off-line paradigm.

An immediate solution to address this problem can be the development of harvest strategies, where the library takes the initiative to identify and simply copy all the publications found meeting a set of requirements. In order to do that, a deposit institution only needs the required legal framework and the technical skills to makes it possible to copy the desired publications that were identified based on its own initiative. However, some on-line publications are based on runtime

Figure 2: The structure of a deposit institution as a use case diagram.

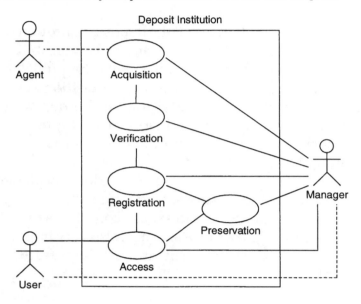

Table 1: Main functional requirements in the management of deposit of digital collections.

Acquisition	Delivery by the publisher	
	Capture by the library	
	Harvesting by the library	
Verification	Medium integrity	
	Content integrity	Logical integrity Authentication
Registration	*Metadata*	Bibliographic and content description Installation and de-installation Preservation Access
Preservation	*Physical preservation*	Medium refreshing Medium migration
	Logical preservation	Format conversion Emulation
	Intellectual preservation	
Access	*Conditions of use*	Local access Remote access

systems, thus requiring also the harvesting and deposit of executable code. Other publications have also embedded components, coded in standard or no standard formats, all of that making it difficult to define generic and technically practicable deposit policies.

These problems suggest to think in alternative strategies for the acquisition of on-line publications based on voluntary and proactive scenarios, for which the institution should develop careful deposit policies, preferably based on agreements and collaborative actions with the publishers and creators in general. In those scenarios it will be then possible for the institutions to conceive systems and strategies to capture, automatically or assisted, desired publications that were previously registered or discovered by automatic processes.

This strategy can be proper for agents producing large quantities of publications, usually in standardized formats (which in some cases are, de facto, "their standards"), or for agents using complex economic models. However, it will not cover the entire spectrum. In fact, it is easy to admit that, due to the increasingly dissemination and user-friendliness of the technology, we will face a future where a huge number of atomic agents will produce (should we say, "will pub-lish"?) sporadic publications and new types of works, most of them also very relevant for deposit. An important part of those works will be produced without any commercial interest, making it easier for the deposit institutions to deal with them, but they will also include proprietary or less common formats, raising completely new dilem-mas to those institutions.

It is not clear what should it be the best strategy for dealing with this problem. Probably it would help if the deposit institutions could take a proactive attitude, such as by trying to identify those potential agents and then trying to influence and educate them for the problem of the long-term preservation of their works, but that would be too optimistic.

In an extreme scenario, this can also be a new opportunity in the missions of institutions such as national libraries and archives, which can propose to those agents, directly or indirectly, pre-prepared "on-line publishing spaces" that they can use as primary targets (especially for cases with no direct commercial interests). By promoting those spaces, these institutions will be in direct contact with the dynamics of the reality, and will have a chance to play an active role in new trends such as the emerging of new publication formats, types, exploitation models, etc.

Verification

The checking of physical media is required to assure the physical consistency of the publications, verifying if all the bits, blocks or files are correct. These are simple technical tasks, required only by off-line media, which can be easily automated.

The quality of the contents can be verified from two perspectives: logical integrity and authentication. The checking of the logical structures intends to assure the logical consistency of the publications, verifying if all the files are present, if they are in the correct formats, etc. Its practical execution can be problematic, since it may require a prior profound knowledge about all the possible technical formats that may be hard to obtain. Publications that incorporate access and usage controls (such as requiring password for access or installation) are other important obstacles, especially for automatic checking.

The authentication checking can be assured implicitly for off-line publications, such as it is done for printed material, but for on-line publications it remains an important issue. It represents mainly a technical problem, inherent to the infrastructure of the Internet, and it will have to be solved in that context. It requires future developments, such as more secure communication infrastructures (secure TCP/IP, HTTP, etc.), authentication services (to be supported such as for example by governmental or specialized agencies), etc.

Registration

Some tasks for the registration of digital publications can be automated, such as identifying and reusing embedded information provided with the publications, or even by using special software applications for automatic analysis of the contents.

However, it is also necessary to address new requirements for new metadata structures. We will need, for example, to register metadata for the installation and removal (de-installation) of some of the publications, especially if important parts of them are incorporating or requiring executable software. We will need also metadata for access (namely decryption keys, passwords, metadata to represent legal terms and conditions of use, etc.). And we will need to register, as much as possible, metadata for preservation (file formats, logical structures of hypermedia publications, etc.).

Preservation

Until very recently, the off-line media for distribution was associated mainly with the diskette, while the designated media for storage was associated with the magnetic tape. Those magnetic media have been showing to be quite fragile, requiring a constant refreshing. Due to that, and also due to the success of the Internet, there is a general speculation about a near future where digital publishing will converge to the on-line paradigm. However, the eternal congestion of the Internet and new reliable off-line storage technology such as the DVD, with a very high capacity, are bringing a new relevance to the off-line model.

This reality will raise a probable scenario favorable to strategies of physical preservation based on media migration, where materials previously "published" on-line will be most likely stored and preserved locally in off-line media using the most recent technology. This scenario will be also favorable to agreements with the publishers in order to assure the deposit of on-line publications in off-line media.

The problem of the logical preservation is associated with the need to assure format conversions when original formats become obsolete or too expensive to maintain. Besides its complexity, this strategy carries other potential problems, namely the definition of the legal status of the new versions of the publications, a potential source of conflicts with the authors and other production agents.

Another problem associated with the format conversion is its effect on the intellectual content of the initial work. This opens a new issue related to the intellectual preservation, since a format conversion can imply a change in the layout, presentation or interaction with the publication, and so a loss of its original intellectual content can be declared unacceptable by the original author. And even if we can demonstrate that a format conversion does not loses content in this sense, it will lose at least the context where the author created the publication.

In some cases emulation would probably be the desirable solution for a correct preservation, especially if the publications are so specific that the migration to other formats would have a significant impact in the intellectual content. However, an emulator is in reality an application for a specific environment (software and/or hardware), so a strategy based on that will in reality just delay the problem for the future, if not making it worst. In fact, after the building of an emulator (usually a very expensive thing to do), it will be necessary to preserve the publication in its original format as well as the emulator.

Access

As referred before, due to the technical complexity of the new paradigm, it is advised for the deposit institutions to seek for agreements with authors and publishing agents in order to lessen the technical and legal difficulties to the deposit. In these cases, to be able to assure the control of the access to the deposited publications becomes a key point in the process, otherwise it will produce negative positions from those authors and publishing agents.

The new problems created by the digital paradigm in this area are related mainly with the control of the copying and the control of the remote access. The copying is much easier here than in the print paradigm, and the right way to deal with it is to restrict the access from controlled terminals or clients. With the actual technology, the only way to observe this requirement safely is to limit access locally or from a trusted network.

This strikes against one important characteristic of the digital paradigm, which is its propensity to promote openness and physical ubiquity, characteristics that give a strong incentive to the deposit institutions to try to extend the range of access to their services in the public interest. If these institutions want to proceed in this way, they will have to conceive it carefully, in order to prevent an excessive "openness" that would be desirable from the social point of view, but would be also a threat to publishers with commercial interests.

A STRATEGY FOR PRACTICAL STEPS

The reality of "digital publishing" has been defined by a constant technological incertitude, instead of a foreseen determinism. This reality is characterized by a large heterogeneity and dynamism of objects and models. To deal with that in a cost-effective way, deposit institutions will need to identify clearly each object and model in order to understand their specific requirements, as also their actual and future impact in the processes. Therefore, the preservation of publications in a digital paradigm is a task much more complex than in the printing one, where classes are fewer and they were usually already defined a long time ago.

In conclusion, for the management of digital publications in deposit institutions, those institutions need to update permanently their knowledge of the reality and adapt their behavior to that reality just like any other technological player in the digital world.

A possible approach for this problem may consist in a strategy for action (implying dynamism) instead of a model or architecture (transmitting the idea of a final and static attitude). That strategy must include a permanent analysis of the problem and be supported by a framework with two tools: publication genre and scenarios.

Publication genre

In our context, a publication genre is defined as a class of publications characterised by multiple common dimensions relevant for a specific stage in their management, handling and access in deposit collections.

Formally, the perspective is to try to describe each digital publication as a point in a multidimensional space, where each dimension represents an important property that has to be taken in account. The purpose of the identification of genres by this way is to make it possible to identify, associated to each genre, the specific requirements for the systems and processes to support and manage them.

This concept of publication genre gives us a tool to address the problem of the identification of the dimensions of the publications which are relevant for a specific institution. As we will see it, this is a problem which is neither stable in time or homogeneous in the way it influences in the problem, therefore requiring a special attention and analysis.

Methodology for application

In each context of application, the concept of genre must be applied independently to each stage of the process. In further steps the results can be then reworked, in order to try to identify compatible genres in different stages that will be merged in order to optimize the overall infrastructure.

This means that a group of genres identified by an institution in its acquisition stage do not need to be, forcibly, the same groups found in the verification, neither in the registration, in the preservation or in the access. A genre can be specific to just one of these stages, or it can cross more than one (a desirable scenario).

In this sense, a system to support digital collections will be based, in the worst case, on a structure of multiple specialized blocks, each one supporting a specific genre in a specific stage of the process. In best cases, merging genres across multiple stages will make it possible to develop, "a priori", common blocks to support them across those stages. New possibly identified genres entering a group "a posteriori" will be processed using those already defined blocks of the system.

One specific genre will represent then a subspace of publications, sharing common relevant properties. By this way we are identifying and naming, in an overall space of digital publications, a specific point, a line, a plan, a volume, etc., depending of the number of relevant dimensions to be considered in each step. The bigger the subspace, the more generic will be the blocks necessary to support it. The smaller the space, the more specific the publications are, thus requiring special attention.

A challenge for the deposit institutions in this area will be the identification of relevant genres and linking them to standard models for deposit.

Analysis of possible relevant dimensions for genres

The main dimensions relevant for the definition of a publication genre, from the point of view of a deposit institution, can be identified as technical factors or contextual factors.

Technical factors are factors related with the technical characteristics of the publication, which can be typically:

- *Publication medium,* referring to the media in which a publication is disseminated, which can be physical, defining an off-line publication (CD-ROM, etc.) or virtual, defining an on-line publication[4].
- *Publication formats,* which are related with the logical and technical formats of a publication, such as the file formats and encoding, the hypertext structures, etc.

Contextual factors are factors related with the context of the publication, which we can group as:

- *Publication type,* which refers to classes of publications, indepen-

Table 2: Simple examples of attributes for dimensions in digital publication genres.

Medium	Formats	Type	Characteristics

- Diskettes
- CD-ROM
- DVD
- Photo-CD
- CD-I
- On-line media
- *Broadcasting media*
- ... etc.
	- ASCII
	- Word processing
	  - MS-Word
	  - Word Perfect
	  - ... etc.
	- Print/view
	  - Postscript
	  - PDF
	  - ... etc.
	- Image
	  - GIF
	  - JPEG
	  - ... etc.
	- Video
	  - MPEG
	  - AVI
	  - ... etc.
	- Multimedia
	- ... etc.
		- Homepages
		  - commercial
		  - personal
		  - governmental
		  - ... etc.
		
		- Digital monographs
		- Digital journals
		- Thesis and dissertations
		- Mailing lists
		- Newsgroups
		- *informational content*
		  - CBT
		  - databases
		  - multimedia applications
		  - ... etc.
		
		- Computer games
		- ... etc.
			- Legal conditions
			  - Publicly available
			  - Commercial
			    publications
			  - ... etc.
			
			- Temporal
			  characteristics
			  - Static publication
			  - Dynamic publication
			  - ... etc.
			
			- ... etc.

dent or not of their media and formats, but related with specific contents, cultural or commercial practices and activities of organizations, institutions, communities, groups, etc. The traditional examples are the common types of newspapers, scholarly journals, theses and dissertations, financial reports, etc.

- *Publication characteristics*, referring to factors of the publication related with the legal and/or temporal status of the contents relevant for its management and access. Examples of such characteristics can be the copyright status of a publication, legal terms and conditions imposed on the publication by its author or publisher, the dynamic or static nature of the publication, etc.

Simple examples of attributes for these factors are presented in Table 2 (it is important to note that those attributes are just tentative examples of possible dimensions and values, to illustrate our actual discussion).

From a generic point of view, it is possible to summarize a relationship model for the genre's factors and the main blocks of the structure of the problem, as presented in Table 3. In this table, the dependencies referred as "dependent" mean conditioning factors imposed on the institution by reasons out of its control, while "relevant" refers to a non-conditioning factor whose impact depend on the strategy of the institution or of its deposit framework.

Based on the framework built until now, we will proceed to the next step of the approach where we will identify relevant scenarios for action.

In a generic perspective, genres are important for the definition of selection criteria for deposit guidelines. Deposit institutions should define deposit criteria related with genres that they can support. The application of selection criteria in a real case, with which the deposit institution will be able to deal, is called a scenario.

The identification, implementation and management of scenarios will be, therefore, the main practical concern of the deposit institution. A scenario must be defined taking in account three factors: a deposit framework, technical factors and the selection criteria.

The deposit framework reflects the local cultural and political deposit perspective. It depends on the library and the legal involving environment (for example, the deposit law and the actual and expected governmental policy, etc.).

The technical requirements are related to local strategic options and/or economic constraints in the technical competence of the institution (hardware and operating systems to use, existing biblio-graphic management systems, skills of the staff, etc.). This is a factor mainly internal to the library.

Finally, the selection criteria are the result of the conjugation of the deposit framework and technical requirements, and its subject is the concept of publication genre. If one new publication can be mapped, in each stage of the process, in one or more genres, then it can be selected for deposit.

The purpose of the identification of real scenarios is to make it possible to proceed in the approach to the problem with the identification of real full sets of functional requirements, their analysis, the design

Table 3: Dependencies between dimension factors for the publication genre and the structure of the problem.

Dimension factors	Acquisition	Verification	Registration	Preservation	Access
Medium	relevant	dependent	relevant	relevant	dependent
Formats	relevant	dependent	relevant	relevant	dependent
Type	relevant	relevant	relevant	relevant	relevant
Characteristics	dependent	dependent	relevant	relevant	dependent

of real systems and their implementation and test in real conditions.

EXAMPLES FOR TESTING

The actual Portuguese legal deposit law does not cover digital publications yet, but a commission worked during 1998 on a new proposal that is under consideration. The new law should give a new framework to the National Library, under which the library will promote the voluntary and the proactive frameworks for on-line digital publications (which has been found as the best strategy to deal with the technical problems inherent to the new paradigm).

Meanwhile, the library already identified a set of scenarios to be tested, in order to understand how they can be fully or partially (sub-scenario) implemented and tested. These are a scenario for the deposit of scientific theses and dissertations, a scenario for on-line serial publications and a scenario for publicly available publications. These scenarios have overlapping characteristics, which we expect will make it possible to identify requirements for common tools, systems and procedures.

Theses and dissertations

The Portuguese legal deposit law requests the deposit of theses and dissertations in the National Library. Due to the traditional advanced usage of the technology in universities, these publications represent an excellent potential scenario for experiments.

This scenario requires a special dedicated system for acquisition and verification, with a strong involvement of the university libraries, are also of the authors themselves. The genre does not require special concern with preservation, but these publications require special requirements for registration and access. The same contents of theses and dissertations are sometimes used to produce other genres, such as books and papers, or they can also include sensitive material related to, for example, patents. This requires the system functionality to make it possible for the authors to declare special requirements for access, which have to be registered and respected.

Serial publications

The scenario for serial publications (magazines and newspapers, etc.) comprises two sub-scenarios based on voluntary deposit, one with the capture of the publications and other with their delivery.

One sub-scenario comprises the capture of the publications from their publishing servers, upon agreements with the publishers. It is expected that the future law will give the National Library a legal framework to harvest those publications, but the Library will try to do it always in a capture scenario, with the previous knowledge, agreement and collaboration of the publisher. A second sub-scenario is based on the delivery of the publications by the publishers, to be used preferably in special cases where the capture would be technically too complex. The delivery of those contents in off-line media is also an open issue to be taken in consideration (especially if they are to be delivered as logically self-contained structures, including for example multiple formats, viewers and other tools).

Public publishing space

The third scenario corresponds to a new public service, offering public space for publishing relevant documents. With this service the library intends to give a formal meaning to the concept of publishing in a digital environment, by assuring the long-term availability to those works. At the same time, the implications of this service can be very relevant to helping define selection criteria and understand the problem of the publication genre in general.

In the context of NEDLIB, the Helsinki University Library identified a scenario for a "blind" harvesting of all the public on-line publications available in the Finnish domain of the Internet. This corresponds to a proactive deposit, for which a robot will search and harvest the publications automatically. This scenario is quite similar to the one identified by the National Library of Portugal, but with different requirements for acquisition, since we are requiring the application of selection rules. This requirement implies the support for a kind of "light-harvesting," where the publication is intended to be discovered (discovery strategies have to be defined), followed by a selection (selection rules will be developed with the experience). Only after this verification the publication is deposited in a capture scenario, and then registered.

OPEN ISSUES

The work discussed here is far from being completed. The approach by scenarios seems to be a very realistic and secure way to address the problem, but the real relevance of the concept of genre, as discussed, needs to be proved in real cases. In this context, there are still several open issues which need to be addressed, namely a more careful revision of the identified dimensions. However, probably more important than continuing an abstract analysis would be to work toward the identification of a relevant set of real heterogeneous scenarios, which could then be reanalyzed for the relevant dimensions for genres.

It is also important to understand that the nuances in the relevant genre dimensions will be dependent not only of the scenarios, but also of the local implementation contexts. This means that the genres and requirements identified by, for example, one specific national library in the context of one specific scenario, will not be forcibly the same as those identified by another national library for a similar scenario. In fact, to be more correct we must say it clearly that the technical context of the deposit institution is in fact an important part of the definition of the scenarios.

In practice, there is a need for experience. That experience can be provided by the identification of "real-life" scenarios, which can be used to give feedback on the presented analysis and provide knowledge to make it possible to revise the presented dimensions and also to identify new ones, and their requirements. Finally, there is also a need to identify and understand the new economic models and the related new publishing formats and media, which represent very dynamic problems and areas, where it is very difficult to foresee the future.

ENDNOTES

[1] José Luis Borbinha is an invited researcher at INESC and a member of the teaching body of IST - Instituto Superior Técnico (Lisbon Technical University). He is commissioned in service at the National Library of Portugal.

[2] The technical responsibility of Work Package 1 of the project NEDLIB was assumed by the National Library of Portugal, with the direct assistance of INESC - Instituto de Engenharia de Sistemas e Computadores and contributions of all the other partners. However, the conclusions and recommendations presented in this chapter may not meet all the points of view of the consortium or of specific partners, so they should not be fully understood as the official position of the

project, but just as the positions assumed by the authors. Updated information and documentation about the project NEDLIB can be found at <http://www.konbib.nl/nedlib>.

[3] NEDLIB target partners are the Koninklijke Bibliotheek (The Netherlands), Bibliotheque Nationale de France (France), Biblioteca Nacional (Portugal), Nasjonalbiblioteket i Rana (Norway), Agentschap Rijksarchiefdienst (The Netherlands), Helsinki University Library (Finland), Die Deutsche Bibliothek (Germany), Biblioteca Nazionale Centrale Firenze (Italy) and the Swiss National Library (Switzerland). The consortium also includes as sponsors the publishers Elsevier Science BV (The Netherlands), Kluwer (The Netherlands) and Springer Verlag (Germany), and as technological partners INESC (Portugal) and CSC Ploenzke (Germany). The project management is assured by Level-7 Ltd (Great Britain).

[4] Other examples of virtual publications can be the broadcast works (radio or TV) that are covered by some deposit frameworks.

REFERENCES

Borbinha, José & Cardoso, Fernando (1998, 25 September). Deliverable D1.2.1 - Functional Specification for DSEP, final version. *NEDLIB Project*. 15.

Borbinha, José (1998, 15 October). Deliverable D1.2.2 - High Level Design. *NEDLIB Project*.

Borbinha, José & Cardoso, Fernando (1999, 8 January). GEN-233 - Document Genre in Deposit Collections. *NEDLIB Project*.

Erikson, Hans-Erik & Penker, Magnus (1998). UML Toolkit. John Wiley & Sons, Inc.

NEDLIB Consortium (1997). *NEDLIB Technical Annex*.

Chapter V

National Library of Korea: South Korean Government-Run Digital Library — RISS and KRIC

Ook Lee
Hansung University

This chapter presents the result of an action research conducted by an IS scholar who was involved in establishing and running a digital library which was government initiated in South Korea. The lessons from the national digital library's case include the issue of the relationship between national IT infrastructure and the success of the national digital library. As a part of building the national IT infrastructure, a digital library that combines all digital libraries which already existed in various universities and that can provide overseas information such as journal articles instantly to every Korean researcher for free was established. An empirical survey was done as a part of the action research which included identifying the user satisfaction rate of the newly established national digital library. After obtaining results out of the survey, the action researcher recommended to go ahead with the current way of running a nationwide government-owned digital library.

INTRODUCTION

This chapter describes a digital library project that was initiated by the South Korean government as a part of building the national information technology (IT) infrastructure. Since South Korea is a developing country, its national IT infrastructure is not well developed to support all aspects of digital library technology unlike developed countries such as the USA. Nevertheless there are many attempts by private entities such as universities which were trying to establish digital libraries on their own in South Korea. Firstly, this chapter introduces the action research method as the research method used in thischapter. The reason for choosing this particular research method is described. Secondly, this chapter introduces the IT environment of South Korea and the argument of inevitability of establishing a nationwide digital library by the government itself. Thirdly, this chapter introduces the concept of the digital library and its development in many countries as another information technology application that makes significant impact on people, and points out that only a few studies on social and user's reaction to this new information technology was conducted. Fourthly, this chapter introduces the national digital library of Korea called RISS (Research Information Service System) which is run by the government agency. Fifthly, the attitude by researchers (users) on the quality of this digital library called RISS, which was run by a government agency called KRIC in South Korea, was identified by presenting the result of an on-line survey with a simple questionnaire, which was conducted by the action researcher as a part of the action research plan. Matters that threaten the success of this digital library such as copyright problems are described based on the observation by the action researcher. As the last step of the action research, the action researcher prescribes the critical success factors for the national digital library.

ACTION RESEARCH AS A RESEARCH METHOD

I chose to conduct this research on the digital library initiative by the South Korean Government by using the action research method since I worked as a senior research scientist at the agency called KRIC which developed RISS, the digital library, from the beginning stage to the testing stage. After I changed my job to professor, I was asked to be a technical advisor to the KRIC especially on user's reaction research. I was supposed to conduct the user satisfaction test and advise on the running of the RISS, the digital library. Action researchers take into account the full richness of organizational interactions (Kock, 1997). Action research studies are characterized by the researcher applying positive intervention to the client organization, while gathering field data about the organization (Jonsonn, 1991). These characteristics of action research provided a particularly solid ground for my decision to use the action research method in this study. I have tried to follow the model established by Susman and Evered (1978) in which the action research comprises five stages: diagnosing, action planning, action taking, evaluation and specifying learning. Firstly, for diagnosing, I had to conduct an on-line survey of users of RISS in order to assess the user satisfaction of the digital library service. Secondly, for action planning and taking, I recommended that KRIC go ahead in maintaining the current system. Thirdly, for evaluating and specifying learning, I had to evaluate the performance of the digital library which resulted in identifying many problems, which in turn, became valuable sources for obtaining lessons in establishing and running a nationwide/nonprofit library in South Korea.

NATIONAL INFRASTRUCTURE AND DIGITAL LIBRARY

I might suggest that running a digital library in a developed country should be different from doing it in a less-developed country; here "development" refers mainly to the level of national IT infrastructure development. National IT infrastructure can be defined as the vision of broadband communications that are interoperable as though they were a single network, easily accessible and widely distributed to all groups within society bringing business, education and government services directly to households and facilitating peer-to-peer communication throughout society (Kraemar, et al., 1996). But this idealistic vision is hard to achieve for countries with fewer economic resources. Nevertheless, South Korea embarked on building its IT infrastructure in 1994 which was officially called the "Korea Information Infrastructure (KII)" project (Jeong and King, 1996). The Korean government committed itself to promoting industries such as computer makers, telecommunication network builders and value-added service providers, Multimedia firms, cable TV industries and Internet-related companies. Since all these projects could not succeed without substantial investment and consumer demand, the recession which started in 1994 halted all these initiatives. With the current economic hardship, the South Korean government's ambitious plans need to wait until the fruit of its investment is apparent.

In the mean time, some government officials of the Ministry of Education thought of establishing a nationwide digital library as a part of building national IT infrastructure. The idea was bought by the government of that time, and the creation of an agency under the Ministry of Education was started in 1996. The compelling reason for establishing the national digital library was that several universities had already started to construct their own digital libraries with very expensive contracts with overseas information service companies, which, as the government official viewed it, could be considered as a big waste of resources for a small country like South Korea. In the U.S., many universities have their own digital library projects and many other public libraries are also wired into digital libraries. This was possible since, simply speaking, the country is such a big and rich country that it doesn't see the benefit of centralizing in order to save resources. In addition to that, the country's national IT infrastructure can sustain such proliferation of digital library projects with high-speed computer networks and relatively low cost of communication, which does not exist in a less-developed country like South Korea. Thus the reasons that the South Korean government tried a central-ized digital library project were the following:

1. By preventing duplication of work which could be done by other entities such as universities and public libraries, saving of re-sources can be achieved.
2. By centralizing, user management can be done more efficiently. For example, only people who are in need of research information should be allowed to use the system; if the system is not central-ized, the criteria on which users should obtain the user privilege could be varied according to different digital libraries in the nation.
3. By representing the entire country, the negotiation and contract with the overseas information service companies can be simpler and easier, i.e., the copyright issue can be negotiated on behalf of the entire country. Otherwise each individual digital library has to negotiate and make contracts, which can be time-consuming and less efficient.

The agency called KIRC (Korea Research Information Center) was established in the beginning of 1997 and embarked upon building an ambitious digital library project which some other Asian countries such as Japan had tried before. Effective digital library activity requires well-developed national information technology infrastructure such as well-connected fiber optic computer networks which cover the entire country, and easy availability of computers and affordable cost of network use among ordinary citizens of the country. Up to now, there has been no attempt to address the difficulties facing digital library activities in those less developed IT infrastructure-based countries which, in fact, covers much of the world. Before all of the world becomes wired to the same extent as the USA, those national digital library projects which try to provide digital documents useful for research through the Internet will face different and difficult challenges compared to their counterparts in developed nations.

DIGITAL LIBRARY AND ITS DEVELOPMENT

The definition of digital library was different according to people who were asked. For example, to some people, the term simply suggests computerization of traditional library catalogs which could be called just "electronic cataloging." To others, it calls for carrying out the functions of libraries in a new way: new approaches to acquisition and storage; new modes of interaction with patrons (Fox, et al., 1995). This new concept of libraries is made mainly possible through the development of IT, especially the Internet.

With this kind of promising technology, the U.S. government paid attention: U.S. government legislation and a number of funding initiatives were launched in 1993 with the digital library as a prominent theme. In 1994, there were numerous talks, panels, tutorials, workshops and conferences on digital libraries (Fox et al., 1995). Lunin and Fox (1993) reported that the 102nd Congress and the 103rd Congress, as well as President Clinton and Vice President Gore, had called for digital libraries to help preserve and extend the U.S.'s global competitiveness. They also called for the creation of an integrated virtual national digital library in U.S. There is a list of many excellent digital libraries already functioning well in the U.S. For example, the list includes the University of Michigan digital library project (Crum, 1995), the Illinois digital library project (Schatz, 1995), the Alexandria digital library project (Smith and Frew, 1995) and the UC Berkeley's digital library project (Wilensky, 1995). This makes sense since in the

U.S. there are already many established digital libraries and coordinating them to be a single, distributed virtual library is technically possible. But in developing countries where only a few digital libraries exist in the country, if any, the physically centralized version of the national library should be the more economical option rather than U.S.-style virtual networked national digital library.

TECHNOLOGY FOR THE DIGITAL LIBRARY

Bill Arms (Anonymous, 1997), one of the world's experts on the current state of research in digital libraries, said in an interview with the Communications of the ACM the following: "The impact of the WWW and open communication has changed our expectations. My own library is the WWW, and almost everything I want is available openly." The national IT infrastructure that supports efficient access to the Web pages with fiber-optic communication lines now opens the world of the digital library as something that an ordinary citizen can touch and feel on his/her desktop computers. In the digital information world compared to the textual world, anything can be a piece of information, including images and sounds.

For example, the growth of the Internet, especially the WWW, has prompted a boom in experimentation with full-image delivery. Schwarzwalder (1995) reports that there have been creations of image-based libraries of scientific and technical documents and that previously the communication among sci/tech people was through e-mail, listservs, and Usenet groups, but now with the Web, which allows graphical, hyper-textual documents with images and direct links, sci/tech people who want to publish something can do it with ease at the Web pages. As a result, these specialized libraries of scientific and technical documents were established on Web pages. This example shows the power of the WWW technology in creating the digital libraries in any form.

While many are interested in establishing a digital library and running it, only a few have the perspective to look at the digital library from the user's point of view. Namely, a user might not want to use the digital library because the interface is difficult to use, not because there are no interesting documents in the digital library (Fox, et al., 1993). The design of the user interface is almost as important as the copyright issue from the user's point of view. As an IS scholar, I see a digital library as an information system, and any information system can have an interface which might have the power to determine the fate of the entire system. That is the primary reason that with Web technology, the digital library has become much more popular especially with users who find the interface easier to use.

Japan's NACSIS (National Center for Science Information Systems), which is the national digital library of Japan, was established in 1986 when there was no Web technology (NACSIS, 1998). Over the years they have provided services in a very cumbersome Unix environment in which one had to telnet from one's home. Thus even in 1997, when I visited, the transition to using the WWW was only initiated, i.e., the telnet Unix system was still the common interface of the national digital library. Naturally they worried about the low subscription rate of researchers in Japan who were the target population, just as Korea's KIRC sees Korean researchers as its primary users. The more astounding fact was that the engineers at NACSIS knew that the real origin of the low subscription rate was related to the cumbersome interface and agreed that they should move into the Web-based system quickly. But the organization became bureaucratic and itself resisted sudden changes. Thus I tried to look into a better example than the Japanese model. There was another Asian country whose national digital library project was farther advanced than any others in the region. The country was Singapore which implemented the national digital library called TiARA (Timely information for All, Relevant and Affordable). This system is a multi-agency collaborative effort by the National Computer Board, the National Library Board, the National Science and Technology Board and participating libraries (TiARA, 1998). It provides users with on-line access to a network of library catalogs, local and international databases, and links to a vast range of interesting and informative Internet Web sites. In other words, this model is the one that combines the Web-based digital library and the Internet information Web sites. Thus I advised people in KRIC to utilize the top-of-the-notch Web technology in creating RISS, the digital library system which should attract people because of its ease of use.

PROBLEMS THAT FACE THE DIGITAL LIBRARY

There are many serious problems for a digital library to succeed. The most serious one is the copyright problem. Samuelson (1995) suggests that pay-per-use style of the copyright enforcement such as done in video-on-demand area cannot be implemented in the digital documents area. Instead she suggested that libraries and consumers of information products should participate in the negotiation of new legal rules and offer proposals that will enhance public access to creative works without undermining the ability of authors and publishers to be compensated for the value they have provided. In most developed countries, there are numerous digital information companies which acquire the digital copyright of the document, and sell the access right to the document to the public entities who are usually universities and public libraries. Then the libraries provide the access to those digital documents to the registered students or residents of that community. But in most developing countries, this option is too expensive. For example, a small university wants to install ABI/ INFORM and the price for the site installation is quite high (especially considering the exchange rate). Therefore the government of developing countries is naturally inclined to seek an alternative solution. A possible alternative is setting up the national digital library and making it act as the representative for all libraries in the country in negotiating the price for digital documents copyright, i.e., a national copyright. As an action researcher, I participated in countless meetings with people from the information companies and they always demanded the "site-based" payment, which means the KRIC has to pay for thousands of university libraries all by itself. The copyright issue is not resolved yet for other Asian countries' national digital libraries such as Japan's NACSIS.

Wiederhold (1995) suggests the digital library as a kind of an enterprise in the market economy, although most digital libraries are supported financially by the government. In the future, firstly, digital revenue collection will become routinely available because having free services will invariably lead to overuse, imbalances and access restriction based on allocation rules. Secondly, problems to be faced will include compliance with standards and protection of intellectual property as works. Thirdly, improved response time will be expected throughout the on-line system. His conclusion is that with responsive and economical services providing quality information, the growth of on-line information use will continue. This optimistic view is, of course, based on the market-oriented capitalism, i.e., the digital library must be a venture that should make money. However, in many countries including the U.S., the digital library is considered to be a public asset which is not interested in collecting revenue. This is especially true in East Asia. The response time will be faster not because of market competition, but because of the advancement of information technology. The standardization and copyright problems should be solved in the international arena so that all the nations should have a consensus on this matter.

SOCIAL AND USER PERSPECTIVES ON THE DIGITAL LIBRARY

Only a few studies have been done for the purpose of identifying new social and user phenomena due to the digital library. Covi and Kling (1996) show that just building a digital library would not be enough; the digital collections, storage and transmission should be useful to people who use the digital library. They show what constitutes effective digital library use; they see the digital library system as the human activity system that unites readers, authors, librarians, and researchers with electronic materials, resource streams, computer equipment and know-how.

An emergent community of research and practice whose members are involved in the social informatics of digital libraries is described in Bishop and Star (1996). They suggest that an inferior IT infrastructure cannot support the active use of the digital library. For example, poor children in a less developed country will find it extremely difficult to experience the world of digital library simply because the national IT infrastructure such as computers and networks is not there to support the use of digital libraries.

As a public asset, the digital library concept has to be examined from the social and user point of view. Namely, people have to feel the need to use a digital library rather than a physical library, which means the digital library has to be at least as good as the physical. There are three critical success factors in drawing people to the digital library. They are as follows:

CRITICAL SUCCESS FACTORS FOR THE DIGITAL LIBRARY

These findings are based on the interviews with KRIC staff and scientists who were involved in creating the digital library (RISS).

1. *Content:* Users need something to find in the digital library which may or may not be in a physical library.
2. *Interface:* The interface must be easy to use. The interface of the digital library is the librarian of the digital library, thus if the interface is easy to use and understand, people will come.
3. *Speed:* The speed is like service waiting time at the librarian's help desk in the physical library; if the digital library is fast enough, people also will come.

All these problems should be solved in order for the users to actually use the system. But as for contents, even though KRIC tried hard to get the copyright matter solved and to provide full-text articles from overseas, it is still unable to reach the agreement with overseas information sellers. Thus even with other interesting information on the Web-based digital library system, I suspected that researchers must be disappointed from the perspective of the contents, which later proved to be true in the empirical survey I conducted. Speaking of speed, when KRIC built our system, KRIC asked for the government to install fiber-optic communication cables to the KRIC. Thus theoretically there should be no speed problem, but many users complain that the system is slow and there are two reasons for that. One is that too many people tried to use a few very popular information services. The other is that Korean national IT infrastructure is still not as good as that in the U.S., i.e., people's home computers will have hard time transmitting and receiving on the Internet due to outdated telephone lines used for data communication purposes.

RISS: A NATIONWIDE, FREE-OF-CHARGE DIGITAL LIBRARY

Bureaucrats of the Ministry of Education thought that valuable resources could be wasted when they realized that many major university libraries were in the process of building digital libraries. Other national institutions such as Library of Congress and National Library of South Korea were also planning to build digital libraries. Unlike in the USA, where many entities such as universities and other institutions created their own digital libraries which are not coordinated or integrated as one giant entity, the South Korean government thought that a nationwide digital library should exist as one entity in the country. It should encompass every type of information necessary for research and its service should be free of charge to anybody who is eligible, i.e., the user must be a researcher.

Following are the objectives and roles of KRIC, the government agency which is in charge of establishing and running the digital library called RISS (KRIC, 1998)

Objectives of KRIC
- To establish a nationwide research information sharing system
- To nourish an advanced research environment through providing up-to-date research information
- To organize a nationwide research information network
- To integrate and maintain the digital libraries of Korean universities and institutions
- To save national budget by efficiently managing research information

Services of RISS
- *Union Catalog Service*
  1. Purposes
     - To develop a Union Catalog of all university libraries in Korea
     - To standardize library catalogs in order to prevent unnecessary repeated cataloging jobs of the same record
     - To provide user-friendly circulation service

  2 Contents
     - Integrated catalogs of all university libraries in Korea on WWW
     - Stable operation of Union Catalog System Service with less erratic information

- *Overseas Research Information Service*
  1. Purposes
     - To provide advanced research environment to researchers in Korea by offering up-to-date overseas research information instantly on WWW
     - To prevent Korean universities from duplicate purchasing of costly overseas research information
  2. Contents

- Abstracts and full-text information
- OCLC FirstSearch
- EBSCOhost
- OCLC ECO (Electronic Collections Online: Electronic Journals)
- Table of contents of foreign journals
- Table of contents and abstracts of foreign proceedings
- Information on newly printed foreign books

- *Journal Article Service*
  1. Purposes
     - To provide full-text information of journal articles published in Korea
  2. Contents
     - Development of a full-text service system for Korean journal articles
     - Technology development for standardization and digitalization of Korean journal articles

- *Research Support Information Service*
  1. Purposes
     - To systematically manage and provide directory and statistical information relevant to academic research
  2. Contents
     - Directory and statistical information on learned societies and research institutes attached to the universities in Korea
     - Information on full-time professors and lecturers
     - Information on domestic and foreign research institutions

- *Internet Classification Service*: provides academic Internet resources classified by Dewy Decimal Classification (DDC) scheme.

- *BBS (Bulletin Board System)*: provides a location for information exchange among users (researchers)

AN EMPIRICAL EXAMPLE: USERS OF RISS SURVEY

RISS, the South Korean government's digital library service's users were surveyed. Total number of registered users is estimated be 10,000. Only people with research needs can be a registered user. For example, university professors, graduate students, researchers at research institutes and undergraduate students with recommendation from faculty advisor can become users. The Home Website (http://www.kric.ac.kr) of KRIC is the starting place for searching information. If he/she is registered, then he/she can go ahead to explore information in RISS.

When he/she registers, KRIC requires him/her to provide a valid e-mail address and an IP address so that they can verify his/her status later. In this survey, since I was able to use the e-mail addresses of all registered users, I sent direct e-mail questionnaire through the Internet. Out of 10,013 users, 5,556 answered the questionnaires completely. Thus the size of the sample was big enough to predict the pattern of the population.

Following are the results to each question in the questionnaire.

1. What is your attitude toward user interface of RISS?
    a) Favorable 90%
    b) Unfavorable 7%
    c) Don't know 3%
- It is clear that most people like this kind of user interface which is based on the WWW and lots of graphical notations to aid the user's understanding of the particular page of the web. Our technology in applying WWW is top-notch and users agree with it.

2. What is your most frequently used service among RISS?
    a) Overseas Research Information Service 72%
    b) Union Catalog Service 13%
    c) Journal Article Service 10%
    d) Research Support Information Service 3%
    e) Internet Classification Service 1%
    f) BBS 1%
- The most important finding of this survey is this fact that most researchers in Korea want overseas information such as foreign journal articles. The reason is that Korea is still a developing country and most of the advanced research information is in English and located overseas. KRIC realizes this fact and intends to upgrade its overseas information service to a higher level by contracting with more overseas information providers and making it possible to download the full-text of foreign journal articles which KRIC cannot do currently due to copyright problems.

3. What is the most inconvenient thing while using the overseas research information service?
   a) The difficulty to get full-text of an article 95%
   b) The difficulty in using the interface 2%
   c) The slowness of the system 3%
- It is clear that people could not get the full-text of the article that they want from the service even if presumably the overseas services are claiming that they also provide full-text for free. From my experience, in most cases, one has to use one's credit card to purchase it so that it can be sent by fax or mail. This difficulty arises from the fact that KRIC did not pay for every article's copyright and does not intend to do so because of the cost.

4. Are you satisfied with RISS overall? Rate your satisfaction from 1 (very negative) to 5 (very positive).
   a) 5 - 22%
   b) 4 - 23%
   c) 3 - 35%
   d) 2 - 15%
   e) 1 - 5%
- Surprisingly high numbers of people answered that they got a positive impression of the service and quite a few users are satisfied. However this is still not a number that KRIC wants to see, i.e., it wants to see higher percentage in the "satisfied" category and no one in the "extreme negative" impression category.

OBSERVATIONS

Full-text of the foreign journal articles could be obtained by purchasing with credit cards individually, but not by the KRIC due to the copyright issue. In other words, KRIC cannot buy full-text articles from foreign journals and then provide them to Korean researchers without charge due to astronomical fees by the copyright holders; The Korean government decided that it could not afford the fee. The overseas information service companies that negotiated with KRIC demanded that they had to be paid by the "number of sites" concept rather than "number of users" concept. In other words, if KRIC intends to provide the overseas information such as a journal article to everybody in Korea, then it must charge all the sites that have the capabilities of providing KRIC's service, namely all universities and research institutions (there are more than a thousand of them). On the contrary, KRIC's position is that there are relatively few users on the system at the given time since this system is only for researchers, thus charge by the "number of users" should be applied here. I observed many fruitless negotiations between KRIC and these information companies. This issue has to be solved in order to achieve the true goal of RISS which is providing all kinds of research information for free. Here are summaries of problems at KRIC and RISS that I observed during this action research.

a) Even though the Web technology is quite state-of-the-art, there are times that the system becomes very slow probably due to large number of users logged on simultaneously. This problem can be solved by limiting the number of simultaneous users at the given time or increasing bandwidth.

b) The BBS should be more frequently used by users and the administrative staffs of KRIC since this is the only place where the user and the system people can interact. Up to now, the usage of BBS is too low probably because of lack of trust between users and KRIC staff, which comes from a cultural aspect of the Korean people, i.e., they do not become friends quickly. My suggestion is that the low usage of BBS should be investigated from the perspective of anthropology and sociology.

c) The critical problem of not being able to provide full-text articles from overseas due to copyright issue should be solved. One suggestion is that KRIC, as a part of South Korean government, can act as a national contractor to these overseas information companies. For example, for the service like FirstSearch, KRIC can pay a certain fee and obtain the right of distribution of all articles from FirstSearch to anybody in South Korea. If the South Korean government is serious about building a digital library system as a part of the national IT infrastructure, it should invest a significant amount of money to pay for a national license.

CONCLUSION

I have introduced the South Korean government's initiative in creating a national digital library as a part of building a national IT infrastructure. As I indicated earlier, since the national IT infrastructure of South Korea is not yet well developed, there are many problems in establishing a national digital library. For example, the service is provided on WWW with top-notch technology, but not many people are using the Internet due to the lack of national IT infrastructure such as fiber-optic cables to connect distant computers. Besides, even if the PCs are widely available at homes and offices, the phone billing system is out-of-date, i.e., there is no unlimited local calling in South Korea. Thus, using the Internet is not only slow but also very expensive at most places in South Korea. This is one of the reasons that only a few people registered for the service considering the significant number of potential users. In conclusion, the success of the national digital library in Korea relies on the following two factors critically:

CRITICAL SUCCESS FACTORS FOR THE NATIONAL DIGITAL LIBRARY IN KOREA

1. The national IT infrastructure should be well developed so that many more people can use the Web easily and at a faster and cheaper rate.
2. The national copyright issue should be resolved before the national digital library can really function as the benefactor to the researchers in the nation by providing free-of-charge full-text articles from overseas.

REFERENCES

Anonymous. (1997). Digital libraries present new challenges: An interview with Bill Arms. *Communications of the ACM*, 40(9) ACMemberNet Supplement)), 1-4.

Bishop, A.P. & Star, S.L. (1996). Social informatics of digital library use and infrastructure. *Journal of the American Society for Information Science*, 31(Annual Review of Information Science and Technology), 301-401.

Covi, L. & Kling, R. (1996). Organizational dimensions of effective digital library use: Closed rational and open natural systems models. *Journal of the American Society for Information Science*, 47(9), 672-689.

Crum, L. (1995). University of Michigan digital library project. *Communications of the ACM*, 38(4), 63-64.

Fox, E.A., Akscyn, R.M., Furuta, R.K., & Leggett, J.J. (1995). Digital libraries. *Communications of the ACM*, 38(4), 23-28.

Fox, E.A., Hix, D., Nowell, L.T., & Brueni, D.J. (1993). Users, user interfaces, and objects: Envision, a digital library. *Journal of the American Society for*

Information Science, 44(8), 480-491.

Jeong, K.H. & King, J.L. (1996). National Information Infrastructure Initiatives in Korea: Vision and Policy Issues. *Information Infrastructure And Policy*, 5(2), 119-133.

Jonsonn, S. (1991). Action Research, Information Systems Research: Contemporary Approaches and Emergent Traditions, Nissen, H., Klein, H.K., & Hirschheim, R.(Eds.), North-Holland, New York, NY.

Kock, N.F. (1997). The Effects of Asynchronous Groupware on Business Process Improvement, Unpublished PhD Thesis, University of Waikato, New Zealand.

Kraemer, K., Dedrick, J., Jeong, K.H., Thierry, V., West, J. & Wong, P.K. (1996). National Information Infrastructure: A Cross-Country Comparison. *Information Infrastructure And Policy*, 5(2), 81-93.

KRIC(Korea Research Information Center). (1998). *http://www.kric.ac.kr*.

Lunin, L.F. & Fox, E.A. (1993). Perspectives on digital libraries: Introduction and Overview. *Journal of the American Society for Information Science*, 44(8), 440-445.

NACSIS(National Center for Science Information Systems). (1998). *http://www.nacsis.ac.jp*.

Samuelson, P. (1995). Copyright and digital libraries. *Communications of the ACM*, 38(4), 15-35.

Schatz, B. (1995). Building the interspace: The Illinois digital library project. *Communications of the ACM*, 38(4), 62-63.

Schwarzwalder, R. (1995). The sci/tech image invasion: Approaches to managing the digital library. *Database Magazine*, (18), 81-84.

Smith, T.R. & Frew, J. (1995). Alexandria Digital Library. *Communications of the ACM*, 38(4), 61-62.

Susman, G.I. & Evered, R.D. (1978). An Assessment of the Scientific Merits of Action Research. *Administrative Science Quarterly*, (23), 582-603.

TiARA(Timely information for All, Relevant and Affordable). (1998). *http://www.digilib.org.sg*.

Wiederhold, G. (1995). Digital libraries, values, and productivity. *Communications of the ACM*, 38(4), 85-96.

Wilensky, R. (1995). UC Berkeley's digital library project. *Communications of the ACM*, 38(4), 60.

Chapter VI

Trends in Web-Based Services in Academic Libraries

Lynn M. Fountain
Russell Public Library, USA

Change is afoot in the academic library world. The World Wide Web has expanded the types of services academic librarians are able to provide their patrons. We can now offer Web-based electronic databases, WebPACS, electronic journals, electronic reserve systems with Web-interfaces and a wide range of specialized digital library collections. Our patrons now have access to a huge variety of information, and they no longer have to leave their offices or homes to obtain it. Future developments include improved information retrieval algorithms, chic user-interfaces, advanced network services and virtual libraries created to serve the growing population of distance and online learners. Academic librarians face a world of exploding digital resources and their assistance in organizing this chaotic web of information is vital.

INTRODUCTION

In 1990, Tim Berners-Lee, a scientist working at the European Particle Physics Lab (CERN), developed a hypertext system—the World Wide Web (WWW)—that allowed more efficient access to the information available on the Internet. Although CERN released the WWW technology in 1992, scientists and engineers remained the primary users and little changed for the general public. Then, in 1993, a graduate student named Marc Andreessen released his creation—an innovative, easy to use Web-browser called Mosaic—and a revolutionary new way of navigating the Web was born. Within two years a newer version of his Web-browser, called Netscape, hit the market and the world hasn't been the same since. In just five years the number of Web sites has grown from approximately 150 to well over 650,000.[1] Today, the number of people connected to the Internet is estimated to be over 40 million.[2]

By the mid-1990s, academic librarians were just beginning to feel comfortable with networked computers, CD-ROMs and a text-based Internet. The majority of electronic databases available to patrons were accessed via stand-alone CD-ROM stations. Electronic journals were rare and not peer-reviewed, and therefore not to be taken seriously. Browsing the Internet meant becoming familiar with unfriendly UNIX commands and terms like gopher, Archie, and FTP. Contact with patrons via the Internet, and Internet-based services, were practically non-existent.

Then, seemingly overnight, everything began to change with the wide acceptance of the World Wide Web and the proliferation of Internet Services Providers (ISPs) ready to provide easy access to the Internet. Suddenly there was instantaneous, global access to a wealth of information. Even slow to move organizations like academic libraries could not help being swept up in the energy of this global information revolution.

Everyone now realizes that the Internet, in whatever future form it may take, is here to stay. As a result, academic libraries are now turning their energies toward offering patrons a slew of innovative ways to access information. This chapter will discuss current trends in Web-based services in small, academic libraries. I do not intend to cover all Web-based services being offered in academic libraries across this country. The trends I mention will be based specifically on services provided at Santa Clara University (SCU), a small, Jesuit university located in the heart of Silicon Valley, in Santa Clara, California. This chapter will also attempt to make some projections about future trends. Where will small, academic libraries be four to five years from now? How will we have improved services to our patrons? Will the Web drastically alter how we provide information? What new tools will be available to us?

CURRENT TRENDS

The Great Migration

Electronic databases are on the move. A couple of years ago the majority of electronic databases and indexes were being released by publishers in CD-ROM format. The mid-1990s saw the arrival of CD-ROM drives as the exciting, new storage medium for PCs. An entire index that would span several volumes in hard copy could be reproduced on a single CD-ROM. Not only was this format less expensive for the publishers to produce, but they could also provide customized, user-friendly search engines such as Folio Views and the SilverPlatter Information Retrieval System (SPIRS) to assist the end-users in locating information within the database. Once the publishers accepted and began pushing this new technology, libraries had little choice but to provide the equipment needed to handle this new format. Computer savvy patrons quickly jumped on the band-wagon.

Stand-alone PCs worked for awhile, but then the lines of patrons waiting to use the electronic databases and indexes began to grow. Librarians soon resorted to sign-up sheets, but this did little to alleviate the real problem. However, libraries could not afford to purchase enough PCs to satisfy the demand, nor did they have the space available to house that many computers.

The solution arrived in the form of local area networks (LANs) and CD-ROM towers. As LANs became more prevalent in academic libraries, it became possible to attach towers to the network allowing access to a single electronic database from multiple PCs (dependent on your licensing agreements of course). Libraries could now provide access to the electronic databases from any networked, public access PC in the library. So if 10 students from a mechanical engineering class showed up at the library at the same time, all wanting to search Ei Compendex, all the students could be accommodated providing the library had 10 available PCs. This was a huge improvement over the stand-alone PC method. The drawback was remote access to these electronic resources was still not a viable option for most small, academic libraries. Most libraries were unwilling, for security reasons, to provide remote access to their LANs.

CD-ROM towers are still in use in many academic libraries. But the publishers are now in pursuit of a new format. Publishers, observing the growing popularity of the Web, have realized there is an easier, less expensive way to provide access to the information they control. Why not publish the information on an in-house Web server and provide Internet access to the resource, instead of updating and distributing new CDs every quarter? Publishers, knowing that most academic libraries are providing Internet-accessible PCs for their faculty and students, also know that Web-based resources are a "sellable" option.

Now, just four years after introducing CD-ROM products to their customers, many of the major electronic resource publishers are providing Web access to their products. Many of them are no longer updating their CD-ROM products. Popular electronic resources such as Infotrac, Business Newsbank, Global Newsbank, Ei Compendex, Medline and National Newspaper Index are now all available as Web-based resources. Huge electronic databases that were once only available via remote dial-up, such as Lexis-Nexis and Westlaw, are now available on the Web.

From the patron's perspective, the greatest benefit to new Web-based resources is remote patron access. Remote access is accomplished in one of two ways. A library can provide their IP range to the publisher. The publisher then authenticates the patron logging into the resource by comparing the patron's IP address with the list of "approved" IP addresses in their database. Alternatively, the patron can be prompted to enter a password, usually the patron's barcode on their student ID card, and the password is checked against a list of valid patron IDs stored in a designated server. In either case, the authentication process is handled in a matter of seconds by a remote server and access to the electronic resource is either allowed or denied.

The benefit to patrons is that they no longer need to be in the library, or even on campus, to access an electronic database. The benefit to the libraries is that staff no longer needs to worry about all the nightmares associated with managing a networked CD-ROM tower.

WebPACS

Another current trend has been the adoption of WebPACs by academic libraries. The late 1980s and early 1990s witnessed a huge movement from manual catalogs to integrated library systems (ILSs). These complex integrated systems were developed at a time when DOS still reigned in the PC world and graphical interfaces were known only to Mac users. The OPACs were character-based and accessed via "dedicated" terminals.

These systems served the libraries and their patrons well throughout most of the 1990s, but change is the only constant in the information industry. In the mid-90s, the graphical user interface, or GUI as it is popularly known, became the accepted interface for the PC world with the infiltration of Microsoft Windows. Libraries slowly became populated by Pentiums running Windows 95, Windows 98 or Windows NT.

The ILS companies, in tune to changes in the market, are now working on next-generation systems. Many have already released WebPAC modules. At Santa Clara University, we deployed the WebPAC from Innovative Interfaces, Inc. in September, 1998. Although we had offered our patrons telnet access to the character-based OPAC for several years, we could now offer an interface with which most of our patrons felt more comfortable. Usage statistics illustrate the popularity of this interface. Despite the relative newness of this technology on campus, WebPAC searches already constitute approximately 40% of all searches done on the OPAC (Fred Gertler, Head of Electronic Services, Orradre Library, personal communication, March 9, 1999). Given that our students arrive at college comfortable with a GUI environment, and with the Web environment, it is only natural that they migrate to the newer interface.

There are additional benefits to the WebPAC. A new MARC tag was created to take advantage of the hypertext nature inherent in the Web. Catalogers can insert an 856 field into a bibliographic record providing a link to a relevant Web page. Librarians can use this new feature to catalog any Web page, or Web site, they deem useful to their patrons. It can also be used to point to an electronic version of an item the library already has in print format. For instance, many of the Law Reviews we have on our shelves in print format are now also available, free of charge, on the Web. By merely adding a single MARC tag, we have increased access to needed resources.

Most WebPACs also allow flexibility in the design and layout of the initial page. The initial page on Santa Clara University's WebPAC (http://oscar.scu.edu) offers several features not available from the traditional OPAC—a link to "more Web resources" and a link to "Orradre electronic journals" (Orradre is the main library on campus). Both of these additional features provide the patron with greater access to needed resources. In many cases, patrons now have access to full-text articles. They also, in some instances, have access to information that is more up-to-date than the information contained in print sources.

Electronic Reserve Software

Librarians are constantly striving to improve the means through which they provide information. Reserve rooms have been an integral part of academic libraries for years. They house an odd assortment of high-demand items—course syllabi, outlines, old exams, photocopied articles, etc. Usually these items are not allowed to circulate for more than a couple of hours and seldom are allowed to leave the building. Reserve materials are a nightmare both for the circulation staff trying to regulate use, and for the frustrated student who is unable to check out material when needed because someone else already has it.

Enter electronic reserve software! Using a Web-based front end, students can now locate reserve material by professor or course name, click on the desired item, and read a full-text copy of the item online. They can save the item to their disk bring it up in their favorite word-processor and annotate it or they can print out a hard copy if they prefer. Students no longer need to be in the library to use reserve materials. They no longer have to sprint to the reserve room in an attempt to beat all of their fellow classmates to the material.

From the library staff's perspective, reserve materials have become easier to manage. At the Law Library at Santa Clara University we are using a software called ERes (http://heaferes.scu.edu). The software was the brainchild of SCU physics professor, Dr. Philip Kesten. The ERes software is made and distributed by Docutek Information Systems, a company founded by Dr. Kesten. It is available for both UNIX/Linux and Microsoft NT platforms, so it fits easily into the network infrastructure of most academic libraries. To date, over 60 colleges and universities are using ERes as their electronic reserve system.[3]

We have found the system tremendously easy to use and customize. Unlike the majority of the 60 or so sites using ERes, the system was not centrally administered by the library when it was first introduced on campus by Dr. Kesten. The system is so user-friendly that faculty began using it on their own. It was a simple matter to have an account setup for their class, and then to upload documents they had already saved in either text, Word, WordPerfect or PDF format to the ERes server. They also had the option of limiting access to that particular class by password if they so desired. Within a year of being introduced onto campus, almost all of the departments were represented on ERes.

Faculty in the Law School were also showing increased interest in using ERes. The number of classes being listed under the heading of Law was growing. In lieu of purchasing Innovative's more expensive electronic reserve system, the Law Library decided to purchase its own copy of ERes and separate the Law School from the rest of the University. We did so to enable us to customize the software in a way that would benefit the Law School community.

Our idea was to turn ERes into an intranet of sorts for the Law School and Law Library. Not only could we provide better management of the materials being added to electronic reserves, but we could also create accounts for each of the administrative departments in the Law School and Library. Staff would be able to put policies, procedures, manuals, memos, etc. onto ERes providing easy, centralized access for everyone. Sensitive material could be secured with a password, allowing access only to a select group.

Just as important as the ease of access ERes provided is the ease of use. The Web interface is familiar to all faculty, staff and students. Anyone with a networked PC on campus, or a PC with an Internet connection at home, can log into ERes anytime of day or night. The Library can now manage the system: creating a consistent look, creating "accounts" for every class at the beginning of each semester to save the faculty from having to do so and keeping the system cleared of out-dated material. Training sessions were provided for any interested faculty and staff members at the beginning of the last semester, and will continue to be provided before each semester as long as the demand exists.

ERes has allowed our library staff to take advantage of two growing phenomena—the World Wide Web and intranets. In doing so, we are providing better service to our patrons.

What's Your URL?

The most obvious way academic librarians have made use of the Web is by creating their own library Web pages. There is probably not an academic library out there without its own web page or site. Web pages can be used to house all sorts of useful information for patrons. On many campuses library staff not only create the library's Web pages, but design and maintain the entire college or university site.

Many academic libraries, including SCU's Law Library, use their Web page to consolidate electronic sources into one, easy-to-find location. Patrons can find links to search engines, general reference sources, specialized collections and Web-based databases and indexes. Our library page includes links to general legal sites, courts, and to sites specializing in international law, intellectual property and elder law. We also provide links to full-text, electronic legal journals. Web pages are also a great way to provide useful information such as library hours, library policies, important announcements and even lists of new books. Most libraries also include a link to their WebPACs, and to their electronic reserve system (if they have one).

Mailing lists and chat rooms are yet another way libraries can serve their patrons. Why not provide an "ask a reference librarian" link on the library Web page? This allows reference staff to provide services to patrons who are unable to make it to campus. Mailing lists are less interactive and immediate, but will allow a student who is working on research at 2:30am to fire off a question while it's fresh in her mind. Chat groups allow for scheduled, real-time interactions between reference librarians and their patrons. Both of these tools are a huge advantage to commuting and part-time, evenings students.

Many academic libraries are also making use of the Web to provide access to local, specialized collections through digitization. This is giving students and researchers, who may not have the time or the funds to travel to that particular library, the opportunity to access a special collection from their office or home. It also gives the libraries the opportunity to create user-friendly search engines for material that may have been more difficult to access in paper format.

On a large scale, there are still many issues and problems with the move toward digital libraries. Interoperability, copyright and fair use issues, friendly user-interfaces and helpful search engines all come to mind. Can we even agree on a working definition for digital libraries? The Digital Library Federation defines a digital library as an organization that provides the resources, "including the specialized staff, to select, structure, offer intellectual access to, interpret, distribute, preserve the integrity of and ensure the persistence over time of collections of digital works so that they are readily and economically available for use by a defined community or set of communities."[4] This is a comprehensive definition to be sure.

Problems aside, digitizing specialized collections and providing access to those collections via the Web has been an invaluable boon to researchers and students. Human rights experts living in Australia now have immediate access to Project Diana, the Schell Center for International Human Rights at Yale Law School's human rights archive (check out http://diana.law.yale.edu/). Priceless manuscripts from the Vatican, rare diaries, historical documents and religious texts are all available on the Web now thanks to teams of dedicated library staff, webmasters and system administrators. For a list of just a handful of digital library sites, check out the WWW Virtual Library at http://www.indiana.edu/~vlib/digital.html

The possibilities for improving access to useful information for our patrons have barely been tapped. The Web has opened up many avenues, but it has also created its share of pot holes and road blocks. There is a seemingly infinite amount of data "out there," but we have barely begun to explore how we are going to organize, weed, maintain and simply *find* the information we need. For each technical breakthrough involving the Web and the Internet, we leave a host of technical, social and organizational issues in its wake. The remainder of this chapter will look at some of those lingering issues and at some possible solutions.

FUTURE TRENDS

Why Can't I Find Anything?

Certainly from a librarian's point of view, one glaring problem with the Web is its chaotic nature. The Web is the repository for an amazingly diverse assortment of information—everything from full-text books and articles, scientific papers, video and audio clips to the threads of Usenet groups. It is also a random collection of data with no discernible organization. The search engines that exist today are of minimal use to the average end-user. For every search engine that exists, there are an equal number of retrieval algorithms employed. Most information specialists can't even keep them straight. How can we expect our patrons to do so? Do we send them to a Web directory, a search engine, a metasearch site? Why should they even be expected to know the difference? Who's there to help when a patron does a search on media and the law and pulls up 450,000 hits?

Fortunately search and retrieval issues have been receiving a lot of attention in the computer and information science fields. There is a wide range of work under way in the area of retrieval (precision versus recall), as well as in the area of user interfaces. Some of this research is being done as part of the "Digital Libraries Initiative" project funded by National Science Foundation, the Department of Defense Advanced Research Projects Agency and the National Aeronautics and Space Administration (http://www.cise.nsf.gov/iis/dli_home.html). Six universities were selected to participate: the University of Michigan, University of Illinois at Urbana, UC Berkeley, Stanford, Carnegie Mellon and UC Santa Barbara. These six universities, in conjunction with a host of other universities and research organizations such as Xerox Parc, are seeking to improve search and retrieval techniques, speech and image recognition, natural language querying, search result presentation and interoperability between heterogeneous systems.

With the exponential growth of the Web, we need to change our focus from simply locating information to locating the most relevant information in an efficient and cost-effective manner. Some researchers feel more sophisticated retrieval algorithms are the answer. Others feel the answers lie in more intuitive, flexible user interfaces.

While I can't possibly mention, even briefly, all the various research groups in this country seeking answers to these issues, I will mention a couple of the more well-publicized ones. Probably some of the hottest work being done right now is in the area of software agents. Agents are small programs that do electronic tasks for the end-user and that can, theoretically, learn from observing and compiling data on the user's habits. Software agents, know-bots, filtering agents, intelligent agents, whatever name you choose to call them, are all the rage. While the concept of smart agents has been around for years in the world of artificial intelligence, no one had ever succeeded in creating a usable agent, let alone marketing one.[5] Now, thanks in part to some pioneering work completed by Pattie Maes and the Software Agents Group in MIT's Media Lab, agents have found their way onto the Web and into the corporate marketplace.

Firefly, AgentSoft, Excite, General Magic and Open Sesame are all companies that have developed some type of software agent. MIT and the Robotics Institute at Carnegie Mellon both have numerous agent projects in process. Some, such as Carnegie Mellon's Webmate, act as personal digital assistants. By accompanying the user as she browses the Web, the agent can provide URL recommendations based on a continually updated user profile, respond to user feedback by selecting features from documents the user found relevant and incorporating these features into new queries, and compile a daily list of new links of interest to the user.[6] Others, like MIT's Let's Browse, act as collaborative Web agents assisting groups of people with common interests to find new material.

But what about user interfaces? Is this where the real answer lies? Some researchers believe so. In her article "Interfaces for Searching the Web," Marti Hearst, a researcher at Xerox Palo Alto Research Center (PARC), describes a new interface she and her colleagues have created called the Information Visualizer.[7] The software draws an animated 3D wheel that links each category with its subcategories. Categories are placed in a branching structure that allows the user to see multiple categories simultaneously. By clicking on one of the labels that appears farther away, it rotates the selected category to the forefront and shows all the sub-categories attached to it.

For instance if a patron searches Yahoo for "multimedia," all the areas where this topic resides in Yahoo's directory structure will appear as subcategories on the wheel. In this instance, the patron may see Computers and Internet, Education and Entertainment appear as relevant subcategories. The patron can then select whichever path seems most relevant and follow those links until she hits a dead-end. The other subcategories are still visible on the screen and are only a click away. Using the traditional Yahoo interface, the patron would have to select one of the three subcategories and follow those links until she hit a dead-end. She would then be "buried" within that subcategory and would have to back out to Yahoo's main page to select one of the other two categories. Visit the PARC site at http://www.parc.xerox.com/istl/projects/uir/projects/InformationVisualization.html to see an image of the Visualizer.

Regardless of whether the best solution to the problem is improved information retrieval software or an improved user interface, part of the answer lies in combining the computer scientist's ability to create, manipulate and automate large databases with the librarian's ability to organize, categorize and locate relevant information. This collaboration has been occurring at universities with both strong Computer

Science and Library and Information Science departments, but academic librarians need to push to become more involved at all levels with this crucially important research.

The World Wide Wait: Is Internet2 the Answer?

So we end up with better information retrieval mechanisms and chic user interfaces—for what? So we can have our patrons waiting for what seems like forever for the information to form on their screen? Will all the information on the Web become useless as people grow tired of waiting to access it? Not if the University Corporation for Advanced Internet Development (UCAID) has their way.

UCAID's project, Internet2, is a collaborative effort of over 130 U.S. universities to develop advanced internet technology and applications.[8] While Internet2 will not replace the current Internet, its goal is to enhance the current infrastructure. Working with the other government and industry initiatives, the Internet2 project is helping to develop technologies such as multicasting (used in teleconferencing and videoconferencing) and Quality-of-Service. Internet2 universities are also busy establishing gigaPoPs (Gigabit per second Points of Presence) that provide regional connectivity among universities and other organizations. Through the gigaPoPs, universities will connect to the federally sponsored Next Generation Initiative (NGI) networks and other advanced Federal networks, including the National Science Foundation's very high performance Backbone Network Service (vBNS), NASA's Research and Education Network (NREN), Department of Defense's Defense Research and Education Network (DREN) and the Department of Energy's Energy Sciences network (ESnet). Internet2 will help ensure that universities and colleges are provided with the advanced network services essential for their research and education missions—missions in which academic libraries play a central role.

Online U.

Better search algorithms, improved user interfaces, digital libraries and increased bandwidth are all going to be of crucial importance in the design of tomorrow's virtual libraries. Although I do not believe libraries as physical structures are going to disappear from our traditional campuses, they are going to be of little use to the growing population of distance and online learners.

A quick search on the Web for distance education or online universities yields a wide assortment of hits. Everything from certificate programs to accredited MBA programs are now offered online. Some are still a mix of videoconferencing and email exchanges. Others, such as University of Phoenix's Online Campus offerings, are a combination of interactive chat-room and e-mail exchanges between students and the instructors.

The numbers are telling: University of Phoenix enrolls roughly 4,000 students in its online campus, UC Berkeley Extension estimates 1,300 students are taking courses via America Online and they hope to have 5,000 by the end of next year, and at Golden Gate University in San Francisco, 600 students are taking courses through the University's CyberCampus.[9] Many of the accredited virtual degree programs are on the West Coast. Two competing virtual universities already exist in the West—California Virtual University (CVU) begun by California Governor Pete Wilson, and Western Governor's University (WGU), a consortium of 17 states and Guam. However, in contrast to WGU, CVU is not a university in and of itself. It does not offer online courses. It is a Web-based catalog of online courses offered at 89 accredited schools throughout the state (http://www.california.edu).

Some universities already provide virtual libraries for their students. As online courses proliferate, electronic access to a variety of reference sources will become crucial. Up until now, special libraries have been the ones concerned with providing increased electronic access for their patrons. But now the academic library paradigm must change. Focus needs to move from the physical collection and storage of huge amounts of paper-based information to easy *access* to all forms of information—increasingly this format will be electronic.

Much of what a virtual library offers is already available to most academic library patrons. An increasing number of electronic resources in the form of Web-based databases, digitized special collections, full-text of thousands of electronic journals, useful links organized by subject on library Web pages and online catalogs with Web interfaces are already accessible. Also available are automated ILL systems. Patrons are able to request an ILL using the OPAC or WebPAC. The next step will be to provide an electronic copy of the information to the patron via e-mail rather than having to ship a paper copy. Fees, if applicable, can be charged to a student account maintained by the library.

CONCLUSION

What does all this really mean for the academic library community? Contrary to what many believe, I do not think this transition to a Web-based universe will bring down the curtain on our profession. Quite the opposite. We are in the best possible position to assist in ushering in a world of improved access for both faculty and students. In the not too distant past, only the most well-endowed research universities could afford to provide access to millions of resources because only they could afford to purchase, process and store such huge physical collections of materials. Now any library, no matter how small or how paltry their materials budget, can afford to provide access to immense amounts of information.

Granted not all of the information currently on the Web is worth accessing. But the trend is toward more digital information, not less. Countless projects are already in progress digitizing materials that are no longer protected under copyright. Publishers are already producing much of the current information in electronic form. This trend will have a positive effect on academic libraries globally, not just within the United States. Researchers, students, patrons of any type, will have access to information from all parts of the world.

So far much of the information on the Web is still free. This may change. Complicated issues such as copyright and other intellectual property issues still need to be resolved. How are publishers going to track who accesses or downloads their publications? How will authors be compensated? How do we afford to digitize all the material that currently exists in paper if we don't charge people to access that material once it is online?

As this chapter discussed, there are still many unresolved issues surrounding the Web and its role in information access in academic libraries. There are also a tremendous number of exciting projects in the works. Our skills as academic librarians are needed now more than ever. We need to become involved at the grass-roots level in finding solutions to many of these problems. We need to take proactive roles within our colleges and universities, pushing for new technology, staff training in technology and reminding the administration that access to information, regardless of where the information resides, is the key.

ENDNOTES

[1] Grey, Matthew. (1996). Web growth summary. [WWW document]. URL http://www.mit.edu/people/mkgray/net/web-growth-summary.html

[2] Zakon, Robert H. (1993-1999). Hobbe's Internet Timeline. [WWW document] URL http://info.isoc.org/guest/zakon/Internet/History/HIT.html#1990s

[3] Docutek Information System. (1999, February). ERes update. [WWW document]. URL http://www.docutek.com

[4] Council on Library and Information Resources. (1998). Digital Library Federation: A working definition of digital library. [WWW document]. URL http://www.clir.org/diglib/dldefinition.htm

[5] Holloway, Marguerite. (1997, December). [Article on MIT professor Pattie Maes]. *Wired*, 237-239, 290-293.

[6] Chen, L., and Sycara, K. (1998). Webmate: A personal agent for browsing and searching. [WWW document]. URL http://www.cs.smu.edu/~softagents/webmate.html

[7] Hearst, Marti. (1997, March). Interfaces for searching the Web. *Scientific American*, 68-72.

[8] Internet2: Frequently asked questions. [WWW document]. URL http://www.internet2.edu/html/faqs.html

[9] Burdman, Pamela. (1998, July). Classrooms without walls: More students are taking college courses online. *The San Francisco Chronicle*. [WWW document]. URL http://www.sfgate.com/cgi-bin/article.cgi?file=/chronicle/archive/1998/07/20/MN87525.DTL

Chapter VII

Impact of the Internet on Malaysian Libraries

Diljit Singh
University of Malaya, Malaysia

INTRODUCTION

The Internet plays a significant role in Malaysian libraries and information centers today. From a humble beginning where computers were a luxury that only the very large libraries could afford, the Internet is increasingly being incorporated into the daily routine of librarians and is being used to provide services that were not possible in the pre-Internet days. Today, Internet services are no longer luxuries, but are being used in management, communication, information access and retrieval, document delivery and personal development by librarians and patrons.

The Internet began in Malaysia in the early 1980s as *Telita*, a two-way commercial tele-text system primarily to exchange e-mail. At about the same time, computer hobbyists started creating local bulletin boards. Through these bulletin boards users could send e-mail worldwide and download freeware and shareware through FIDONet, a global network of bulletin boards. The first Malaysian network connected to the Internet was set up in 1983 from the University of Malaya's Faculty of Engineering. In 1986, a Malaysian computer network (*Rangkaian Komputer Malaysia* or RangKoM) was established linking the main universities in the country. This network offered e-mail facilities and access to the USENET newsgroup. However, it was expensive to use since connections were through dial-up lines to gateway countries. On January 24, 1990, a Joint Advanced Research Integrated Network (JARING) was launched to optimize the use of data communications, which became the base for Internet services in the country. In 1992, the Malaysian Institute of Microelectronic Systems (MIMOS), which was the only Internet Service Provider in the country at that time, obtained a 64Kbps leased line to the United States, thus marking the beginning of the real Internet connections (Wong, 1998).

Since then, the use of the Internet has increased by leaps and bounds. With an estimated 10% of the Malaysian population having access to the Internet at the end of 1998, the popularity is evident in the number of seminars and conferences, exhibitions, publications, cybercafes and from conversations among the ordinary person-on-the-street. Malaysia's aim of attaining a developed nation status by the year 2020 (commonly referred to as Vision 2020) is expected to further enhance the use of Internet. Furthermore, the commitment of the government towards setting up the Multimedia Super Corridor (MSC), a 15km by 50km corridor as a multimedia testbed incorporating electronic government, a national 'smart' card and world-wide manufacturing webs, is expected to be a further boost for the Internet in the country.

The use of the Internet among Malaysian libraries took off in 1994, when the National Library introduced the *Jaringan Ilmu* (Knowledge Network) project to link libraries using the Internet as a platform. Under this project, the National Library, all 14 state public libraries and 35 special libraries in federal government ministries and departments were provided with computers linked to MIMOS. By early 1995, a few libraries had started developing their own Web sites, and in early 1996, it was estimated that about 60 libraries had set up their own Web sites (Mohamad & Fadzil, 1996). Today, it is estimated that more than 500 libraries have access to the Internet. This number may appear to be small for a country with approximately 10,669 libraries (Singh, 1998a), but considering the large number of school libraries in rural areas which only have basic infrastructure, this figure is commendable. A quick search of the Internet also shows that approximately 100 libraries have their own Web sites that are easily located by the major search engines, with an unknown number having their Web site on free Web hosting services.

This chapter describes the use of the Internet by Malaysian libraries and information centers, and looks at the impact of this usage. The chapter represents a synthesis of ideas gained from the author's observations, and from conversations and interviews with librarians in and around Kuala Lumpur. In sharing the experiences of Malaysian libraries, this chapter hopes to provide a developing country perspective on the role of Internet, the impact on libraries and some of the challenges faced. The ideas and views presented here are by no means comprehensive, but represent a sample of the issues faced by Malaysian libraries that may also apply to other developing countries.

THE USE OF INTERNET IN MALAYSIAN LIBRARIES

The need to access and use information in this competitive world, the influence of developed countries, the demands of patrons and the networked nature of libraries are some of the factors that have resulted in many Malaysian libraries using the Internet. An increasing number of libraries and information centers are getting connected to the vast electronic resources, and have benefited from the access, organization, storage and publishing opportunities provided by the Internet.

While no precise statistics could be located on the number of libraries that use the Internet, a 1997 survey among Malaysian librarians indicated that 90% of them use the Internet, primarily from their place of work (Singh, 1998b).

Conversations with long-established users suggest that in the early days, librarians used the primarily text-based Internet to:

- communicate with colleagues, academics and researchers on the availability of resources through e-mail;
- access academic institution sites overseas through gopher;
- search foreign library online public access catalogs (OPACs) through telnet;
- download files, software programs, documents and directories through file transfers (ftp); and
- enhance their current awareness by subscribing to the limited newsgroups available.

The above survey also suggests that librarians today use the Internet for basically the same purposes but on a wider scale. Some of the specific uses mentioned in the survey included:

- corresponding through e-mail, primarily with overseas colleagues, and answering queries from patrons, sending out notices and minutes of meeting, communicating with publishers, interlibrary loan and document delivery matters. Other uses included tracing local newspapers in foreign countries and arranging schedules for overseas visits;

- retrieving information, checking cataloging data from other library catalogs, seeking answers to reference queries and keeping current with developments through the World Wide Web (WWW). Other uses included evaluating Web sites for linkage to the library's own site, searching materials for inclusion in library's own newsletter and evaluating electronic journals;
- keeping abreast with current developments in the field and seeking information on common problems faced through newsgroups;
- connecting to remote computer resources, exploring other library catalogs, and accessing database services through telnet services;
- obtaining software programs through file transfers for use within the library, and obtaining text, image or sound files for their work, e.g. in developing their own Web sites.

However, conversations and observations suggest that the Internet has allowed libraries to expand their programs and services as well as initiate new services and programs. In many cases, the Internet has been integrated into promotion and marketing, public services, technical services and research activities. Some of the more prominent examples of Internet use include:

- *Library promotion*: Almost all Malaysian libraries that have Web sites provide general information on location opening hours, library rules and the services provided. This helps to reach a wider section of the population at low cost, something which was not possible in the pre-Internet days.
- *Current awareness*: Many libraries use the Internet and intranets to provide selective dissemination of information and current awareness services to their users. The Universiti Multimedia Telekom Library (*http://library.unitele.edu.my/*) provides awareness on current news, business and information technology matters to all users. Similarly, the Malaysian Securities Commission Information Resource Center (*http://sc.com.my/html/information/ f_inform.html*) provides Current Contents and SDI services to its

members through its Intranet services.

- *Public Services*: In addition to providing reference services through e-mail, users are able to renew books, request for consideration to purchase and request for interlibrary loans through the Net. Such services are available at the Universiti Multimedia Telekom Library, the University of Malaya Library (*http://www.umlib.um.edu.my/*), and the Universiti Utara Malaysia Library (*http://www.uum.edu.my/*). The Perak State Public Library (*http://spl.pnm.my/~perak/*) allows registered users to e-mail their requests for loans, and books are then sent to them by regular mail.

- *Announcements*: The National Library of Malaysia's opening page (*http://www.pnm.my/*) maintains a section on announcements from the library. The Sabah State Library (*http://www.sbh.lib.edu.my/*) has a Special Features of the Month link to current happenings.

- *Subject Libraries*: As a result of access to a wider range of resources, libraries are able to compile bibliographies on specialized subject areas, thus making them available to a wider audience. For example, the University of Malaya Library maintains a Malay Studies Web site (*http://lontarweb.umlib.um.edu.my*) which contains an on-line bibliography, directory of expertise and Internet resources. The Science University of Malaysia (USM) Library (*http://www.lib.usm.my/*) identifies Internet resources and creates virtual subject libraries (VSL) in subject areas relevant to the teaching and research at the university.

- *Virtual Libraries*: The UNITAR Virtual Library (*http://vlib.unitarklj1.edu.my/*) is a rare set-up for a university library, as its contents and services were designed and planned from the beginning to be in the virtual mode. Furthermore, there was no physical library to start with. Using available technologies and incorporating as much as possible of its contents in digital format, it aims to provide library and information services to its users anywhere, anytime and in many forms mainly through the Net.

- *User Education*: Some academic libraries also place their course materials on the Net. For example, the Putra University of Malaysia Library makes available its Information Literacy course (*http://lib.upm.edu.my/pg291.html*) in this manner. The Science University of Malaysia also keeps a set of past examination papers in electronic format at its web site.

The use of the Internet is not confined to any particular type of library, for all libraries use it based on their needs and priorities.

The National Library of Malaysia has always been at the forefront in the use of the Internet. In addition to providing information on its resources and services, the library offers access to users, conducts seminars and workshops for librarians. The National Library generally acts as a catalyst for the development of other libraries by providing leadership, material assistance and serving as a model to follow.

Academic libraries are perhaps the most prominent Malaysian libraries on the Internet. Almost all university libraries have their own Web site, as do many of the established colleges. Those that do not have a Web site of their own, have at least a page on their parent institution Web site. Based on their content, visual appeal and currency, the academic library sites are among the better developed ones compared to other libraries.

Public libraries may have been slow to integrate the Internet into their services due to financial and human resource constraints, but many of them do provide browsing facilities for patrons. In some cases, such as at the Kedah State Public Library (*http://kdh.lib.edu.my*), there is such a heavy demand on the terminals that users are limited to only one hour of use. At the British Council Library (*http://www.britcoun.org.my/*) in Kuala Lumpur, usage is also heavy as students use it for information searching and communication with their professors in Britain.

Special libraries, partly as a result of strong support from their parent organizations, have been strong users of the Internet. The Forest Research Institute of Malaysia Library (*http://library.frim.gov.my*) for example, provides concise information on its services and collections thus enabling patrons to know in advance if their needs are likely to be met.

School libraries have perhaps been slow at adopting the Internet due to the high costs, but this is changing. With the launching of the Smart Schools project in 1999 by the Ministry of Education, electronic resources are being integrated into the teaching and learning process, and information literacy is being incorporated into the curriculum. Some schools' libraries have been using the Internet for instructional purposes for a number of years. In 1996 and early 1997 when the country was enveloped by a haze from forest fires in a neighboring country, teachers at the International School Kuala Lumpur (*http://www.iskl.edu.my/*) used the Internet to their advantage. The school set up its first Web page then, and placed their lessons and worksheets on the Internet for students to access from their homes (which in some cases were in another country).

As a developing country, Malaysia depends on access to information from the outside. For a long time, more information flowed into the country than out of it. Now, with the publishing opportunities provided by the Internet, Malaysian libraries are also becoming producers of information. A number of local databases, such as AGRIMAL (on Malaysian agriculture), PALMOLIS (on palm oil) and SIRIMLINK (Malaysian standards) are becoming available to subscribers through the Internet. For example, PALMOLIS is of immense value to those seeking information on palm oil, as they are able to tap into the knowledge base of one of the world's largest palm oil producing countries.

It is interesting to note that most of the Malaysian library Web sites have been developed in-house by librarians. Only in a few cases has the development of the Web site been contracted out. Librarians who developed the sites were in many cases already involved with library automation, and picked up the additional Web-development skills either through self-study or local in-service courses. For this reason, the cost of developing library Web sites has been kept low. The basic costs included that of acquiring the necessary hardware, and the librarian's time. The software has been obtained either through freeware and shareware sites, or purchased locally. The technology employed has been simple, with many libraries starting with a donated computer to provide access for patrons.

In looking at the development of Internet among Malaysian libraries, a pattern seems to emerge on the stages that they have gone through. While this is not a formal model of development, it does represent the steps that many Malaysian libraries have gone through. The first stage was the creation of awareness among librarians on the need for the Internet. This was accomplished by seminars, study visits, readings, etc., and was primarily catalyzed by one or more librarians who had seen the development elsewhere and became aware of the potential. This stage was followed by the acquisition of one or more computers, either donated or obtained from the parent institution. These computers were used for two purposes, by the staff to perform library technical services and by the patrons to access Internet sites. As these few terminals became popular, more computers were obtained, specifically for the purpose of patron use. User education resulted in even greater usage. This led to libraries setting up their own Web site. Initially this was a passive site, conveying basic information on the services provided, library hours and regulations. This stage was followed by integration of Internet services into traditional library services, such as answering reference queries through e-mail. As more sophisticated technology was acquired, it enabled libraries to make their online catalogs available through the Net. The final stage involved the development of new programs and services, such as online requests and renewals.

IMPACT OF THE INTERNET

The use of the Internet has had a significant impact on libraries and information centers in Malaysia. While the actual effects vary depending on the availability of facilities, usage by the librarians and patrons, quality of communication links and other factors, the Internet has in many cases resulted in new roles for librarians, provided them with new opportunities and led to a more efficient library.

The Internet has forced libraries and librarians to review their roles. With library patrons becoming more Internet literate and being able to access information themselves, there was a stage where libraries feared they would become dinosaurs. This proved to be a 'wake-up call' for libraries, and many of them have now adopted the Internet as a tool for providing better services. The role of the librarian has changed from guardians and organizers of information, to that of access providers, navigators, educators, evaluators and organizers of information.

While librarians see their existing roles changing and new roles emerging, nevertheless they believe that the role of the library as an information repository will not diminish. A study that partly touched on the role of library in the Internet era noted that while librarians expected the library to continue purchasing materials in print format, they also expected the nature of their jobs to change in the future. Librarians saw the Internet enhancing their roles to become information searchers, evaluators and verifiers (Elbakhiet, 1998).

The Internet has also enabled libraries to expand their services.

Where previously libraries were open only during certain hours of the day, online materials are now accessible 24 hours a day. For example, the Putra University of Malaysia Library and the University of Malaya Library allow for their users not only to access their online catalogs to check the availability of materials, but also to check the status of a loan and to make online renewals.

The Internet has also shifted part of the responsibility of collection development from the librarian to the user. Where previously librarians decided on which resources should be placed in the collection, today patrons are able to bookmark regularly used sites and access them when needed. Collection development is thus based on the patrons' usage patterns rather than the librarians' perceptions of the users' needs. Libraries have been proactive in meeting the users needs for frequently accessed resources by examining these user-created bookmarks. The Virtual Subject Libraries of the Science University of Malaysia and the National Library of Malaysia are two examples where libraries have identified and organized Internet information resources relevant to the needs of their patrons.

The Internet has also been a boon to technical services librarians, especially in processing and cataloging. The availability of MARC records from the Internet enables catalogers in smaller libraries to access full cataloging information. This has been of tremendous help, for example, to the Kuala Lumpur Securities Commission Library which is now able to catalog between 25–30 books per day as compared to 8-10 books earlier.

Public services have also benefited from libraries using the Internet. For example, users can e-mail questions to the Reference Division, and get answers to their queries. The author's personal experience at using this service provided by the National Library has been generally positive, with replies to queries being received within 48 hours.

DIRECTIONS FOR THE FUTURE

As use of the Internet increases, there is a move towards integrating Internet resources and services with traditional library services, and the development of new services. Libraries, at least in Malaysia, appear to move in phases of adoption, integration and innovation. There are many libraries that are just beginning to use the Internet, while others have integrated it into traditional services, and a few are beginning to provide innovative Internet-based services.

Many libraries that use the Internet have integrated it into answering reference queries, communication with vendors and suppliers, interlibrary loans and other services. Libraries have also placed subject bibliographies on their Web sites, and Internet-based virtual libraries are beginning to emerge. At the time of writing this chapter, at least two digital libraries with considerable digitized resources are also functioning. The MIMOS Digital Library (*http://www.digilib.mimos.my/*) has made available part of their collection of research, conference and technical papers on information technology to persons in pursuit of knowledge enrichment. Similarly, the Subang Jaya Hypermedia Library, which is designed as a digital public library, provides access to its digital collection of materials through the use of its "smart card."

While progress in the use of the Internet has been admirable, there are still many challenges ahead.

One major challenge for Malaysian libraries is to increase the local content on the Web sites. Many library Web sites provide links to information sources that are based in other countries, while the number of local databases and locally produced materials is still small. This results in a continuing dependence on information from outside sources, a situation that the country must address if it is to become a developed nation by the year 2020. However, there are rays of hope, for with greater research and development, and with more users learning the techniques of placing information on the Internet, local content and locally produced materials will improve.

Another challenge is for Malaysian libraries to further invest in technology. Many Malaysian library Web sites are slow, and this frustrates the users, especially those with older computers. Some of the librarians involved with development of Internet services indicated they would like to, for example, place their catalogs on the Web but were unable to do so because of the lack of equipment. Librarians also faced the challenge of keeping up with the latest in technology, as many indicated that Internet technology kept changing so fast, it became difficult to keep up with the changes. The economic problems in the region have slowed the acquisition of better technology, but with improvements in the economy, it is hoped that this problem will be overcome.

The training of users is another challenge that needs to be addressed. While most librarians have mastered the skills for using the Internet, either through formal training programs or learning on-the job, the skill level of most users is very low. A brief observation of users at one public library and one academic library in Kuala Lumpur showed that many users did not have the searching skills. Students were found to be randomly browsing, and many ended up frustrated at either not being able to find what they were looking for or being overwhelmed with too much information.

Another challenge is to maintain the Web sites and keep them current. A quick search of Web sites showed that in some cases the dates of last change were more than a year old. While this could be the result of the date not being physically changed, it could also be attributed to a lack of human resources, as few libraries have a Webmaster specifically to look after the Web site. The task of maintaining the site is usually assigned to a librarian with a great deal of enthusiasm, some knowledge on Web maintenance, and little time.

Malaysian libraries also need to ensure continuous access to their Web sites. A project carried out as a class exercise by an MLIS student at the University of Malaya over December 1998 - January 1999 showed that some of the Malaysian library sites were not accessible during the public holidays. This could have been due to servers being deliberately shut down during holidays or staff not being present to restart the system when it automatically shut down.

As the Internet becomes more popular and heavily used, new buildings will have to be designed with electronic access in mind. Most library buildings existing today were designed for a print environment, with a limited number of power points and appropriate cabling. The International Islamic University Library in Gombak, Kuala Lumpur, does address some of these needs by having a very large number of terminal points, but rapid changes in technology make this a difficult task for older libraries.

CONCLUSION

In conclusion, it can be safely said that the Internet has brought about many positive developments in Malaysian libraries and information services. Libraries have benefited from the increased access to resources, the opportunities for communication and the facilitation of new services that were not possible in pre-Internet days. The Internet has in many cases been integrated into administration, public services, technical services and research. While problems and challenges still exist, primarily of high costs, limited local content, rapidly changing technology and insufficient human resources, there is little doubt that a developing country like Malaysia has done quite well.

REFERENCES

Elbakhiet, A.B. (1998). *The impact of the library on the Internet: Usage patterns and perceptions of postgraduate students at the University of Malaya*. Unpublished master's thesis, University of Malaya, Kuala Lumpur, Malaysia.

Jaafar, S.B. (1998). *Marketing information technology (IT) products and services through libraries: Malaysian experiences*. Paper presented at the 64th IFLA General Conference, August 16-21, 1998, Amsterdam.

Mohamed, A.R. & Fadzil, G.M. (1996). Internet in Southeast Asia: The development of Internet in Malaysian libraries. In Congress of Southeast Asian Librarians, *Libraries in national development: papers presented at the tenth Congress of Southeast Asian Librarians, Kuala Lumpur, 21-25 May 1996* (pp. 309-333). Kuala Lumpur: CONSAL.

Singh, D. (1998a). Library and information services in Malaysia. In K. de la P. McCook, B.J. Ford and K. Lippincott (Eds). *Libraries: Global Reach-Local Touch* (pp. 60-69). Chicago: American Library Association.

Singh, D. (1998b). The use of Internet among Malaysian librarians. *Malaysian Journal of Library and Information Science, 3*(2), 1-10.

Wong, S.L. (1998). *The Malaysia Internet book*. Singapore: Addison Wesley Longman.

ACKNOWLEDGMENTS

I would like to thank the Faculty of Computer Science and Information Technology, University of Malaya for providing an environment conducive to publishing. I am also grateful to my students of the Management of Internet class 1998/99 for their ideas, comments and remarks, some of which have been incorporated into this chapter.

Chapter VIII

The University of Queensland Cybrary: A Virtual Library in a Wired University

Janine Schmidt, Jennifer Croud and Deborah Turnbull
The University of Queensland, Australia

Students discover short cuts to scholarship
Any place..... Any space..... At any pace..... At any time
The University of Queensland Cybrary – Australia's first – makes travel to a new world of knowledge easy. Students can plan their route and take advantage of short cuts, or if they prefer, take a leisurely meander and discover exciting new places off the beaten track. The Cybrary integrates state-of-the-art information technology with traditional services to create a "virtual library" in a "wired university." From any of hundreds of high-end Pentium computers within the Library, and day or night from home or office, students can explore or target the world of information as they wish. The Cybrary pushes out the boundaries of information gathering and gives students new scope for synthesizing and processing the material they discover. The Cybrary is an indispensable, integrated approach to meet the information demands of lifelong learning and problem-based teaching. It is a powerful support for flexible learning and an enhancement to flexible teaching. The Library has taken a leadership role in applying this innovative approach to addressing the real needs of students in the 21st Century, and is working collaboratively with students and teachers to develop and refine the Cybrary as new possibilities open.

INTRODUCTION

Cybrary, or virtual library, services have been discussed in the literature for many years. However it is only in recent years that it has become technically possible to achieve the vision.

The University of Queensland Library is leading the way in developing cybrary services in Australia. Its Cybrary is an innovative, ongoing project. Other libraries have some components but the University of Queensland Library is the first in Australia to integrate its information technology support services with traditional services to provide cybrary services.

These services are accessible from lecture theatres, offices on all campuses and homes. Access is available any time of the day or night; 24 hours per day access from students' own terminals, 81 hours per week in the Library.

Bauwens (1996) states a virtual library "is still a place, albeit a virtual one. The whole secret of interactive marketing is to become an invited persuader. In general it will be imperative to motivate the users to visit even though there will be enormous competition for their attention." This paper describes the University of Queensland Library's efforts to capture that attention and become an invited persuader in students' learning journeys.

HOW THE CYBRARY BEGAN

The University of Queensland Library is the largest library in the state of Queensland and one of the largest in Australia. It contains 1.8 million volumes, 11,000 videos, 20,000 journal titles and extensive microform, multimedia, digital and primary source collections. It provides services to students and to their teachers through 13 branch libraries located on several campuses, in a number of teaching hospitals and the University's Dental School, as well as other scattered sites throughout the State. The collections are housed in branch libraries, and in a warehouse on the main campus which provides cost-effective storage for less used material. Each branch library includes similar facilities and provides similar services, although there are some variations due to client need.

The Library's very size can be confusing to students and finding a way through the many resources to the few that are needed for a particular purpose is not easy for many. Services are designed to assist

The University of Queensland Library – Cybrary Web Page (http://cybrary.uq.edu.au/)

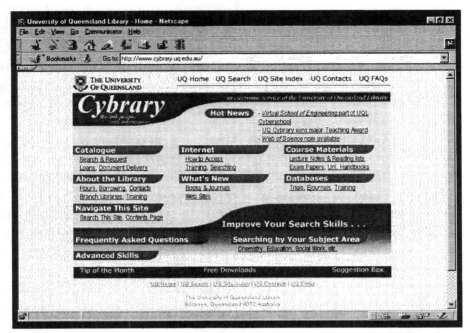

students as much as possible. Surveys of students are regularly undertaken to ensure feedback and to assist in planning and design of services provided. Services to assist students range from one-on-one inquiry services to Internet training in classroom situations. While the services are designed for the benefit of students and staff of the University, these same services are appreciated by members of the wider community who regularly use the Library.

Like other libraries, the University of Queensland Library has provided automated catalogue and lending services to students for many years. Students have come physically to the Library to access the automated systems and to locate known items, under authors or titles, to look for materials on topics of interest and to find items on the shelves, primarily books and videos. They then borrowed or photo-copied them. Students used printed indexes to access the journal literature to enhance their learning experiences.

As some of these printed resources moved to electronic forms, the newer versions were first accessed by librarians off-site on behalf of users and then purchased for local use. CD-ROM indexing services were acquired and made available at individual workstations. With improvements in technology and communication, these electronic databases were gradually networked. Students began to use them to conduct their own searches. The University of Queensland Library was the first in Australia to install a SilverPlatter ERL (Electronic Reference Library) network to make databases, indexing thousands of journals, available from a single interface. The databases were initially used by students in all campus libraries and then by dial-up access from all kinds of personal computers located in laboratories, offices on campus and homes.

The University of Queensland Library participated with other CAUL (Council of Australian University Librarians) libraries in the consortium purchase of some databases. The statistics on use of these consistently shows the University of Queensland as the heaviest user of all databases throughout Australia. The University of Queensland Library has steadily increased the databases networked and now has the highest number locally networked of any university library in Australia.

The advent of the Web changed forever the approach to locating information. Web navigational links and alternative structures facilitated new access possibilities. The University of Queensland Library was one of the first to mount a Web version of a library catalogue in Australia. Its ease of use and its popularity with students being demonstrated by use that has doubled each year since 1996.

The Library has continued to add other electronic services as they have become available – electronic journals obtained either individually or as part of "umbrella" services from specific vendors, electronic versions of textbooks and multimedia formats. Projects have been carried out on the construction of electronic reserves and the scanning of examination papers, and Web pages outlining library services were constructed as the technology changed. Library staff were trained in the effective use of the new technology and some were also trained in the use of HTML. Increasing numbers of classes were held to explain the use of the new services to students who greeted both the classes and the services enthusiastically.

During 1997, the Library realized that its Web pages needed restructuring. The incremental growth had led to an array of ill-assorted data. The Web site had been designed from the library perspective rather than a client's, and was internally, rather than externally, defined. It did not have an overall plan, subdirectory structure tended to be uneven and idiosyncratic and the standard for site structure, style and presentation of Web pages was an ad hoc one that had evolved over time. Also, there was no means of navigation or a search facility. A survey of library Web pages throughout the world revealed some good ideas but no innovative model worthy of emulation. In late 1997 a market research consultant was engaged to conduct focus groups with library users to assist in the development of an ideal approach.

The findings were invaluable in redesigning the Web site. Specifically, the focus group research was to:

- determine the existing client needs in relation to the library Web site
- obtain client reaction to the model under construction
- explore a number of existing library Web pages to determine patterns of usage and reaction to layout.

The results of the research revealed that most people know only a little about the Library, and that few would ever acquire an in-depth knowledge. Their approaches to the Library Web site are task-oriented and frequently crisis-driven. Many users lack computer skills, Internet skills and information-seeking skills. For these clients, the Library is a source of frustration. Most students approach the Library in search of reference material for assignments, theses and papers. Hence, their primary need is direct access to the catalogue and databases. Whether experienced or inexperienced, they are interested in learning how to search more effectively. They need details about the Library including the hours of operation, borrowing rules, the location of library branches and facilities available in each branch. Undergraduate students particularly are interested in access to examination papers.

Level of experience and degree of confidence impact on the ability of people to explore a Web site, and experienced users are more likely than inexperienced ones to use search engines. Experienced users agreed a good Web site is one that is updated regularly. To summarize, students want speed of access, instant comprehension of link words for efficient browsing, the ability to navigate/explore the site, help with searching, information on University courses and essential information on the Library.

In consideration of the findings, work began on a new design of the Library's Web pages and the University of Queensland Cybrary was born. The Cybrary's Home Page address is *http://cybrary.uq.edu.au/*

. In building the Cybrary, the results of the student input were used. Essential items of communication were placed at the first level of the web pages as few students bother to develop an understanding of what is on offer throughout the site. Information categories were made as clear and concise as possible. Statements were designed to be immediately clear to the lowest level of user and details kept as brief as possible but not, hopefully, at the expense of understanding. Layout was standardized across all pages. Given the access speed required, non-essential graphics were avoided to reduce the time taken in downloading.

HOW THE CYBRARY WORKS

To develop the Cybrary, the Library has invested heavily in information technology hardware and software infrastructure. The Library has: linked component parts via a local network and the University's wide area network; developed its staffing resources to provide extensive informative technology expertise at the planning, implementation and support levels; provided Electronic Information Centres in each branch library with sophisticated training facilities, data manipulation software and multimedia support software; allocated significant funds to electronic resources and negotiated appropriate multi-user licenses; and implemented standardized interfaces (e.g. Z39.50) to external databases.

It has developed services with the equipment and facilities students are likely to have in mind. Many Web developments use complicated Java script and other interfaces requiring sophisticated hardware, software and browser plug-ins for access. The Library has chosen to develop interfaces requiring only widely available hardware and software, and new services have been worked up from prototypes. Projects have been undertaken in consultation with user groups where possible to ensure their relevance. Services have been developed with students' time constraints and pressures in mind, and are simple and user friendly as possible. Personal assistance is available 81 hours per week, during library opening hours.

The information technology infrastructure of the Cybrary comprises:
- a leading edge integrated library management system (purchased from Innovative Interfaces, Inc.) with a 350 simultaneous user license running on a DEC Alpha computer.

- 10 file servers using Unix, Novell Netware and Windows NT, with over 200 gigabytes of storage for data. Two of these support the SilverPlatter ERL (Electronic Reference Library) databases for up to 100 simultaneous users. One fileserver acts as the Library file server to provide ease of access to all resources.
- 750 public and staff personal computers, most being high-end Pentium workstations (100mb/sec ethernet network adapters), some with soundcard and CD-ROM drives.

STUDENT DESTINATIONS

Through the Cybrary, students are able to navigate their way to new sources of information. Use of the journal collection has doubled and students and staff have registered their appreciation through increasing use of the services provided. Students have taken control of their own learning.

Students begin with a single integrated web interface to all library collections and services, including library opening hours, staff contacts, branch library layouts and details of facilities and training programs. From here, they can travel to the local catalogue of on-site holdings of books, journals, videos and other resources. Occasionally textbooks are available in electronic form, for example Harrison's *Principles of Internal Medicine*. Students are also able to view their own borrowing records and renew their loans.

To gain further knowledge from the journal literature, students can continue their voyage of discovery by searching over 250 locally held databases indexing thousands of journals.

Databases indexing the journal literature cover all subject areas. The most heavily used databases are *Medline, ABI-Inform* (a business database), *Biological Abstracts, CABI* (agricultural and biological information), *Current Contents* (all disciplinary areas) and *APAIS* (Australian Public Affairs Information Service). Approximately 60% of the databases are networked using SilverPlatter ERL (Electronic Reference Library) software, rendering them accessible via a wide range of workstations located on all campuses and from homes. These databases are available via dialup 24 hours a day. Other databases are networked from several Novell netware servers and are accessible from workstations both within the Library and in departments across the University.

Students can then find the printed journals on the shelves or use electronic versions. The Cybrary provides access to over 3,500 electronic journals. All are listed in the Library's catalogue under title, and direct links made to them. The Library obtains electronic journals either in association with subscriptions already paid for printed services, or as part of umbrella services which include a large number of journals. These services typically are provided by publishers, or by subscription agents who provide interfaces to a large number of journals, usually in a specific disciplinary area. Electronic journals range from individual titles like the *Medical Journal of Australia* to large-scale services such as IDEAL, IAC Searchbank and SpringerLink. IDEAL: Academic Press journals on-line indexes and provides full-text access to 175 Academic Press journals. IAC Searchbank consists of a number of databases: *Expanded Academic ASAP International Edition*, which indexes 1,580 journals providing full-text of 527; *Computer ASAP*, which indexes 150 journals and provides full-text articles from 103; *Health Reference Center – Academic*, which indexes 205 journals and provides full-text articles from 150; and *LegalTrac*, which indexes 800 journals. SpringerLink provides full-text articles from 117 journals published by Springer Verlag.

Students can continue their voyage of learning by checking catalogues of other libraries either locally or internationally, or by using the Internet. The Cybrary provides access to millions of information services on the Internet and some are licensed by the Library for direct use by students. These include databases identifying relevant articles in printed journals, which in some cases are linked to the electronic form of the journal itself.

Specialist assistance is available to undergraduates via the Cybrary. Students can find sub-sets of information in an electronic reserve collection. They also heavily use electronic versions of examination papers, subject guides, subject and course notes and reading lists. An electronic reserve program has been implemented for the Graduate Medical Course (GMC) and approximately 100 articles are available on a GMC Intranet. Electronic versions of examination papers are being placed on the Web and ultimately, all papers will be available electronically. The Library has developed a range of "Find-Its" which are guides to sources of information in particular subject areas. These guides begin with introductory sources of information on a specific subject area and outline how they can be found and used. Over 160 of these are available on topics ranging from anatomy to philosophy. Appropriate subject headings in the catalogue are listed and "hot links" made to them. Internet sites are included and "hot links" provided. "Use-Its" are the companion guides to the "Find-Its." They cover topics such as evaluating and citing Internet resources, and the use of specific databases. Subject and course notes are available electronically and some lecturers' notes have been placed on the Library's Web-server. Links are also made from the Library's Web-server to departmental Web-servers where appropriate. Electronic reading lists have been prepared for a number of departments. They include "hot links" to entries on the Library's catalogue and give clear indications to the students of the availability of materials in high demand. Also provided is easy access to various Internet search engines and direct links are made to the best of these.

As not all Cybrary services are immediately easy to use, the Library assists student learning through the provision of specially tailored information skills training programs. They focus on effective access to, and use of, information. Programs are provided in the classroom and also interactively via the Cybrary. The content of the programs emphasizes effective search strategies and effective use of resources, and many are designed in partnership with teaching staff and relate to specific assignments.

The range of information skills courses includes:

- Effective searching on the Library's Web-site.
- *Winning with WinSpirs,* which focuses on generalized approaches to searching databases on both the SilverPlatter ERL and Netware servers. There are also specific programs relating to the use of individual databases. Many of these are conducted during lunch times to facilitate student attendance. Others are provided in partnership with departments and emphasize resources relevant to specific subject areas.
- *Navigating the Internet,* which provides basic skills in the use of standard Internet tools, and *Research on the Internet,* which provides instruction in the use of search tools and indexes to locate relevant information on research topics.
- a 10-hour course, *Information Skills for Researchers and Postgraduates,* offered to postgraduate students and researchers is a comprehensive program addressing all aspects of services provided

via the Cybrary. Initially designed in cooperation with the Dean of Postgraduate Students, it has proven extremely popular. It is delivered by library staff who are frequently assisted by postgraduate students.

- *Endnote* courses. The Library worked with the Office of Research and Postgraduate Studies within the University to obtain multiple copies of the personal reference database *Endnote* and provide it to students and researchers. The Library provides free training to users.
- Research Methods in English. A significant component of the course is conducted by Library staff over a four-week period detailing not only the printed materials held in the Library and accessible via the Library catalogue, but also the indexing and abstracting services available across the University's network. Valuable sources on the Internet and the use of Internet tools to locate resources are also described.

The Library also provides a number of information skills programs via the Web. For example, in collaboration with the School of Computer Science and Electrical Engineering, the Library has produced "QUIK-IT," an interactive Internet training kit available freely across the Net. It includes all aspects of use of the Internet, including e-mail and use of Internet search engines. An interactive information skills program using WebCT, Webbook for Engineers, was developed for first-year Engineering students by library staff in conjunction with academic staff. Library staff have worked with teaching staff to prepare effective search strategies for the location and effective use of information on particular topics. Programs are delivered interactively via the Web, and students are assessed on the quality of information located as part of the assessment in the subject area.

For postgraduates the Cybrary provides additional specialized services such as an electronic current awareness service and an electronic document requesting and delivery service. Electronic current awareness services are provided to postgraduate students via the *Uncover Reveal Service*. Profiles of specific subject interests are developed and up-to-date information automatically e-mailed to clients. With regard to document delivery, the University of Queensland Library was successful in obtaining a Federal government RIEFP grant (Australian Research Council Research Infrastructure Equipment and Facilities Program) in association with other Queensland libraries to develop an electronic document delivery site. The University of Queensland Library was the lead site, and one of the world's first electronic document delivery services REDD (Regional Electronic Document Delivery) was developed. It facilitated electronic requesting, using a Web form, and delivered journal articles via e-mail. The Library is now using an integrated document delivery service, based on the Innovative Interfaces, Inc. Inter-Library Loan module that has the same look and feel as the catalogue, with a choice of telnet and Web interfaces.

The **Cybrary** assists students to access information equitably and progress in higher education. As Internet passwords are available free to all students, equitable access is assured. While many students own their own PCs or have access to PCs through family or work (80% on a recent survey), the University Library has taken equity issues seriously and provides Electronic Information Centres for student use, free of charge, in all branch libraries. These Centres are equipped with high end PCs that are loaded with a variety of software, including word processing programs. The Library is open up to 81 hours per week and access is also available from lecture theatres, tutorial rooms and offices on all campuses, and dial-up use 24 hours per day, 7 days per week, 365 days per year further assures equity. The Cybrary's universal availability makes it accessible for students at their own pace, in their own place, and in their own time. Learning support for students with a range of abilities is provided. Services are available to on-campus students and to those undertaking flexibly delivered programs.

Students come with varying levels of information skills and training provided by the Library is available without charge to all. This also facilitates equitable educational progress. Students who are under-prepared for university are able to obtain the skills they need to operate at the same level as others. Programmes are provided in classroom situations, in the Electronic Information Centres and also interactively via the Cybrary. Many programmes are designed in partnership with teaching staff and relate to specific assignments - all students are provided with the opportunity to do well and to gain lifelong learning skills.

Lifelong learning is a major objective of information skills programs. Students leave the university equipped with the means to continue their own education. Classes are voluntary, available to all and provided at a range of times, days and locations. The sessions are structured to provide a forum in which discussion and question and answer clarify students' understanding. There is a general belief that attendance by students at information skills programs leads to effective use of the Cybrary and that effective use of the Cybrary ensures better performance by students. Postgraduates attending classes have rated their own improvement as significant. Academic staff working with library staff consistently report that students who use the Cybrary's services effectively perform better than those who do not. While hard evidence is difficult to provide, there is nothing to suggest that the anecdotal reports are invalid. Students who use the Cybrary's services effectively progress through their education more easily than those who do not. Students are also able to build on their information skills as they progress through their studies. The classes are extremely popular, and in 1998 over 24,000 students and staff attended various information skills programs.

The Cybrary is not only for students, and the University of Queensland Cybrary's services are available via the University's Home Page to all within the community. Alumni are also users, and anyone with Internet access can use the Cybrary. Some of the Cybrary's services are IP and/or password protected as licenses restrict useage to University of Queensland students and staff. The University of Queensland Library has also worked with other organisations to provide direct links from their organizational Web sites to the Library's Web page. For example, a direct link is made from Queensland Health Information Network (QHIN). Many other university libraries in Queensland provide direct links to the University of Queensland Library, and other links are made through a variety of umbrella and directory services. The 24-hour nature of the service makes it easily accessible by members of the community.

The University of Queensland Library is also currently working with several secondary schools in Queensland on a trial basis to provide access to one particular database on its network. This work involves subsidized use by the vendor who is providing the database free of charge during the course of the trial. A gateway is provided for schools' access to the database, and it is hoped that the trial will extend to a full service during 1999. Special training also has been provided in support of university programs for gifted and talented children.

Training sessions on use of the Internet were held for over 100 school teachers in 1997, and many school tours are conducted throughout the year.

Special relationships have also been established with particular sectors of the community. The Commonwealth Scientific and Industrial Research Organisation (CSIRO) and small research arms of local companies are heavy users of the Cybrary. Programmes in Internet training are also provided to members of the community at a small charge and have been well received.

THE STUDENT LEARNING JOURNEY

Over 28,000 students, many of whom are postgraduates, come to the University with a variety of experiences. They have different learning styles. Some are young and some are mature age students. They pursue their chosen courses of study in different ways. Some are thirsty for knowledge, seeking as much as they can. Others are doing the minimum amount to obtain the qualification they need to get a good job. While all receive the same type of teaching, each individual student conducts his or her own learning. Students receive guidance and input from teaching staff, from the content of textbooks, from discussions with fellow students, from completing assignments and group work, increasingly from the Internet and from the body of knowledge contained in the heart of the University, the Library. The Cybrary places control of learning in the hands of students. Students describe the Cybrary as:

- Indispensable
- Helps me write my assignments
- Always available
- Saves time
- Helps me to research
- Helps me learn
- It's great to use from home
- Easy to use; a one-stop shop

They use the Cybrary to interact with the world of knowledge to improve their learning experiences.

How does this work for each student? The following brief narratives, one undergraduate and the other postgraduate, demonstrate how integral the Cybrary is to student work.

Travel with an Undergraduate

- *Katherine is a first-year undergraduate studying Journalism. She is at home; it is early evening and she has an assignment due in three days. Her assignment is "Ethics in Journalism."*

Katherine logs onto the Cybrary's web page to check the title of a book mentioned in her lecture. Katherine finds *Lecture Notes* on the web page under *Course Materials*. The Lecture Notes refer to the Reading List for more information. Reading Lists are also listed on the Cybrary's web page under *Course Materials,* and the link for the book is there. The book is listed as available on the shelves and she can pick it up in the morning. She also checks her loans on the library system to make sure there is no overdue material that would block her from borrowing the book tomorrow. There are two books due back today and Katherine renews them.

Katherine then starts to work on her assignment. She clicks on the Cybrary's link *Searching by Subject Area*, then on the "Find It" (a guide for finding subject information) for Journalism. Katherine checks which databases to search for information under *"Journals – Current Information on your Topic."* The databases are all on the Cybrary's *Silverplatter* Electronic Reference Library (ERL). Katherine then logs on to the databases, searches and finds three appropriate articles. She reads the abstracts and decides to photocopy two of the articles when she goes to the library in the morning. The third article she needs is in the newspaper, *The Australian*. There is a Web link for Australian newspapers listed on the Find It, and she clicks on it, finds the link for *The Australian* and then retrieves the article. Assignment preparation done, she logs off, reads the article and commences the draft of her assignment.

The Postgraduate Route

- *Michael is a postgraduate student beginning the second year of his PhD on "Alexander the Great's military policy in India". He shares a PC in the department's postgraduate common room. He has recently modified his topic and is checking references for his thesis. He needs two crucial journal articles to show his supervisor.*

Michael logs on to the Cybrary's Web page and clicks the link for the Catalogue. He does a Title search for the two journals he needs. The first one, *The Historical Journal*, is listed in the catalogue. It is available both electronically and in print in the library collection. He clicks on the Web link and connects to the Web journal site. He reads the abstract and decides to download the full text. This needs *Adobe Acrobat* software, but Michael doesn't know what that is. He returns to the Library's Web page and clicks on the Search this Site link, then searches for information about *Adobe Acrobat*. He finds a FAQ (Frequently Asked Questions) file "Adobe Acrobat & PDF Files" which explains what to do. He downloads the *Adobe Acrobat* software, and then the article. The second journal is not listed in the catalogue, so Michael clicks on the Document Delivery link. Michael had attended a postgraduate information skills training program and knows he can request items not held. He fills in the form, decides to get it fast-tracked and submits the request.

Michael continues his search for information for his thesis by clicking on the Databases link to obtain a subject list of databases to search. Under History, *Current Contents* and the *Humanities Index* look the most promising and both are available via the Library's Silverplatter ERL (Electronic Reference Library). He logs on to them using the Silverplatter WinSpirs software loaded on the PC. He searches the databases and finds three relevant articles in *Current Contents*. Michael then cuts and pastes the journal titles into the Library's Web catalogue to see if they are available locally. One is a recent book review in *The Times Literary Supplement* and it is listed in the Library's catalogue as being available on the Web. He clicks on the link and is taken to the Web version of the journal, reads the article and decides to print it.

His supervisor had also mentioned checking for further information on the Internet. He checks the Library Web page for help with searching the Internet and clicks on the link for Internet. He doesn't know where to start, so he runs through the free self-paced Internet tutorial QUIK-it! He now knows he needs to use a search engine, so he clicks on the link for Search the Internet, then on Search Engines. Michael reads the library information about the search engine *Hotbot*, and decides to use it to start his search. He clicks on the link for *Hotbot*, and spends the next hour scanning documents on his subject. He then logs off, and begins work on redrafting Chapter 2 of his thesis.

CONCLUSION

The University of Queensland Library's Cybrary is integrating state-of-the-art information technology with traditional services to create a "virtual library" in a "wired university." It is an ongoing project, constantly being modified as technological progress is made and new service possibilities become viable. The emphasis is on serving student and staff needs and meeting their expectations. In some cases these expectations exceed what is currently possible. While the Cybrary has attained Bauwen's (1994) second level of virtuality, "electronic access to virtual collections but with delivery of real documents," the third degree of virtuality, of complete "electronic access to virtual collections consisting of electronic documents" is not yet a reality. While the Library is working towards this and continuing to acquire electronic materials (within budget constraints), the hybrid library will be with us for many years – the bookless library is as real as the paperless office.

The University of Queensland Cybrary services are well received. Student response to cybrary services has been extremely positive with very high use indicating extensive adoption by many students. The number of logins per month to the catalogue has doubled each year over the last two years. The database network component of the Cybrary has experienced similar heavy use and growth. Compared with other university libraries in Australia, the statistics supplied by the various commercial services show that the University of Queensland Library is still consistently the highest user of all databases for which consortium purchasing agreements have been received. The e-mail discussion list set up by the Library to provide information on the availability of new services is well subscribed and high attendance at voluntary information skills training sessions evidence a thirst for knowledge amongst the student community.

The University of Queensland Library's Web site is the most heavily used site at the University of Queensland. That the University's Home Page has a direct link to the Library on all pages that are part of the Web site evidences the significance of the Cybrary to the University. Many positive comments are received through both solicited evaluations, particularly in relation to information skills classes, and spontaneously through suggestion box comments. Further work is being done on Web-CT approaches with information skills programs in several subject areas, e.g. social work, engineering. Approaches to "virtual reference" are being explored – the Library's suggestion box is already being used in this way. A project for 1999 relates to customization of services with students creating their own virtual libraries.

The Cybrary is pushing out the boundaries of information gathering and giving students new scope for synthesising and processing the material they discover. Where both cybrary and traditional services are available students are choosing the flexibility of the former. The Cybrary is meeting the information demands of lifelong learning and problem based teaching and is a powerful support for flexible learning and an enhancement to flexible teaching.

REFERENCES

(1998). eLib: focus on the 'hybrid library'. *Library Association Record,* 100(1), 17.

Bauwens, M. (1997a). Marketing the cybrary (reprinted from Marketing Library Services Je '96), *Marketing matters* (pp. 93-4.): Special Libs. Assn.

Bauwens, M. (1997b). What is cyberspace? (reprinted from Comput Libr Ap '94), *The Cybrarian's manual* (pp. 395-403.): American Lib. Assn.

Cronin, B. (1998). The electronic academy revisited. *Aslib Proceedings,* 50(9), 241- 254.

Ensor, P.-L. (1997c). Why can't a user be more like a librarian? (With apologies to My Fair Lady's "Why can't a woman be more like a man?") (reprinted from Technicalities May '93), *The Cybrarian's manual* (pp. 297-300.): American Lib. Assn.

Ensor, P.L. e. (1997d). *The Cybrarian's manual*: American Lib. Assn.

ILCSO Electronic Resources Committee. (1999). *Illinois Digital Academy Library: A Request for FY 2000 Funds*, [Internet Web Page]. Available: http://www.lis.uiuc.edu/~sloan/idal.html [1999, 29/01/99].

Kovacs, D.K., & Kovacs, M.J. (1997). *The cybrarian's guide to developing successful Internet programs and services*: Neal-Schuman.

Myers, J.-E. (1997b). Reference services in the virtual library (reprinted from Am Libr Jl/Ag '94), *The Cybrarian's manual* (pp. 418-25): American Lib. Assn.

Olsen, M. (1997). *Library WebSite: Client Attitudes and Requirement* . Brisbane: Durham Kelly and Olsen, Market and Advertising Research for The University of Queensland Library.

Owl, R., & Morgan, R. (1997). Seven buttons: a user-friendly, patron-appropriate technique (reprinted from Audiov Libr Ag '94), *The Cybrarian's manual* (pp. 309-11.): American Lib. Assn.

Saunders, L. (1998). MCI announces Cybrarian of the year award winners. *Information Today,* 15(8), 26+.

Schankman, L.-H. (1997). Beyond surfing: serving information to our patrons, *The Cybrarian's manual* (pp. 283-94.): American Lib. Assn.

Strangelove, M. (1997). Using the Internet for promoting your skills and services: two basic techniques (reprinted from Business Finance Div Bulletin Spr '94), *The Cybrarian's manual* (pp. 404-7.): American Lib. Assn.

Chapter IX

Towards the People's Network: UK Developments and the Work of the EARL Consortium

Helen Baigent and Chris Moore
EARL Consortium, London

This chapter explores Web-based public library networking developments within the context of the United Kingdom. The political context in recent years has led to plans to deliver a national Public Library Network, promising innovative new services to combat social exclusion and facilitate lifelong learning. The road to realizing the vision of a People's Network is still far from a reality and many of the issues currently facing the sector demand enormous amounts of coordination and cooperation in order to ensure that public libraries remain at the heart of the political agenda. It is suggested that the work of the EARL Consortium, its achievements and approach to library networking present an important model to shape the roll-out of the national network. Once delivered, the United Kingdom will arguably hold a place amongst the world leaders in the global information society.

INTRODUCTION

Until recent years networking developments such as online access to a range of services including data hosts, view data systems, local systems, interlending and document delivery had been the focus of public library research and implementation in the United Kingdom. As such the development of Internet-based technologies has entered the scene far later than our counterparts in the academic sector and other countries such as the United States. This chapter explores the shift in focus towards Internet-based technologies within United Kingdom public libraries, which has been largely driven by a huge political movement to ensure that the United Kingdom holds a place on the global information stage. Plans to implement a national Public Library Network and deliver innovative new services to the nation and beyond promise to promote the role of public libraries to previously unimagined levels and arguably place the United Kingdom among the world leaders in the global information society.

In the last 18 months or so, public libraries in the United Kingdom have witnessed unprecedented levels of government support, undoubtedly confirming that this is the most radical and dynamic phase in the entire history of the public library service. The first part of this chapter introduces the political context which led to the publication of several key reports subsumed within the wider political shift towards an "information society." Dominant themes in these reports, which are central to the public library movement, have highlighted the importance of lifelong learning and social inclusion, and emphasize the role that public libraries will play within the United Kingdom and in the global information society. An overview of the most critical of these reports is used to demonstrate the timeliness of delivering a Public Library Network.

This is followed by an exploration of early experiments in public library Web-based networking that have helped to propagate this defining moment, focussing in particular on the work of the EARL Consortium. It is shown that EARL, the Consortium for Public Library Networking, has played an important and sustained role in lobbying for the network and has contributed towards achieving the vision of the Public Library Network. The work of the Consortium has also developed a showcase of Web services, to demonstrate that public libraries and their valued cultural assets form a fundamental component of the information society and the global information superhighway. Much of the success of the Consortium is attributed to its unique national yet local perspective, drawing upon the collaborative efforts of nearly 75 percent of library authorities in the United Kingdom. An overview of the range of services which aim to show the potential for using the Internet demonstrates an approach to library networking that serves as a model for others to follow.

The general state of development nationally, however, shows that we still have a long way to go and there are many important issues and considerations that need to be addressed by the profession as a whole, central and local government and the private sector. There is still much to be done to ensure that the network is delivered in a cohesive and sustainable way, demanding new ways of thinking and working together to the mutual benefit of everyone involved. In essence, a shift is required from political rhetoric to actual implementation, and later seamless interconnection and access to networked public library services.

It is argued that the solutions to these challenges demand a national policy framework which coordinates collaboration and development on local, regional and national levels. Consideration is given as to how this framework might be achieved. It is shown that the EARL Consortium will continue to play a vital role in this process, bridging the gap between local authorities, the wider library and information community and central government as the network develops. Only then can the future of public library networking in the United Kingdom and the global information society be secured.

HARD TIMES

Developments in Web-based public library networking in the United Kingdom began to take place from 1995 in response to a number of wider political and cross-sectoral influences. In order to appreciate this phase it is necessary to understand the political climate that the sector faced at that time. No one could ever have imagined that these experimental beginnings would metamorphose into the greatest public library revolution ever to be experienced in the United Kingdom, leading to a new age of public library services.

For more than a decade public libraries had faced enormous challenges in a climate of economic recession, resource cuts, downsizing and reorganization of local government services (Dolan, 1997). In contrast, to amplify this difficult period, the academic sector had already been exploiting the benefits of Internet-based networked services for many years through the establishment of a nationwide computer network, the Joint Academic Network (JANET), to deliver services and resources within higher education institutions. The earliest experiments in public library Web-based networking were therefore poised to explore the potential of information and communications technologies (ICT) in order to share resource development within an era of harsh financial constraints (Hare, 1995).

ENVISIONING AN INFORMATION SOCIETY

At the same time the wider political climate was establishing a vision to attain an "information society," embracing the fact that world economies were increasingly being built on information exchange and transfer. The concept refers to a society that "has an economy which is dependent on the creation, storage and accessibility of information on a national and global scale. Typically this information is transferred and accessed using the latest communication and computer technology" (Ormes & Criddle, 1997:3), and increasingly through the use of the World Wide Web.

WHY AN INFORMATION SOCIETY?

In line with government policies from around the world, the benefits of developing an information society are perceived to lie in improved global economic positioning and increased competitiveness in and through the expansion of knowledge-based industries (Library & Information Commission, 1997). As the industrial landscape moves into the business of teleworking on an increasingly global scale, small and medium-sized enterprises especially in the United Kingdom are increasingly dependent upon electronic access to information either from the office, the home or other public access points such as libraries.

Also embedded in the vision of an information society is the changing nature of education. A global shift towards lifelong learning has necessitated changes within the formal education sector, offering students greater independence to learn in more flexible and imaginative ways to cater for the dramatic growth in the number of nontraditional students. Reports such as *Our Information Age* (1998), *University for Industry* (1997), *Learning for the Twenty-First Century* (1997) and *The Learning Age* (1998) in the United Kingdom have argued the need to acquire new skills and competencies throughout people's lives:

> Learning is the key to prosperity, for each of us as individuals, as well as for the nation as a whole: "for individuals, learning offers excitement and the opportunity for discovery;" for businesses, learning helps them to be more successful; "for communities,

learning contributes to social cohesion;" for the nation, learning is essential to a strong economy and an inclusive society" (*The Learning Age*, 1998: Introduction).

Similarly the vision addresses the issues of democracy and social inclusion. Bringing the citizen closer to local and central government is central to these agendas. Plans to deliver 25 percent of their services and communication electronically by the year 2002 (government.direct, 1996), set a clear example to other public services that this is a matter of priority. The issue of social inclusion was most explicitly addressed in *The Net Result* (1997), when it was argued that providing access to technology was vital to ensuring that individuals and communities are not excluded or alienated from the information society, failure surely resulting in a society of information-haves and have-nots. Access to these technologies therefore offer opportunities to deliver information to those who are housebound, such as the disabled or infirmed, the geographically isolated and those who are unable to purchase their own.

Finally, an information society envisions a culturally enriched nation, opening up our cultural warehouses to all via computer networks. Local and national treasures from libraries, museums, galleries and exhibitions can be dynamically exploited and delivered to experience culture, entertainment and learning in new ways.

A TIME FOR CHANGE: THE VISION OF A PUBLIC LIBRARY NETWORK

In order to embrace the information society, the public library community was encouraged to consider completely new ways of thinking and operating library services. Their involvement in this movement was seen to be critical to the success of this vision, as well as the changing information needs of customers, and in the light of a sustained period of economic hardship, to the survival of the public library service itself.

Attempts were made to obtain lottery money to develop public library networking in a proposal submitted by Information for All in 1996 (Information for All, 1996). The bid was unsuccessful, but in 1995 the United Kingdom's Government's Department of National Heritage (now renamed the Department of Culture, Media and Sport) set up the Library and Information Commission (LIC) (in order to advise Government on library and information issues and to promote cross-sectoral cooperation and collaboration) and commissioned them to develop a plan to network all public libraries in the United Kingdom to the Internet.

By October 1997 the Commission, skilfully led by Matthew Evans (Managing Director of Faber & Faber Publishing) had delivered its vision to government. The report, *New Library: The People's Network* (1997), stunned the public library community with its revolutionary and innovative appeal, and marked a critical turning point in the development of services when it argued that,

> The networking of public libraries will place them in the forefront of the drive to create an educated, informed and ICT-literate society "The library is an enormously powerful agent of change: accountable to and trusted by people, and integral to education, industry, government and the community" (*Library and Information Commission*, 1997: Introduction).

The aim of the Public Library Network is to connect all public libraries in the United Kingdom to each other, to the Internet and other networked resources. Each library within a local authority will be networked at a local level and then these local networks will be in time connected to a national network. The infrastructure is seen to be an integral part of a parallel initiative for schools, *The National Grid for Learning* (1997), enabling a cross-fertilization of learning resources to be accessible via schools and libraries.

At the heart of *New Library* is the immense opportunity not just to provide access to the wealth of resources currently held within public libraries, but to develop and deliver dynamic new content and services on a global scale. The initiative is popularly referred to as the People's Network, surely a more appropriate metaphor than the Public Library Network which imagines a network for all citizens, not limited within the walls of public library institutions, or indeed those within the United Kingdom. Five key areas were identified as critical to its development, building on existing central public library services: education and lifelong learning; citizens' information; business and the economy, and training and development; community history and identity; and the development of a national digital library. Significantly each area fitted perfectly into the current political climate, mirroring several of government's agendas (highlighted below).

At last the vital role that public libraries play in the delivery of information and learning support had been fiercely advocated by the library community, and critically it was argued that as a result these institutions must be placed center stage to deliver the information society agendas of lifelong learning and social inclusion.

THE GOVERNMENT'S RESPONSE

The government's response in the spring of 1998 continued the emphasis on the importance of public libraries stating that:

> Libraries contribute to four of this government's most important policy objectives. They underpin *education*, providing essential support to school children, students, and lifelong learners; they enhance *public access* to the world's storehouse of knowledge and information; they promote *social inclusion*, by helping to bridge the gap between those who can afford access to information and those who can't; and increasingly, they have a role to play in the *modernization* and delivery of public services (Department for Culture, Media and Sport, 1998:1, original italics).

Crucially the government's support for public libraries was demonstrated by its proposal to channel 50 million pounds sterling into the digitization of educational and learning materials held within public libraries, and a further 20 million pounds sterling to ensure that all 27,000 library staff throughout the United Kingdom would receive adequate training to develop and deliver these networked services to the public. Financial investment would be allocated through the New Opportunities Fund in close liaison with a specific body set up to oversee the delivery of the People's Network.

The government had already provided 9 million pounds sterling to fund pathfinding network projects within libraries (DCMS/Wolfson Challenge Fund), and additionally two further sums of New Opportunities funding, amounting to 600 million pounds sterling have been committed to a number of initiatives including community access to lifelong learning (New Links for the Lottery, 1998) and the creation of IT-based learning centres (Chancellor's budget speech, 1999).

Further support from the government was demonstrated through its pledge to negotiate for reduced telecommunications tariffs on behalf of the public library community. At present the United Kingdom does not benefit from free local telecom calls as the United States does, and as such the profession has welcomed this promise, as library budgets leave little or no room to implement networked services alongside traditional services. Whilst the outcome of these negotiations is unknown at the time of writing this chapter, it is felt a favorable outcome to these discussions will go a long way to ensuring that the People's Network will be sustainable in the long-term.

THE NEW LIBRARY BLUEPRINT: REALIZING THE VISION

The government charged the LIC working party with the task to develop a framework for delivering the network. By November 1998 the Commission had presented its proposals to Government in the report: *Building the New Library Network* (1998). Now hailed as the blueprint for future public library services in the United Kingdom, this report presented recommendations as to how the network should be built and delivered, and how the proposed funding should be administered and awarded.

Three broad strands of content, training and infrastructure were addressed in the report. For content it was suggested that funding should be awarded to projects holding national relevance and significance within the areas of cultural enrichment, citizenship and reskilling, encompassing lifelong learning in its broadest sense. It was stressed that *New Library* would require new librarians, equipped with skills in Information and Communications Technologies, and recommended that funds should be allocated to train all public library staff accordingly.

On the issue of infrastructure, the report did not propose a specific networking model; instead it suggested that it should be for local authorities to decide which approach would be best for them, but to give consideration to interoperability at the national level. Various avenues for funding to implement and sustain the network were identified in the report, including public funding from local and national streams, lottery funds, privately financed initiatives and third-party revenues, such as user fees. It stated explicitly, however, that access to the People's Network must be free at the point of use.

Since the publication of *Building the New Library Network*, the entire public library community has been waiting in anticipation of the funding guidelines so that the initiative can get underway.

THE BEGINNINGS OF THE WORLD WIDE WEB IN PUBLIC LIBRARIES

Amongst all the hype and activity currently taking place, however, it is easy to ignore the roots of these developments, which predated the publication of *New Library* and the political thrust behind its realization. A number of research projects began to explore the potential of the World Wide Web from 1995. Among the first of these were ITPoint and the Croydon Libraries Internet Project (CLIP) (Dick, 1995; Batt, 1996; Kayam & Turner, 1996). Each of these experiments aimed and succeeded in demonstrating the value of providing Internet-based services at local authority levels and arguably acted as a catalyst for other local authorities to follow suit.

At the same time others in the public library community (including representatives from the aforementioned projects) invested in a completely different approach to networking. The basic principle behind this approach was not in itself unique, merely a translation of the ability of public librarians to collaborate with each other in the delivery of library services through a national consortium. What was significant about this approach, however, was the imaginative forethought in developing and delivering shared library services within an environment which by its very nature necessitates an intrinsic level of cooperation: that environment being the Internet. Though undoubtedly each of these pioneering projects did much to chart the course, in this chapter it is argued that the collaborative approach developed through EARL has played and will continue to play a central role in the development of the People's Network.

THE EARL CONSORTIUM

As evidenced in its name, EARL was conceived in 1994 to develop and deliver Electronic Access to Resources in Libraries. Quite simply, the aim was to develop and deliver World Wide Web networked services to public libraries through collaboration (Woodhouse, 1998). The original scoping study and project received funding from a number of interested public library authorities, the British Library

Research and Development Department and the London and South Eastern Regional Library System (England is divided into broad regional groupings of library authorities for interlibrary loan purposes, LASER being the largest), and was largely driven by the imaginative flair of Frances Hendrix and Peter Smith of LASER and consultant Peter Stone (Dolan, 1995).

EARL ran as a research project for two years and achieved formal Consortium status in 1997. Since that time the number of local authority partners has grown to nearly 160, with widespread geographical representation from around the United Kingdom. Partners pay a contribution fee to EARL in order to share costs and contribute expertise in the management, development and delivery of a growing range of Web-based networked services designed specifically with the public library community in mind. Most importantly, though, the Consortium represents a unified voice to advocate the need for the People's Network, in raising awareness and providing practical advice to the public library community on all aspects of networking.

NEW WAYS OF WORKING: EARL TASK GROUPS

Public libraries in the United Kingdom are learning to manage and deliver networked services on local, regional and national levels, to reflect the dynamic environment in which they must now operate. At the heart of public library services is the importance of local identity, and at the heart of EARL's approach to service development is the fundamental belief that the key to delivering these networked services is collaborative working. Through collaboration, EARL partners are developing services at a national level, which at the same time embrace and underpin the importance of local identity (Woodhouse, 1998).

The mechanism of collaborative working and the fruits of cooperation are realized through the work of several task groups. The groups represent a unique and important model for future service development and delivery which embraces the national dimension of a People's Network. Members of task groups participate voluntarily, signalling an increasing recognition within library authorities that management of staff and resources must encompass a broader perspective than they are traditionally used to. Much of the credit for EARL's achievements, though, is owed to its task group participants, who have shown tremendous levels of commitment to the challenges of working in a networked environment. However, collaborative working has also relied on champions from within the profession. Particular credit must be given to Peter Stone, EARL consultant for four years, who was the inspiration behind task groups and indeed much more, and to the enthusiasm and voluntary commitment of Robert and Sheila Harden, who have been largely responsible for the success of two of EARL's demonstrator services: *EARLweb* and *Ask a Librarian.*

Undoubtedly, though, these groups have recognized the enormous benefits to be gained from working collaboratively: for it encourages a coherent approach to services delivery, it provides a cost-effective way of exploiting content, it provides a valuable training opportunity for staff in the use and understanding of networking tools, it pools experience, ideas and expertise and its national focus adds value to the exploitation of local resources.

EARL'S ACHIEVEMENTS

It is not possible to list every achievement of the Consortium in this short chapter. Since the genesis of EARL, task groups have collaboratively developed a growing number of Web-based services and resources which aim to demonstrate the potential of using the World Wide Web to deliver public library services to users. In support of these developments, EARL has also been delivering a program of events and publications to assist the transition to a networked environment, which serves to facilitate the roll-out of the People's Network. The first part of this section highlights some of the service examples currently available from the EARL Web site (http://www.earl.org.uk), and is followed by an overview of the wider facilitating role of EARL.

DEMONSTRATOR SERVICES

EARL's demonstrator services are available to everyone who has access to the Internet, not restricted by passwords or to partners who have paid contributions to the Consortium. Many of the services were groundbreakers within the United Kingdom and have succeeded in opening up public library resources to many: not all traditional library users, and not all from the United Kingdom.

Ask A Librarian (http://www.earl.org.uk/ask/index.html) was launched in November 1997 and has attracted a good deal of praise and acclaim. The idea was simple enough: to provide a service for users which translated the primary skill of librarians in finding, assessing and then passing on information directly to a Web environment using email.

A link from the Ask A Librarian homepage to a page of links to the participating library authorities demonstrates the truly networked nature of the service. Each participating library takes questions for 24 hours on a rota basis and provided guidelines on how to tackle reference enquiries. The source of the answer is always provided in a reply e-mail to the enquirer and often suggestions for other potential sources of interest are included. Where possible the source is Internet-based not only to demonstrate the amount of useful information already on the Web but to allow the enquirer potentially immediate access to the source consulted. This unique approach offers the same service a user would expect to have in a face-to-face situation but adds an extra dimension to the reference situation by allowing questions to be asked at any time from potentially anywhere.

While *Ask A Librarian* demonstrates how Internet users can interact with librarians through the Web, two more of EARL's services demonstrate how the holdings of UK public libraries can be exploited through the Web to enhance services provided to users. *MagNet* (http://www.earl.org.uk/magnet/index.html) and *Familia* (http://www.earl.org.uk/familia/index.html) are both directories of public library holdings that draw together local holdings into a national database which means that authorities are providing local information but at the same time presenting a national focus.

MagNet, developed by the Serials task group, is a distributed search service which allows users to find magazines, journals and newspapers in public libraries throughout the United Kingdom. The task is not yet complete, but it is already a useful and practical finding aid. In the future the aims are to develop this location tool to include full-text, representing a fundamental shift towards creating a virtual hybrid library serials service.

Familia is a Web-based directory of family history resources held in public libraries in the United Kingdom and Ireland. Updated and maintained by the Family History task group, *Familia* provides an online starting point to find information about materials held in public libraries which help to trace family history. The directory offers information on different kinds of materials and services in British libraries, maps to aid location, a developing search interface, and a gateway to other Web sources to aid research. The guides section also points to some excellent online guides to family history research, and gives useful hints and tips on how to make the most of these library resources.

EARLweb (http://www.earl.org.uk/earlweb/) and *Euroguide* (http://www.euroguide.org/) are both examples of public-library-purposed Internet gateways to help guide users through cyberspace. More than a gateways to links, however, users can be assured of the quality of resources being accessed because they are evaluated by librarians and presented as themed sections, which reflect public library collections. Because these sites are the result of collaboration it avoids duplication of effort by library authorities as they can all contribute to and link to one central Website. Another benefit is that the serendipitous discovery of one librarian can be used to the benefit of many. *EARLweb* is increasingly being adopted as a common reference tool and is featured on many public access homepages to the World Wide Web, while *Euroguide,* developed by the European Information task group aims to increase the accessibility to the mass of European information available on the web.

These are just some of the examples which prove that collaboration at a national level to provide services with national context does not mean ignoring the needs of local users. Clearly the lessons which have been learned through this mechanism of working and delivery provide one model for delivering the People's Network.

BRIDGING THE GAP BETWEEN POLICY AND IMPLEMENTATION OF THE PEOPLE'S NETWORK

EARL has played an important and sustained role in advocating the People's Network and has lobbied on national and local levels to enhance and maintain the momentum for change. EARL has practically advocated the importance of *New Library*, by being involved in the publication of *The Speakers Presentation Pack* (Ormes and Criddle, 1998) (in association with UKOLN - the UK Office for Library and Information Networking, and the Library Association) which provided all library authorities with a toolkit to cascade the vision and implications of the People's Network to library staff. Plans to publish a similar pack for *Building the New Library Network* are well underway.

The role of EARL as supporter and facilitator, though, has been most explicitly embraced by the Networked Services Policy task group (hereinafter Policy task group). The importance of their work is widely supported by the LIC, government, and public library community as a whole, and has helped the community to get to grips with this defining moment. The Policy task group (with support from UKOLN, and the Library Association) has developed their own Web site, (http://www.earl.org.uk/taskgroups/policy/issue.htm) to help the community translate the management and delivery of services to a Web environment.

The group anticipated a growing need for a simple way to share information about networked policy developments, and to learn from each other's experiences (Ormes and Potts, 1998). One of the group's primary aims, therefore, is to build an archive of existing policies for the Community to refer to. It is hoped that by sharing information, the public library community will therefore be able to make informed policy decisions. The number of policies currently listed demonstrates the state of infancy of public library networked services development and policy making in the United Kingdom, but in time this archive could present models of best practice, in an effort to attain a national networked policy strategy.

To assist the public library community further, the group has been involved in the delivery of a series of workshops and discussion forums, providing a necessary forum to debate key issues involved in the development of networked services. Issues such as assessing information quality, providing equality of access and charging have been the subjects of debate so far, with plans to deliver many more in the future. The events have proved to be highly successful and most welcome to those who deliver library services and those involved in the decision-making process, not just to those within library authorities, but also to representatives from government and the private sector.

Outcomes from these workshops have provided the group with a great deal of information which are fueling the publication of a complementary series of issues papers. Papers on filtering, quality of information and charging have already been published and are available from their Web site (http://www.earl.org.uk/taskgroups/policy/issue.htm) and others are in the process of being completed.

Together, the archive of existing policies, the workshops and issue papers are building a collaborative *New Library* "think-tank," to ensure that services are developed and delivered efficiently and effectively throughout the United Kingdom. The work of the Policy task group represents an important bridging process between local, regional and national levels involved in the delivery of *New Library* and is helping to link policy-making to implementation of the network.

PUTTING THINGS IN PERSPECTIVE: THE CURRENT SPREAD OF DEVELOPMENT

Despite the fact that there are examples of excellent public library Web services, it is important not to lose sight of the broader picture of development across the United Kingdom. Until recently, the existence of these services was so insignificant that it was not until the end of 1995 that the first Internet survey of public libraries was produced (Ormes and Dempsey, 1995). In 1998 two further snapshots of activity were published by Batt and on a smaller scale by EARL's Policy task group (Batt, 1998; Ormes and Potts, 1998). Both of these findings suggested that a growing trend in activity had taken place since the first picture was presented just over a year before that, and that the public library community was indeed undergoing a process of change.

At first glance, the Policy task group's survey presented a very impressive 90% of local authorities having some form of staff Internet access (compared with 53% in the first survey by Ormes in 1995), and just under 70% providing some form of public Internet access (compared with 17% indicated in Ormes survey in 1995) (Ormes and Potts, 1998). However, as Batt's survey shows, just 9% of the actual service points in the United Kingdom provide public Internet access (Batt, 1998).

An assessment of the kinds of connections used by libraries, highlighted in each of these surveys also confirms that public library networking is still in a state of infancy. Each show that the most popular method of delivery of networked services is via dial up access, as opposed to more sophisticated methods such as leased line and ISDN provision. Dial up limits the type of access available and therefore the types of services that can be offered due to limited bandwidth capabilities (Ormes and Dempsey, 1996). Each of these surveys paints a fragmented picture of development and a very inconsistent approach to delivering networked services. The bottom line is that these surveys show that there is still a long way to go and there are many issues to be resolved before attaining the vision of the People's Network.

ISSUES TO ADDRESS

Clearly the unevenness of development suggests that the road to *New Library* will not be an easy one. There are still many issues to be addressed and resolved before attaining a national Public Library Network (and this must come before the Community comes to terms with delivering services specifically with the global information society in mind), and yet at the same time it should not be forgotten that the public library community has come a long way in a very short period of time.

One of the current concerns of the Community, for example, is the lack of certainty about the exact interrelationship between the People's Network and other initiatives, such as the National Grid for Learning and the University for Industry. Questions relating to the interoperability and seamlessness of these networks must clearly be addressed. Similarly, the exact roll-out of the People's Network must be determined to ensure that appropriate interrelationships between local, regional and national developments are established and maintained. Will the diversity of approaches to accessing Internet services currently in existence, for example, present too fragmented an approach? How can duplication of effort be avoided and what will the primary focus of networking within library authorities be (local, regional, national or global)? Concerns like these require further guidelines from government and the LIC to ensure that these issues are adequately and quickly resolved.

Funding and sustainability of the network is also a hot topic amongst the public library community. How is it that such a vision can be delivered in a climate of bidding for funds, with no guarantee that future funding will become available to deliver and sustain these services? Moreover, if the network must be delivered free at the point of use, how is it that libraries will be able to continue to develop and deliver these services?

These hurdles must be overcome in order for public libraries to remain at the heart of the government's agenda to create an information society. Many believe that this window of opportunity will soon pass and yet public librarians are asking how on earth are they going to deliver? Many of these concerns are indeed justified, given the enormity of change that they are currently facing. Certainly a number of the answers to these questions, though, can be found in the blue-print document: *Building the New Library Network*, and arguably through the work of the EARL Consortium. Let us now turn to the future and consider how these issues might be resolved.

THE WAY FORWARD

In terms of the infrastructure of the network, *Building the New Library Network* (1998) placed the nuts and bolts of the decision-making in the hands of local authorities, providing a number of alternative models for them to choose from. Some commentators are unhappy that a managed broadband network will not be imple-mented from the network's inception, suggesting that this presents too fragmented an approach to deliver such an ambitious project. It has been argued throughout this chapter, however, that EARL has shown that even without specific government funding and a broad-band network, that a bottom up approach to networking services can be achieved on a national scale, without sacrificing the importance of local identity. Moreover EARL believes that over time, as the value of the network is fully realized, the ideal infrastructure will be supported through financial backing from both the public and private sectors, and that the shift to a networked environment is by its very nature subject to an evolutionary process of development. Additionally, the Community will most likely be provided with technical guidelines from the Public Library Network Team which will help authorities to implement network strategies.

Ironically, it seems, that whilst the public library was heralded as an enormously powerful agent of change in *New Library*, the public library community must undergo a radical process of change them-selves. This must be achieved at deep and pervasive levels to ensure that the management and delivery of services encompass a broader national perspective, and that staff and resources are divulged accord-ingly. EARL's collaborative approach provides a useful model for achieving this but requires further attitudinal change from the public library community as a whole to fully integrate this approach into routine procedures, rather than relying on the good will of a minority of public library staff. The proposal to train all public library staff in the use of networked services within *Building the New Library Network* will go some way to ensuring that this shift is achieved.

At the same time, EARL recognizes the need for local and regional developments to parallel this national perspective. The People's Network cannot be developed from one central place: its appeal is derived from the vision to collate the abundance of unique resources which all public libraries hold. Together, though, local, regional and national initiatives can be united to form the most remarkable collection of services the public library community has ever known. This, of course, will require tremendous amounts of coordination from all levels of the Community.

In terms of the sustainability of the network, partnerships are the key to ensuring that the network is continuously maintained and developed. Enormous amounts of money have already been promised by Government to help build the infrastructure and content of the network. It was explicitly stated, though, that further sources of funding must be secured at local, regional and national levels to ensure that the necessary infrastructure is in place and appropriate forms of content developed. Libraries must cultivate partnerships within and between local authorities, the private sector and most especially with telecommunications providers, to supplement what will hopefully be fruitful negotiations between the government and telecommunications providers at a national level. Working together will be a prerequisite, avoiding duplication of effort and collaboratively rolling-out the network.

Once the network is established, it will be necessary for public libraries to continue to lobby for support in order to update and develop services delivered over the network. The People's Network must prove to be indispensable to our society, attaining support from key players in local and national government to secure the future of the network. Partially, at least, the key to achieving this will require the Community to foster and embrace a global perspective in the development and delivery of services to ensure that the United Kingdom holds a place within the global information society. In the shorter term, though, a shift from political rhetoric to actual implementation of the network must take place.

It has been suggested that there are solutions to many of the issues already present themselves in the form of existing documentation and networked services delivery. The final section of this chapter proposes how these solutions might unfold.

CONCEIVING A FUTURE STRUCTURE FOR THE PEOPLE'S NETWORK

The proposed Scottish model provides a clue as to how the national network may develop. Here the Scottish Library and Information Commission (SLIC) has the task of coordinating developments across the board in this "region" (region is used here to define each of the four United Kingdom home countries). The model proposes to provide comprehensive access by building partnerships to ensure that regional sustainability is achieved. A strong regional strategy will complement telecommunications deals that are being established at a local level.

As regional and local strategies develop across the United Kingdom, it will be possible to tie them into a higher strategic, or national, level to deliver the People's Network. This method of delivering the network will require a process of symbiosis between a number of different levels. It seems likely that the LIC will oversee the sustainability of the network at an overarching national level (in association with the SLIC) by coordinating strategies at each of the regional levels (i.e. Scotland, Ireland, Wales and England). Below this various 'pressure groups' could be held responsible for coordinating current regional (hereinafter subregional) library system developments. Below this the subregional library services could be commis-

Figure 1: The People's Network

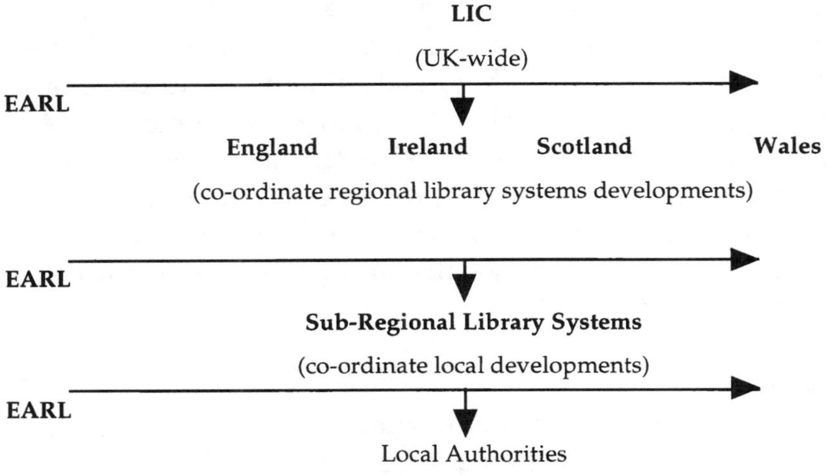

LIC

(UK-wide)

EARL

England   Ireland   Scotland   Wales

(co-ordinate regional library systems developments)

EARL

Sub-Regional Library Systems

(co-ordinate local developments)

EARL

Local Authorities

sioned to coordinate local authority-level activities within each subregion. These interrelationships assume that there would be overlapping developments between all levels, which would be strategically managed by the LIC (and SLIC), and practically held together by a facilitating body, such as EARL. Figure 1 shows how together these interrelated levels could form the People's Network.

EARL AS FACILITATOR

At the same time it will be important for the public library community to have access to models of best practice within national, regional, subregional and local levels of the network. It will also be vital for communication to flow between each of these levels to support the overseeing role of the LIC and SLIC. Critically too it will be important to ensure that a body continues to advocate the importance of the Public Library Network on behalf of local, regional and national levels. This means convincing Local Authority Chief Executives, politicians and the private sector that it is in their interests to continue to support the network.

It is conceivable for EARL to extend its practical commitment to advocacy by continuing to act as this national facilitator. In the long term it will be possible for EARL to benchmark networking achievements and provide case studies to demonstrate what works and what doesn't work. This will help authorities put together successful bids for future funding and therefore contribute in a practical way towards the sustainability of the network. In effect, EARL would be acting as the glue that holds the People's Network together.

In the future, EARL envisages an expansion of its existing Web site, to act as virtual centre to public libraries networked resources in the United Kingdom. Plans are already underway to develop this interface, which could also act as the point of reference to EARL's national facilitating role. As with all of EARL's achievements, this will require enthusiasm, commitment and collaboration to succeed, but if the past is anything to go by, EARL is confident that however the network actually rolls-out, they will continue to play a central role in its development and looks forward to doing so.

CONCLUSION

In this chapter it has been demonstrated how the momentum for the development and implementation of the People's Network in the

United Kingdom has grown from government policies of social inclusion and lifelong learning to secure economic and social prosperity. A strong recognition from Government of the vital role that public libraries play in tackling these issues has led to plans to develop and deliver new and innovative services to our information society, and the global information society at large.

It has been argued that EARL has played, and will continue to play, a central facilitating role in providing practical help to the public library community, which is evolving to form the New Library "think-tank." At the same time it was proposed that EARL is well placed to contribute to the strategic roll-out of the network at a regional level to support the national objectives outlined by the LIC. Moreover, it was demonstrated that EARL's national-local philosophy and self-help approach through collaboration illustrates an important model for actually delivering the People's Network. The significance of EARL's approach was eloquently encapsulated in Batt's most recent Information Technology survey of public libraries in the United Kingdom when he said that:

> EARL ... demonstrates the transition of the public library from simple storehouse of other people's information into mediator of access and coordinator of resources "and presents an important exemplar of the public library as proactive agent for change." The work EARL has started is but the first hint of what the future landscape will be like" (Batt, 1998:56).

REFERENCES

Batt, C. (1996). The libraries of the future: public libraries and the internet. *IFLA Journal*, 22(1), 27-30.

Batt, C. (1998). *Information technology in public libraries*. 6th Edition. London: Library Association Publishing.

Chancellor's Budget speech. (1999). Available: http://www.hm-treasury.gov.uk/budget99/speech.html [1999, Mar 9].

Department for Culture, Media and Sport. (1997). Connecting the learning society: national grid for learning. Available: http://www.dfee.gov.uk/grid/consult/index.htm [1999, Jan 15].

Department for Culture, Media & Sport. (1998). New library: the people's network. The Government's response. London: The Stationery Office Ltd.

Department for Culture, Media and Sport. (1998). The learning age: a renaissance for a new Britain. Available: http://www.lifelonglearning.co.uk/greenpaper/index.htm [1999, Feb 20].

Department for Culture, Media and Sport. (1998). New links for the lottery: proposals for the new opportunities fund. Available: http://www.culture.gov.uk/NOFINFO.HTM [1999, Feb 2].

Department for Culture, Media and Sport. (1998). University for industry. Available: http://www.dfee.gov.uk/ufi/index.htm [1999, Feb 22].

Dick, J. (1995). The Croydon libraries internet project (CLIP). *The New Review in Information Networking, 1,* 99-103.

Dolan, J. (1997). The EARL experience. In Ormes, S., & Dempsey, L. (Eds), *The interent, networking and the public library* (pp 91-99). London: Library Association Publishing.

Fryer, R.H. (1997). Learning for the twenty-first century. Available: http://www.lifelonglearning.co.uk/nagcell/index.htm [1999, Feb 13]

Government.direct. (1996). *Government.direct.* London: The Stationery Office Ltd.

Hare, G. (1995). The EARL consortium: the evolution of the public library internet project. *New Review of Information Networking, 1,* 89-98.

Information for All (1996). *Millennium libraries: A national public library network.* Cambridge: Information for All.

INSINC. (1997). The net result: social inclusion in the information society. Available: http://www.uk.ibm.com/community/uk117.html [1999, Jan 27].

Kayam, G., & Turner, S. (1996). IT Point: internet in a public library context. *The New Review of Information Networking, 2,* 55-67.

Library and Information Commission. (1997). New library: the people's network. London: Library and Information Commission. Available: http://www.lic.gov.uk/publications/policyreports/newlibrary/index.html [1999, Apr 02].

Library and Information Commission. (1998). Building the new library network. London: Library and Information Commission. Available: http://www.lic.gov.uk/publications/policyreports/building/index.html [1999, Apr 02].

Ormes, S. (1998). Public libraries corner: Ask a Librarian. Ariadne, 13. Available: http://www.ariadne.ac.uk/issue13/public-libraries/

[1999, Feb 23].

Ormes, S., & Criddle, S. (1998). *Speakers presentation pack.* Bath: UKOLN.

Ormes, S., & Dempsey, L. (1995). The Library and Information Commission public library internet survey: first public report (December 1995). *New Review of Information Networking, 1,* 71-87.

Ormes, S., & Dempsey, L. (1996). Net use in public libraries. *Library Association Record, 98*(4), 200.

Ormes, S., & Potts, D. (1998). Public libraries corner: the work of the networked policy taskgroup. Ariadne, 18. Available: http://www.ariadne.ac.uk/issue18/pub-lib/ [1999, Feb 23].

Woodhouse, S. (1998). EARL: setting the agenda for the future. *Impact: the Journal of the Career Development Group, 1*(1), 12-15.

Chapter X

Providing Multilingual Internet Services in the Global Information Environment: WorldLinQ™ Project, Queens Library's Practices

Xuemao Wang, Malabika Das,
Maria V. Sunio and Andrew N. Schlein
Queens Borough (NY) Public Library, USA

This chapter describes the Queens Borough Public Library's WorldLinQ™ (URL: http://www.worldlinq.org), a unique Internet-based multilingual information system to provide user access to global and local information resources, currently in English, Chinese, Korean, Spanish, Russian and French. WorldLinQ™ comprises a multilingual Web resource collection, multilingual access to the Library's online catalog (InfoLinQ™) and international resource sharing. The W-Team selects and maintains the content, with a goal of covering the major languages spoken by immigrants in Queens. Content includes topics academic, business, technology and entertainment, in multilingual and multimedia format, from anywhere on the Internet. Alliances with corporate (AT&T) and library partners (the Shanghai Library and the National Library of China) have played a crucial part in the project's development. The network configuration of the Queens Library and the software setup of WorldLinQ™ are also described.

INTERNET—A GLOBAL PERSPECTIVE AND ITS IMPACT ON LIBRARY SERVICES

There has, perhaps, been no phenomenon with a more significant impact on public library services than the advent and subsequent astounding growth of the Internet. The public demand for access to the Internet, especially in economically depressed communities, puts a new and different strain on libraries and their human and fiscal resources. It has become the public libraries' responsibility to provide this access where schools and other public institutions have been unable or unwilling to commit the necessary funding. As is so often the case, this responsibility is a double-edged sword. The availability of high-speed access to the global resources of the Internet in a library draws more people to use a library's services. At the same time, however, it raises the question of whether this access should be part of a public library's offerings. Free access to the public at a large urban library carries with it a significant drain on resources. Internet access with insufficient bandwidth is worse than none at all, as the result is dissatisfied and underserved customers. It has been the policy at the Queens Borough Public Library (also known as the Queens Library or QBPL) that offering free access to the Internet will go a long way toward leveling the playing field for our customers, most of whom would have no other entrée.

The World Wide Web provides an incredibly abundant variety of information, which is available in an easily accessible, usually user-friendly and media-rich format. On a daily basis the number of available sites increases to the extent that only the most powerful search engines can keep up with the proliferation. The quantity of information available grows exponentially and apparently without limit. Whether one looks for song lyrics, government documents, reviews of the latest technological advances or a partner for a game of backgammon, the resources are available. As amazing as this rate of growth is, it is equally surprising that the cost of the variety of information is virtually nil. While the cost of access may be high, the increase in variety does not carry with it a concomitant increase in cost. The late science fiction writer Robert A. Heinlein was fond of including the acronym TANSTAAFL in many of his books: There Ain't No Such Thing As A Free Lunch. This thought may well apply to the World Wide Web as well. With the vast amount of data available, how does the naïve Web surfer determine the validity of the information that she finds? We believe that libraries and librarians can provide the added value that will greatly enhance the value of the Internet to our customers. As is the case of WorldLinQ™ (see below), Web sites can be cataloged and referenced and can gain the de facto imprimatur of the host library. Just as an experienced librarian will recommend one book over another to a customer seeking information in the more traditional way, the library's customized web site can point the user to a set of information. This method is particularly useful with our younger customers. One of the Queens Library's sites is KidsLinQ™, a selection of pre-screened, age-appropriate web sites. KidsLinQ™ has been very well received by professional children's librarians as well as the children and their parents.

THE QUEENS LIBRARY: ITS BACKGROUND, INTERNET INFRASTRUCTURE AND SERVICES

The Queens Library is the sixth largest public library system in the country in terms of population served (Public Library Association, 1998). It has generated the highest circulation of any city library system in the United States since 1989, circulating more than 15.5 million items in 1998. The Library's holdings comprise over 9.5 million items. In its capacity as a public library, the Queens Library serves far more than its 847,000 cardholders. Each year, eight million people walk through the doors of the Queens Library's Central Library, 62 community libraries and six adult learning centers. High circulation and attendance may be attributable to merchandised collections, which make popular materials easily accessible to customers; technological innovation; an emphasis on meeting the needs of neighborhood residents; and strong outreach programs to potential library users.

In 1996 as part of the Queens Library's Centennial celebration, a wide area network (WAN) was installed throughout the Borough of Queens. Funded by the New York City Executive Budget, the Queens Borough President, and the Library's own resources, with the cooperation of NYNEX (now Bell Atlantic) and with the project management of Digital Equipment Corporation, the 63 locations of the Queens Library became united. Each of the 62 branch libraries was given a network file server, Pentium-class personal computers (PCs) and laser printers. The branch libraries were connected to the NYNEX Frame Relay cloud via either 384Kb/sec. or 56Kb/sec. lines depending on the branch size. Each location also had an ISDN connection for backup when the frame relay connection was out of service. All lines come into the Central Library's Data Center and are routed to the Internet through the City University of New York on a pair of T-1 lines. Initially, 400 PCs were deployed across the borough.

As a result, InfoLinQ™, the online catalog of the Library's holdings, has been available for public access within all 63 Library locations since 1996. Prior to InfoLinQ™, most Library customers visiting the branches could only check a CD-ROM catalog, which could be updated only quarterly, or request Library staff to conduct a search of the character-cell (text-only) online catalog at the reference desks. InfoLinQ™ gave Library staff and customers better tools for searching and checking the availability of the Library's holdings. In addition, via InfoLinQ™, customers can research periodical and newspaper databases, with many full-text articles available online; look up community resource information, with details of more than 1,000 programs offering health and human services to Queens residents; and explore the Internet.

Since then, public demand has necessitated adding more computers which, in turn, have demanded increased bandwidth allocations. The Library's connection to the Internet has been upgraded to a DS-3 connection running at 45Mb/sec. The branch connections to the frame relay cloud are now T-1s (1.544Mb/sec) at all but the 10 smallest branches, which are running at 384Kb/sec. As of this writing, there are approximately twice the number of PCs and printers as in the original network design. This network configuration should be sufficient for the next couple of years and will support new PCs, which are likely to be added during that time. After that, however, bandwidth demand is expected to outstrip the current technology and an alternative will have to be found. In view of the current state of technology, an Asynchronous Transfer Mode (ATM) network will most likely be the next step. Aside from the increase in available bandwidth, the ATM WAN would be able to carry the Library's voice and video traffic as well as the data traffic.

THE QUEENS LIBRARY'S WORLDLINQ™ PROJECT

Project Overview

The Queens Library's WorldLinQ™ project is a unique Internet-based multilingual information system to provide user access to global and local information resources, currently available in English, Chinese, Korean, Spanish, Russian and French. It is accessible over the Internet via the URL http://www.worldlinq.org. The goal of the project is to offer library services in the major immigrant languages spoken in Queens. The project is sponsored by a $500,000 AT&T grant, which is the largest grant given by the company to a public library. While the World Wide Web has largely been developed by and with regard to the English-speaking world, the Queens Library believes that only providing a service in English is inadequate to serve a community as diverse as Queens (Marriott, 1998). WorldLinQ™ is a significant strategy of the Queens Library for providing access to these global information resources. Customers can search internationally published information resources on topics academic, business, technology and entertainment, in multilingual and multimedia format, from the Internet. There are three major components in this project: a multilingual Web resource collection, multilingual access to the Library's online public access catalog and multilingual international resource sharing.

Community Profile and Project History

The Borough of Queens, New York, is one of the most ethnically diverse counties in the United States. According to the 1990 U.S. Census, the population of Queens reaches almost two million people, of which 36% were born in a different country and 44% speak a language other than English at home. A recent study conducted by the New York City Department of City Planning examining the flow of legal immigration between 1990 and 1994 revealed similar findings: 30% of New York's recent immigrants have chosen Queens as their new home. More than 120 countries and 100 languages are represented among Queens residents. Trying to serve the needs of this microcosmic community, the Queens Library maintains collections in more than 40 languages other than English and operates the second largest program of English-for-speakers-of-other-languages in the country. Many programs are geared to recent immigrant arrivals on topics like citizenship or how to get a driver's license and are often presented in a language other than English.

While many library customers in Queens may not be fluent in English, they are frequently literate in other languages. Applying the

Library's outlook on collection development and outreach practices for serving these groups to technology seemed a natural progression. The popularity of the InfoLinQ™ stations had already demonstrated how technology could attract people into the library, physically and virtually. The Chinese-Japanese-Korean (CJK) project began in 1995 with a small-scale prototype of a Web interface displaying the Chinese, Japanese, and Korean characters. At its inception, Queens Library staff knew of no other information system of its kind in the nation for providing access to library electronic resources in a multilingual format. Recognizing a potential to add more languages to this project, the Library renamed the CJK project as "WorldLinQ."

It became clear that more funding would be needed to support the development of such an ambitious project. To do this, the Library would need to secure a sponsorship with an organization that would want to align itself with a valued public institution. To the Library's credit, it could offer the sponsor positive public recognition, widespread throughout the borough. In March 1995, the Queens Library Foundation wrote and submitted a grant proposal to the technology giant AT&T. In November 1996, the partnership was forged: AT&T would sponsor the Queens Library's WorldLinQ™ project by giving $500,000 over three years of development. This grant has been the largest amount of money that AT&T ever awarded a public library. Soon after, the Queens Library officially registered the name of the project as a trademark.

By the middle of 1997, the WorldLinQ™ started to provide access in four languages: English, Chinese, Korean and Spanish. The Russian module was added in December 1997, the French module in January 1999. By summer of 1998, the multilingual online catalog component was linked to WorldLinQ™. (This component is described in greater detail later in the chapter.) In recognition of its service to users and for its inventive use of technology, WorldLinQ™ has gained attention nationally and internationally, receiving several awards, including the Highsmith Library Innovation Award (1997), the Joseph F. Shubert Library Excellence Award (1998), and the ALA/Information Today Library of the Future Award (1999).

Project Team

The content of WorldLinQ™ is developed and maintained by a special project group known as the W-Team in the Library, which consists of 21 professional employees with diverse cultural and language backgrounds. Including mostly librarians and some paraprofessionals, the W-Team members come from different departments and internal agencies but collaborate toward the same purpose. The W-Team members are required to work five hours per week to search, evaluate, select and annotate Web resources published in languages other than English, and finally add these resources to the WorldLinQ™ site. The basic characteristics required of a W-Team member are Internet savvy, fluency in English and the other language(s) in which the member is working, as well as a willingness to learn new technology. The W-Team is organized into subgroups by each language. Each subgroup consists of three members, including a coordinator.

WorldLinQ™ Technological Infrastructure

WorldLinQ™ runs on DEC/Alpha computer hardware, with Microsoft Windows NT 4.0 and Internet Information Server 4.0 software. The PCs on the Queens Library network use the Windows NT operating system. Microsoft Internet Explorer 4.0 is currently the Library's default Web browser, selected for its capacity to display different languages in the Library's Web catalog. Instead of running an international-language operating system on public stations, the Library enables an additional multilingual function on PCs running an English-language operating system. This configuration minimizes the costs of technical support and optimizes the functionality of the station. For example, the display and input of Chinese characters is easily handled if Microsoft Chinese Windows™ is run on a station. However, the technical staff would have to be literate in Chinese in order to maintain the station. Also, if international-language operation systems were used, the Library would have to designate a number of stations per language and the location of each station.

There are two ways to implement an additional multilingual feature, described here as a browser add-on feature and an operating system add-on feature:

Browser add-on feature:

By using a Unicode-based browser application like Internet Explorer 4.0 with the appropriate language fonts and input method editor (IME) installed, users can display and input multilingual characters from the Web pages. The Library installed and enabled all multilingual functions of Internet Explorer 4.0, especially for non-roman languages like Chinese, Japanese, and Korean. This implementation includes Microsoft Global IME and Microsoft true-type fonts in Chinese, Japanese and Korean. The advantages of the browser add-on feature are that it is easy to implement and that the demands of learning to use this technology are relatively low, compared to the challenge of learning an entirely new software package (see next paragraph). In addition, the browser add-on feature does not consume too many systems resources. The disadvantage of the browser add-on feature is that it only works in the browser environment. It does not work for other multilingual applications running under Windows. For example, if a user wants to search a multilingual CD-ROM database on a PC that has a browser add-on feature, that user would only be able to search this database in English because the PC is accessing the database via a non-browser connection. Also, the Microsoft Global IME employs low-end implementation, limited to the Pinyin for simplified Chinese and ZuYing for traditional Chinese scripts, lacking functions of other commercially available IMEs for PC users that offer more choices in transliteration or scripts. (See the Access Variables section of this chapter for more discussion of the IME.)

Operating system add-on feature:
Because of the limitations of the browser add-on feature, the Library also utilizes another option known as the operating system add-on feature. This feature is especially useful for non-roman languages like Chinese, Japanese and Korean. By using commercial third-party software like RichWin97, Twin Bridge4.0 or AsianSuite97, users can display the CJK characters, but also can enjoy additional features of those IMEs that come with other commercial software. Also, since those software products run on top of English-language Windows, the software works alongside other Windows-based applications. Some of them even include a handy feature that allows a user to customize the standard English-language Windows menus into another language. For example, by using the RichWin97 for NT, readers of Chinese can turn the browser menu "File," "Edit" and "View" into the corresponding Chinese characters.

Usage Analysis

To understand how the WorldLinQ™ has been used by the customers and to enhance this service, the Library uses Microsoft Site Server's Usage Analysis module to analyze the Web server logs. Any connection to an Internet Web site is counted as a hit. According to the data gathered in 1998, the WorldLinQ™ Web site gets 100,000 hits monthly, and an average of 3,000 hits a day. Web usage analysis has shown that WorldLinQ™ visitors originate from within and without the local neighborhoods of the borough. In November 1998 users from these countries visited the WorldLinQ™ site: the United States, Canada, Australia, China, Finland, Singapore, Malaysia, Hong Kong, Japan, Sweden, Taiwan, United Kingdom, Brazil, New Zealand, South Korea, France, Netherlands, Portugal and Spain.

WorldLinQ™ Components

WorldLinQ™ serves three functions: access to a multilingual Web resource collection, multilingual access to the Library's online catalog and international resource sharing.

Multilingual Web resource collection:

Mainly, WorldLinQ™ arose of the Queens Library's goal of exposing Internet resources to all its customers, especially those who are more comfortable with languages other than English. With this audience in mind, selection and annotation of globally available multilingual Web resources are chosen for timeliness, accuracy, and value of the content to the user. Currently WorldLinQ™ has Web sites available for public access in six languages: Chinese, French, Korean, Russian, Spanish and English. All resources are arranged by subject categories, such as business or arts. There is also an integrated component known as "Queens Local Resources," which lists local information resources for ethnic communities. The non-English Web pages are designed in a bilingual format, for example, Spanish/English or Russian/English, to offer an easy reference format for the Library staff who may not read or write a language other than English, but need to help those customers trying to locate information with WorldLinQ™. The consistent site design incorporates Web frames in such a way so that a content page will point to the main resources page, guiding the user, whether staff or customer, whether literate or untrained in the language being displayed on the screen.

The following figures show the opening pages of WorldLinQ™ in four of its six languages:

Figure 1. WorldLinQ™ opening page.

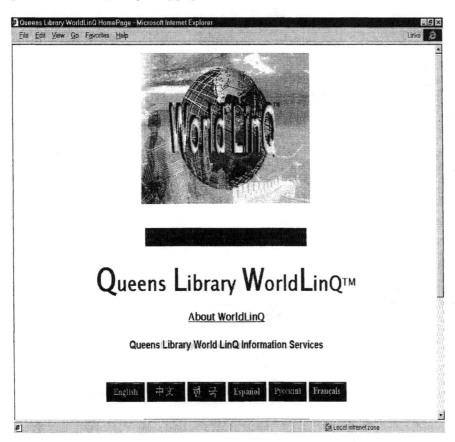

Figure 2. WorldLinQ™ Chinese opening page.

Figure 3. WorldLinQ™ Russian opening page.

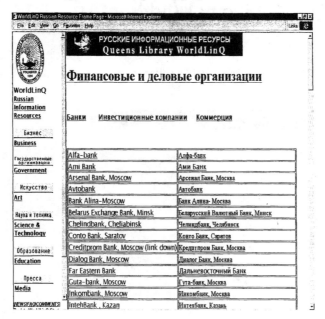

Figure 4. WorldLinQ™ Spanish opening page.

Multilingual access to the Library's online public access catalog:

The Queens Library not only needed to expose its immigrant customers to Internet sources, but to ease their searching of the Library's catalog, InfoLinQ™, via a Web interface. Library catalogers had to be able to catalog, store and search in different languages, especially by non-Roman languages, like Chinese, Japanese and Korean, so that users could search for those bibliographic records in the online public access catalog (OPAC). The AT&T grant partially allowed for the Library to contract customized programming from Data Research Associates, Inc. (DRA) to enhance the existing DRA Classic integrated online library system already in use by the Queens Library. With this implementation, the DRA software could map an OCLC East Asian Character Code (EACC)-based bibliographic record to the international Unicode standard. It subsequently stores and indexes it within the DRA database, working from the 880 field of the MARC bibliographic record. The Library OPAC is searchable by using a Web browser. Now, with the appropriate configuration, the CJK bibliographic records will be displayed and are searchable within the Library's Web OPAC. The Library has created its own Chinese and Korean interface by customizing the English-language DRA Web2 interface. Currently, Library customers can search the online catalog in English, Chinese, Korean, Japanese, French and Spanish.

The following diagrams demonstrate the Library's customized user interface for the Chinese language and an example of search results in Chinese:

Figure 5. Opening page of Queens Library multilingual OPAC, InfoLinQ™.

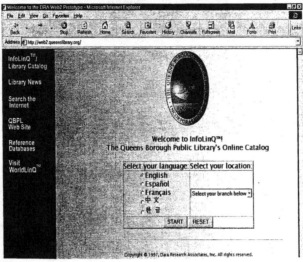

Figure 6. InfoLinQ™ title search in Chinese.

Figure 7. InfoLinQ™ search results display in Chinese.

International resource sharing:

Another purpose of the WorldLinQ™ project is to construct a technological infrastructure to increase the exchange of international resources via the Internet. Resource sharing includes the building of dedicated Web sites for international exchange programs, an Internet connection with library partners around the world and the use of technological standards like Z39.50 to integrate the different library systems for resource sharing.

Under the exchange agreements the Queens Library has signed with National Library of China (NLC) and with the Shanghai Library of China, two dedicated Web sites have been established under the WorldLinQ™, known as the Queens/Shanghai Library Site and the Queens/National Library of China Site. As part of the technology exchange initiative, NLC also agreed to allow QBPL to use its National Bibliographic Database free of charge. As of this writing, the NLC's National Bibliographic Database known as China BIP is up and running at QBPL's International Resources Center at QBPL's Flushing Library. The Queens Library is also working with the Shanghai Library of China to share the electronic resources by linking the two library systems with Z39.50 technology.

Figure 8. WorldLinQ™ Queens Library/Shanghai Library Web site.

Figure 9. WorldLinQ™ Queens Library/National Library of China Web site.

Figure 10. Sample screen of National Bibliographic Database of China from NLC.

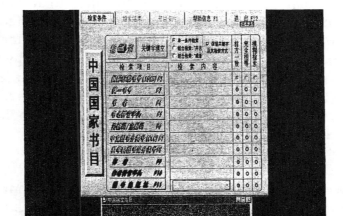

Access Variables

Providing computerized user access is a major challenge in a multilingual environment. It becomes even more challenging for the library that does not opt to install a localized-language operating system. As another course, vernacular scripts could be converted into and displayed as image files in the Web environment. However, when factors of page load speed, network bandwidth and indexing issues are taken into account, this option of distribution using image files is not practicable. Providing a true vernacular text-based access will not only speed up the development process, but also make the multilingual Web pages load faster.

The following discussion of access variables is based on the assumption of using a Web browser as the user interface to access multilingual Web-based information resources.

Roman characters vs. other vernacular characters:

Display and input of roman alphabetical characters has never been as difficult as the display and input of the non-roman characters like Chinese, Japanese, Korean, Arabic, Hebrew, etc. Currently, since most Western languages have been included in Internet Explorer 4.0, there is not much that users need to do other than modify the "Language" option to choose the language that they wish to display on the screen. Some Web pages have included the "Character Setting" tag into the metatag inside the HTML code. In this case, the users do not need to take any action at all; the non-English characters should be displayed in the language as the tag was being set. However, things are not always as simple. For most languages other than English, there are more variables to be considered.

Fonts:

The Microsoft Windows system comes with basic fonts for English and some additional fonts for other Western languages. Microsoft also provides more language fonts on its Web site for downloading, which are not included with Windows as shipped. The instructions on how to set up these fonts with the Windows system should be included in the font package.

Operating system:

The computer's capability of handling the multilingual display depends on the operating system running on the computer. For example, there are basically two versions of Windows systems: one known as 16-bit Windows system, which includes Windows 3.X; another is known as the 32-bit Windows system, which includes Windows 95/98 and Windows NT/NTWS. For the user who wants to implement multilingual access on her own desktop computer, then 32-bit Windows system is the recommended direction.

Language codes:

Both software developers and users should be aware: Language codes is one of the most complex issues in configuring computerized multilingual access. For some languages that use a multi-codes scheme, the code being chosen to develop the Web page will affect the user's access of multilingual resources. For example, the Chinese language has two different code schemes, one known as Big5 code for traditional Chinese and the second known as GB for simplified Chinese. To display Chinese language characters correctly, users need to have a basic knowledge of the characteristics of Big5 and of GB. The latest technological trend to deal with these codes is the international

Unicode standard, which tries to handle all languages in one code scheme. As a result, users do not need worry about what language code is being used to switch from one language to another. The Unicode standard specifies the rules describing the shapes and positions of characters or glyphs that may not have the horizontal and vertical lines of Western characters. It makes the Web design possible of combining different languages in a single Web page, which was impossible under the exclusive code used for specific languages.

Input method:
The basic function of the input method editor (IME, sometimes also referred as the input method environment) is to provide users with a way to key in the vernacular text-based characters by using a standard English keyboard. To use the IME for inputting vernacular characters, one has to know the script schemes of a particular language (as the roman character relates to the non-roman character) or other methods of inputting the characters. For example, to input Chinese characters, you have to know the schemes of at least one of those romanization or input methods, namely, Pinyin (also known as the Chinese Phonetic Alphabet), ZuYin, CangJie, Internal Code, Cantonese, Symbol, etc.

FUTURE DIRECTIONS OF WORLDLINQ™ PROJECT
The direction of future development of WorldLinQ™ project will focus on three aspects: adding more languages, expanding the sharing of international resources and creating an online virtual community.

Adding More Languages
The Queens Library has a goal to offer library services in languages spoken by the immigrant communities in Queens. So far, some of the larger ethnic communities of Queens have been represented in the language module of WorldLinQ™. The languages of Chinese, French, Korean, Russian, Spanish and English are used in the multilingual Web resource collection, and the languages of Chinese, Japanese, Korean, French, Spanish and English for multilingual access to the Library's OPAC. However, the addition of Greek, Russian, Hebrew, and Indic languages to these modules would serve more of the Queens communities. A major factor determines which languages will be developed in the future: the availability of in-house talent that

the Library can locate within its own staff. At this time, the Library is not considering outsourcing of this aspect of WorldLinQ™ development. However, partnerships with other organizations, such as the other library systems in the New York City area, could be fostered. The enhancement of multilingual access to the Queens Library's online catalog is also bound by Data Research's capacity of adding other language sets to its cataloging and OPAC software products.

Online Virtual Community

To provide people access to multilingual electronic resources is only the first phase of the WorldLinQ™ project development. WorldLinQ™ grew out of the Queens Library's existing mission to serve its public, and it will continue to grow under this mission. The Library is planning to go beyond the one-way communication for access by creating a multilingual online community. The online virtual community could host services like online bulletin boards or discussion lists, online chat, video-teleconferences, an online interactive multilingual and multicultural learning center and online multicultural exhibits. The purpose of providing two-way communication with the ethnic communities of Queens is to serve them better. Again, the Queens Library would have to explore ways to build the systems and staff support for this endeavor.

Multilingual Community Network

The combination of WorldLinQ™ with the establishment of a multilingual catalog has gained Queens Library recognition with both its customers and other agencies. The expertise gained by developing WorldLinQ™ as an electronic resource has created an interest for future partnering with the government, information providers and local community groups to enhance WorldLinQ™ in areas that are not presently covered.

As a meta-guide that annotates and reviews multilingual resources, there is room for additional multilingual enhancements, for example, creating special guides for users in both English and other languages. Recently, a partnership was formed with the Queens County Overall Economic Development Corporation to develop an electronic format for their booklet *Minding Your Own Business: A Guide to Starting a Business in Queens*. It is currently available in English, Chinese, Korean and Spanish. This Web-based addition is a useful extension to WorldLinQ™, where users already have the expectation that resources found there are in their native languages.

Expanding International Resource Sharing

Having the Queens Library's system linked to the Internet does not necessarily mean that all these resources can be shared internationally. There are still too many areas that need improvement, e.g., differentials on the issues like network protocol, bibliographic standards and database format. The purpose of international resource sharing of WorldLinQ™ is to create a solid technology base by using open standards technology. Open standards technology allows different libraries, no matter where they are, to use this infrastructure to develop their own sharable components. The Queens Library will continually build this infrastructure by using the emerging technologies in both Web and library automation areas.

CONCLUSION

The WorldLinQ™ project serves as a link between local and international communities, using language and technology to connect people to the information they need. A library interested in beginning a similar language-technology program should begin at home. By learning the makeup of the communities it serves and by gathering information from census data and frontline staff who are in daily contact with the public, the library can determine what languages that are spoken in different neighborhoods, who comes to the library and who stays at home. A library could also evaluate language needs and gauge community support by distributing questionnaires or conducting surveys.

Teams and partnerships are essential for the success of any effort to reach different groups of people. Personnel with the language and technical skills necessary to begin and maintain this project may come from various job classifications within the library or from library volunteers. The firm support of the library administration cannot be stressed enough. Queens Library Director Gary Strong has played a crucial role in forming alliances with international libraries. These alliances have created access to information resources that have enriched WorldLinQ™. He has also worked diligently to garner support for projects from local government officials, neighborhoods and businesses. Library trustees and library friends' groups may also be enlisted to bring public and commercial backing to a project.

Libraries should also plan for and implement the most advanced technological applications and systems available. Given how quickly technology changes, this can be tricky. While the appreciation of the end-users will be high, initial investment in systems could also run high. Besides funding from a local tax base, a library should seek applicable grants and corporate sponsors. Monetary gifts can lower the financial hurdles of any project with technology-related expenses, reinforce the value of the project to others and often advertise the availability of the program. Without the foundation of the Library's vision and mission statements, and without the support of both internal and external sources, the project might have collapsed under the weight of its endeavors. Instead, with teams to share the load, this WorldLinQ™ project is growing to fulfill its name.

REFERENCES

New York City Department of City Planning. (1997, December). *Community District Needs, Queens, Fiscal Year 1999* (NYC DCP #97-16). New York: New York City Department of City Planning.

New York City Department of City Planning. (1996, December). *The Newest New Yorkers, 1990-1994* (NYC DCP #96-19). New York: New York City Department of City Planning.

Public Library Association. (1998). *Public Library Data Service Statistical Report.* Chicago, IL: American Library Association.

U.S. Bureau of the Census. (1992, September). *1990 Census of Population and Housing Summary Tape File 3A, New York Counties* (CD90-3A-40) [CD-ROM]. Washington, DC: U.S. Government Printing Office.

Chapter XI

An Analysis of Using Expert Systems and Intelligent Agents for the Virtual Library Project at the Naval Surface Warfare Center — Carderock Division

Jay Liebowitz and Monica Adya
University of Maryland Baltimore County

The Virtual Library Project[1] at the Naval Surface Warfare Center/Carderock Division (NSWC/CD) is being developed to facilitate the incorporation and use of library documents via the Internet. These documents typically relate to the design and manufacture of ships for the U.S. Navy Fleet. As such, the libraries will store documents that contain not only text but also images, graphs and design configurations. Because of the dynamic nature of digital documents, particularly those related to design, rapid and effective cataloging of these documents becomes challenging. We conducted a research study to analyze the use of expert systems and intelligent agents to support the function of cataloging digital documents. This chapter provides an overview of past research in the use of expert systems and intelligent agents for cataloging digital documents and discusses our recommendations based on NSWC/CD's requirements.

The explosion in the use of the Internet for information exchange and retrieval has significantly increased the production and distribution of digital information. This has increased our reliance on rapid information availability and exchange for decision making. The benefits of such technology motivated trends are several. Information is available globally within seconds. Multiple users can view the same information in the same format all over the world. More importantly, this data exchange is not limited to text but extends to audio, video and pictorial data exchange.

As with any situation, the above benefits are tempered by the challenges that accompany such technological advances. The volume of digital data available is increasing rapidly. Consequently, the Internet has become a library without a catalog. Although several search and retrieval functions are increasingly becoming available, their effectiveness is dependent largely on the effectiveness with which digital documents are cataloged.

Digital documents are being generated and propagated at tremendous rates. In fact, in our daily experience, we find that our exchange of paper-based documents has been reduced to the minimal. Most of the documents are exchanged via e-mail or through the Web and are stored electronically. The challenge then is ensuring that each document being generated and exchanged digitally be effectively and rapidly cataloged and archived. How can the cataloging function be automated such that a document is cataloged as soon as it's received electronically? In this study we explore the use of Artificial Intelligence (AI) techniques for cataloging. In particular, we examine the use of Expert Systems at the Naval Surface Warfare Center/Carderock Division (NSWC/CD) which is actively exploring the storage and exchange of their books, drawings, manuscripts, documents and photographs digitally so that they can be transmitted at high speed to computer screens anywhere in their original format

THE CATALOGING FUNCTION

According to Anderson (1990), the Head of Cataloging Services at Virginia Commonwealth University, cataloging is, arguably, among the most complex of library processes. Typically, as with NSWC/CD, a cataloger provides both the descriptive and the subject cataloging for each item handled and must also be able to use appropriate classification "schedules" and subject heading thesauri. Familiarity with the principles of uniform headings and the application of name authority control procedures are also standard aspects of the cataloger's responsibilities (Anderson, 1990).

Because the cataloging function is very labor-intensive and costly, many organizations are looking at alternative ways to either aid or automate this function. Some libraries, like at NSWC/CD, are looking at providing a system that helps the contributors catalog their own documents. According to Ruschoof (1995), Head of the Cataloging Department at Georgetown University, the various approaches to cataloging fall into four categories:

- streamlining cataloging through curtailing procedures and simplifying records,
- sharing cataloging through cooperative enterprise,
- obtaining cataloging through contracting schemes, and
- automating cataloging through artificial intelligence or "expert systems."

Chander, et al. (1997) built an expert system to aid cataloging and searching electronic documents on digital libraries. While understanding the domain, they found that to catalog and describe the document, reference librarians relied on their knowledge of classification schemes, terms, indices, structures and resources available in the domain of the user's needs.

Cataloging digital documents is different from cataloging traditional documents in several ways. According to Gaynor (1994), Head of Original Cataloging and in charge of the Cataloging Electronic Texts Project at the University of Virginia Library, the issue with digital documents is that of what constitutes an edition or version or state of an electronic text. Digital documents are more dynamic than traditional documents particularly when they are in print. Once catalogued, traditional documents become a static entity in the catalogs. This does not hold true of digital documents which can change frequently. Another pressing concern for the cataloging community in particular is the relationship, both short and long-term, of the TEI (Text Encoding Initiative) header to the MARC record. Gaynor (1994) states that in the short-term, the cataloging community needs to reevaluate its tools for cataloging electronic texts.

In spite of these concerns, the need for document cataloging is unquestioned. The trend though is to use non-traditional techniques for such cataloging particularly those that rely on Artificial Intelligence (AI). The use of such automated techniques can support the dynamic nature of the task more effectively and cost-efficiently than traditional cataloging. An example of the use of AI techniques for cataloging is from the University of Exeter. The University is exploring the use of expert systems for cataloging digital resources.

Efforts at OCLC have been directed at automated descriptive cataloging. According to Weibel (1987), the head of the Automated Title Page Cataloging project at OCLC, automated descriptive cataloging entails three broad functional activities: (1) capturing a page image in machine-readable form; (2) identifying functionally related text strings from the page image; and (3) assigning these text strings to appropriate bibliographic fields, e.g., title, statement of responsibility, publisher.

Assigning subject fields entails the following: selecting from a document certain words, phrases or sentences that may suitably represent its information content; if necessary, transforming these sets of words into a standard terminology and casting them into standard form; if necessary, translating the text words or standard terms into a code; and choosing some of these words, terms or codes as access points for the information search. The inherent problem in automated indexing is that the meaning of a word depends on the context in which it is used (University of Texas Report, 1998).

Automatic summarizing is another technique that may help in cataloging. Automatic summarizing is the process by which a computer creates a condensed version of a text. The new version should well represent the original in meaning and scope.

In order to see what has been done in terms of developing expert systems for the cataloging function (Michaelson 1991, Palmer 1990), the next section highlights projects that have been accomplished in this area.

EXPERT SYSTEMS FOR CATALOGING

In reviewing the literature, a number of expert systems have been developed for cataloging documents. However, most of these expert systems are in the prototype or conceptual stages and have not been developed and implemented as *fully operational systems*. This section will highlight some of the leading projects in this area.

Chander et al. (1997), at Concordia University in Montreal, developed an expert system to aid in cataloging and searching electronic documents on digital libraries. For cataloging and searching, they used a metadata description called a "semantic header" to describe the document. The expert system is designed to mimic the behavior of a reference librarian. This system was built using CLIPS, a rule-based expert system shell.

SKICAT, developed by Usama Fayyad at the Jet Propulsion Laboratory and CalTech Astronomy, includes tools for the analysis and exploration of a large catalog database—namely, a comprehensive northern sky survey catalog that will ultimately contain on the order of one billion entries.

At Northwestern University, several expert system projects were developed for cataloging. CLARR is an expert system to assist in MARC field validation. DELICAT (Data Enhancement of Library Catalogues) is an expert system capable of automatically detecting errors in library catalogues and drawing these to the attention of library staff. IESCA (The Interactive Electronic Serials Cataloging Aide) is a tutorial which assists libraries in cataloging electronic documents. It guides the user through the process and includes most applicable rules and standards from cataloging organizations.

OCLC has developed the Automated Title Page Cataloging System. This prototype is a rule-based system, written in PROLOG, which interprets typographic files and builds an approximation of an AACR2 first level description. In preliminary tests, 75% of the fields in a sample were identified correctly; half of the title pages were captured correctly in their entirety.

Another OCLC-sponsored project by Svenonius focused on the problem of automatically deriving name access points. She found that 93% of all personal names and 80% of all corporate names assigned by the Library of Congress (LC) and the National Library of Medicine (NLM) could be successfully assigned by an expert system.

A newer research project at OCLC is called Scorpion[2]. Scorpion explores the indexing and cataloging of electronic resources. The primary focus of Scorpion is the building of tools for automatic subject recognition based on well-known schemes like the Dewey Decimal System. According to the project leaders on Scorpion, Scorpion cannot replace human cataloging. There are many aspects of human cataloging that are difficult if not impossible to automate, according to the Scorpion research team.

At Exeter University in England, an expert system was developed for cataloging. The system used AACR2 and the MARC manual as sources of rules for the knowledge base. In a keynote address, Tillett (1995) discussed the following conclusions from the University of Exter's efforts:

- rules for determining access points could be reinstated as production rules,
- rules governing bibliographic description could be entered through the use of templates,
- local rules could be accommodated,
- menus and screen forms could be designed which would act as a user-friendly interface between a cataloger and an expert system, and
- explanation facilities, in terms of the systems' attempt to decide which rules from AACR2 (Anglo-American Cataloging Rules, 2nd ed.) apply, could easily be incorporated.

At UCLA, MAPPER was an expert system designed for the descriptive cataloging of maps. This doctoral project used AACR2 cataloging rules for maps and knowledge contributed by expert catalogers. A similar project called ESSCAPE (Expert Systems for Simple Choice of Access Points for Entries) was developed at Linkoping University in Sweden. ESSCAPE was designed for the cataloging of books versus maps.

The University of Michigan Digital Library (UMDL) project is an agent-based approach for rendering library services in a digital networked environment.

It is worth noting that even though expert systems are being prototyped, built and designed for cataloging, their full potential in the cataloging function is questionable. Even if the development of such a system is possible, the complexity and expense of encoding current processes will be a deterrent. Furthermore, the expert system should be customizable so that it may observe local practices.

NSWC/CD'S REQUIREMENTS FOR AN EXPERT SYSTEM FOR CATALOGING

Based on discussions with the Virtual Library project leaders at NSWC/CD, the following requirements for an expert system for cataloging digital records emerged as follows:

- the Virtual Library project will be operated over the Web with a Web interface;
- documents will ultimately be added to the Library by individual users over the Web (thus, a cataloging expert system should be able to catalog these documents automatically or at least aid the user in the cataloging process);
- Center reports are accessed the most so the expert system should focus initially on cataloging Center reports;
- for digital document check-in, the following fields are **required** to be cataloged, according to NSWC/CD officials:
  - corporate source
  - title
  - personal author
  - publication date
  - series numbers
  - major descriptors (thesaurus terms)
  - identifiers (keywords that are not in the thesaurus)
  - barcode
- the following fields would be **desirable**, according to NSWC/CD officials:
  - pagination
  - subject descriptors (thesaurus terms)
  - circulation restriction
- cataloging should follow acceptable standards and guidelines (e.g., American National Standard's Scientific and Technical Reports—Elements, Organization and Design—adopted by the Department of Defense).

IS A CATALOGING EXPERT SYSTEM FEASIBLE FOR NSWC/CD'S NEEDS?

It appears, on paper, that expert systems technology should be suited for descriptive cataloging (not subject cataloging) due to well-established rules. However, in reviewing the work that has been done over the past 15 years in applying expert systems to cataloging, very few systems, if any, have been implemented beyond the prototyping or conceptual stage. As Lancaster and Smith (1998) point out, most of the studies have provided conceptual models of expert systems rather than actual implementations. They cite several studies that have revealed that tasks that are very easy for human catalogers are difficult to delegate successfully to automated routines. For instance, the distinction between title and subtitle may not be as evident to the machine as to a human cataloger (Lancaster and Smith, 1998).

None of the experiments on the automation of descriptive cataloging has produced a significant prototype system, much less a truly operational one (Lancaster and Smith, 1998). The costs involved in developing a complete and comprehensive cataloging system are prohibitive. The National Library of Medicine abandoned a $130,000 project for identifying the correct form of an author's name since it was determined that putting an operating tool out would be too expensive an undertaking. Similarly, the QUALCAT project, which identified duplicate records and selected the one that was of superior quality, was declared infeasible due to the limitations of MARC records (Lancaster and Smith, 1998).

Although, Clarke and Cronin (1983) suggested 16 years ago that an appropriate application of expert systems might be to catalog electronic publications as they are generated online, in light of the findings and conclusions discussed above, it does not seem promising to develop an expert system for the cataloging function. Poulter (1994) also confirms our findings.

Based on the above analysis, we reiterate the infeasibility of developing an operational expert system for cataloging. We base our conclusions on the following reasons:

- In an earlier publication, Liebowitz (1998) identified several criteria for expert system problem selection. They are:
  a. the task involves mostly symbolic processing,
  b. test cases are available,
  c. problem task is well-bounded,
  d. written materials exist explaining the task,
  e. task requires only cognitive skills,
  f. experts agree on the solutions to the problem,
  g. at least one expert exists and the expert is cooperative,
  h. the expert is articulate,
  i. the expert's knowledge is based on experience, facts and judgment,
  j. a need exists for developing an expert system for the problem,
  k. the task will be provided with the necessary financial and moral support,

l. top management supports the project,

m. the domain-area personnel have realistic expectations regarding the use of an expert system,

n. users would welcome the expert system, and

o. the knowledge used in the expert system is not politically sensitive or controversial.

It appears that an expert system for cataloging digital documents could meet many of these criteria. However, the key deterrent is that many leading authorities have tried to develop expert systems in the cataloging area over the years, and have only produced mainly prototypes versus real, fully operational systems.

- It might be possible to develop a *limited* version of an expert system for **descriptive** cataloging of digital documents, but it would be difficult to develop a system for automatic **subject** cataloging.
- The expert systems that have been developed so far in cataloging have had very limited success.
- There are more viable AI technologies versus expert systems that could have a greater likelihood of success for handling library functions.

In the following section, we propose a preferred solution as the next step for rendering library services in a digital networked environment as part of the Virtual Library project at NSWC/CD.

INTELLIGENT AGENTS FOR SEARCHING MULTIPLE SITE DATABASES

One of the recent trends in Artificial Intelligence has been the use of intelligent agents for searching and indexing functions, particularly over the Internet for Web-based documents. Intelligent agents are software that assist people and act on their behalf. They can automate repetitive tasks, remember things, intelligently summarize complex data and learn from and make recommendations to the users (Russell and Norvig, 1995). Agents are:

- autonomous, that is they have control over their own actions;
- goal-driven, in that they have a purpose and act in accordance with those actions;

- reactive, in that they sense changes in their environments and respond in a timely fashion to these changes;
- adaptive, that is they change their behavior based on previous experience.

Intelligent agents can be classified in a number of ways based on the functions they perform (Gilbert):

- *Interface Agents:* These are used to decrease the complexity of the increasingly sophisticated and overloaded information systems. They may add speech and language understanding to otherwise dumb terminals.
- *System Agents:* These run as integrated parts of operating systems or network protocol devices and help manage the complex distributed computing environments.
- *Advisory Agents*: They are used in complex help or diagnostic systems.
- *Filtering Agents*: These agents reduce information overload by removing data that does not match the user profile. Agentware and InfoMagnet provide more general kind of filtering capabilities.
- *Retrieval Agents*: These agents search and retrieve information. ATI, Bullseye, Go-Get-It and Surfbot are some of the tools that provide these capabilities.
- *Navigation Agents*: Navigation agents are used to navigate through external and internal networks, remembering short-cuts, pre-load caching information and automatically bookmarking interesting sites. IBM's Web Browser Intelligence is an example.
- *Monitoring Agents*: These provide users with information when particular events occur, such as information being updated, moved or erased.
- *Recommender Agents*: They are collaborative agents that need many profiles to be available before an accurate recommendation can be made.
- *Profiling Agents*: These agents are used to build dynamic sites with information and recommendations tailored to match each visitor's individual tastes and need.

For digital library initiatives, most of the research and interest lies in the areas of filtering, retrieval, navigation, monitoring, recommender and profiling agents. In the section below, we discuss briefly some research in the design and use of intelligent agents in these functions.

Research on Intelligent Agents

In the context of digital libraries, several studies have indicated their findings with the use of intelligent agents on online databases and on the Internet. Harvest was developed to index topic-specific collections rather than to locate and index all HTML documents it can find (Information Interchange Report). It allows the users to control the enumeration in several ways by including stop lists, depth limits and count limits. Searchbots are a simple example of a cooperative multi-agent approach to information retrieval. To satisfy one's query, multiple agents perform search at heterogeneous remote sites via the Web. Some of the search methods may include using existing database search engines. Domain experts determine what sites to search and the path to the best solution. The best solution is the one with the lowest search cost (CIG).

Newt is an example of an information filtering system utilizing a society of agents that inhabit the user's computer (Beerud, 1994). Each agent is a user profile that searches for documents that matches the profile and recommends these documents to the user. The user can provide feedback to the agent for the documents recommended. User feedback changes the fitness of the profiles. If the user provides positive or negative feedback for a document, the fitness of the profile that retrieved the document is either increased or decreased. Second, user feedback modifies the profile. Therefore, each agent learns and adapts during its lifetime to the changing needs of the user.

Rapoza (1996) describes the use of filtering agents for feeding corporate intranets. Such agents push news items or other information to network users within selected categories such as sports, financial news and others. Richardson (1996) provides a discussion of an agent that indexes a local database maintained on a Web server. This tool though has limited text capabilities.

Certain commercial products provide several facilities for document management. AppleSearch is an agent system that searches and retrieves text from computers linked together by AppleShare, Apple's file sharing application, or by System 7's personal file sharing capabilities. Up to 50 users can operate on a network as AppleSearch clients. AppleSearch uses agents to examine text and to read and index documents that exist in a variety of formats (Valauskas, 1994).

The University of Michigan, as an undertaking in NSF's Digital Libraries Initiative, has created a digital library for science in the schools, grades six through nine. The project was a vehicle for investigating the use of ontologies and intelligent agents, as well as for creating economic incentives for use[3]. They now have an operating model that includes age-appropriate materials, as well as tools for working with the information.

A comprehensive review of agent use can be found in Lancaster and Smith (1998) and Liebowitz and Beckman (1998).

Issues with Agent Technologies

Research on the use of intelligent agents for information retrieval and management is in its infancy. As with most new technologies, there are some concerns with using intelligent agents over the Internet:

- they can generate a substantial amount of load on servers;
- sites can block out access by agents (Eichman, 1995);
- agents roaming the server can threaten the server with theft of resources, assets and reputation (Ordille and Travis, 1996).

Most of the initiatives are in preliminary stages although commercial products using agent capabilities are emerging rapidly. Despite its recent emergence, agent-based technologies are gaining popularity in document retrieval and management, as the next section reveals.

Ongoing Research on Intelligent Agents in Digital Libraries

STARTS—Stanford Protocol Proposal for Internet Search and Retrieval—is a project initiated at Stanford University to develop an agent-based protocol that text search engines should follow to facilitate searching and indexing multiple collections of text documents. Research and development of intelligent agent technology, particularly in the areas of digital libraries, document and workflow management, and computer games, is underway at Mitsubishi Electric Digital Library Group in London. The largest current undertaking is the NSF-sponsored Digital Libraries Initiative (DLI). Under the DLI, six universities, including the University of Michigan and Carnegie Mellon University are exploring various new information technologies to support various functions within digital document management. All six universities involved in the DLI are utilizing intelligent agent technologies in one form or another.

RECOMMENDATIONS FOR THE NSWC/CD REQUIREMENTS

Instead of using expert systems technology, a preferred approach to aiding the Virtual Library Project at NSWC/CD may be the use of intelligent agents for searching multiple site databases and acting as a virtual TIC user agent. Intelligent agents are already being applied in a number of digital library initiatives. For example, the University of Michigan Digital Library project designs and builds a flexible, scalable infrastructure for rendering library services in a digital networked environment. In order to meet this goal, intelligent agents are utilized for representing the library as a collection of interacting agents, each specialized to perform a particular task and all of them acting in an artificial economy.

Other projects like WebSEEk have been developed at Columbia University as a content-based image and video catalog and search tool for the World Wide Web. It has already catalogued over 650,000 images and 10,000 videos from the Web. Netscape Communications Corporation also has an agent-based product titled Catalog Server where catalog agents gather resource information from a variety of primary sources (including Web servers, end users, archivists and legacy systems). The agents communicate indexing information to one or more Catalog Servers via an open standard. For other projects, the reader may want to consult the National Science Foundation's Digital Library Initiative[4] and Project Aristotle[5].

The goal of digital libraries, according to the University of Michigan Digital Library, will be to provide mechanisms by which a digital library can continually reconfigure itself as users, contents and services come and go. Challenges for digital libraries include: digitizing contents, particularly a variety of forms such as documents and images; computerizing services to support this digitization; and networking users.

The NSWC/CD Virtual Library initiative could require several of the following components: document acquisition, document cataloging and management, document retrieval and other services (e.g., library security, bibliographic information, copyright protection). Each of these areas will be discussed next.

Document Acquisition

Since Internet access and input is a projected goal for the NSWC libraries, one of the challenges will be the identification of remote documents in addition to the local documents. Presuming the local acquisitions will be supported by traditional library functions, support for extracting indexes from suitable sites on the Internet and cataloging and managing these resources will be critical. For this task, the research team proposes the use of a multi-agent architecture.

Document acquisition via the Internet can take on two aspects. The first would be input from users of the Internet. These would be documents created by users as well as those found over the Internet via traditional search mechanisms. In the latter case, to help users search over heterogeneous information services that support nonuniform query languages, users will be allowed to compose simple boolean queries in a front-end natural language interface that may be interfaced with an intelligent agent that will then take on the task of searching the Internet.

For automatic search of the Internet, we propose the use of an intelligent agent that would take initiative in searching the Internet for relevant resources. It may be beneficial to promote communication between this agent and the one discussed in the above paragraph to enhance this agent's search capabilities.

Once retrieved, some mechanism for rating and recording the contents of digital documents will be required for facilitating the cataloging functions. This may be best supported by some parsing mechanism.

Document Cataloging and Management

The cataloging and management of documents obtained through various sources discussed above can be supported by traditional keyword indexing, knowledge-based systems and an agent-based architecture. For documents that are input by users, titles and keywords can be used for supporting cataloging and management functions. This will typically require traditional indexing capabilities. A knowledge base for known indexes or analogous terms may also be maintained.

For documents searched via the Internet, some parsing mechanism will be required to determine keywords from frequently occurring phrases in the document. An intelligent agent may be able to support this function most effectively by filtering out nonsignificant characters and strings. SGML tags from these documents can provide further insights into the nature of the documents.

Document Retrieval

The digitization of libraries will be able to enhance the search and document facilities provided by traditional library functions. These can be supported by simple query functions that will allow, among others:

- author search for authors who have produced a document, have cited certain other authors, have a name in the body of the text, etc.;
- search on keyfields, titles, bibliographic information and their combinations;
- modifying searches based on search results;
- Boolean searches;
- full-text SGML retrieval;
- rating and site information.

Other Services

Library Security

Traditional library functions have been open with security issues, particularly with the intention of promoting usability. In the NSWC / CD libraries, security becomes a concern since the libraries will contain both public and private documents relating to naval warfare. In particular, security architectures are required for mobile computing to allow the frequent migration of computers in and out of security enclaves and wide-area collaboration and to create dynamic sessions that stretch across organizational boundaries (as done in the University of Illinois Digital Library Initiative).

In response to the security issues, we propose the development of a system access and encryption mechanism. This mechanism will undertake the process of verifying the authority and validity of new security services and policies and enforcing the restriction of system resource access by these services and policies. It will provide basic public-key encryption and authentication. Together, these components will restrict access to the system and will determine if a user should be allowed access to a particular operation. Simple Java applets can be used to provide the support for this part of the initiative.

However, to promote flexibility and extensibility of this system, a mobile agent may be used.

Bibliographic Information and Copyright Protection

A tool for maintaining bibliographic information should be able to support various formats and provide a uniform searchable database of bibliographic information. Simple SQL query mechanisms that permit searches on authors, journals, documents/reports and keywords would be able to address the needs for the NSWC/CD digital libraries.

The generation and distribution of illegal copies of digital documents is an issue. Some mechanism will be required to track the unauthorized distribution of illegal versions of documents.

Next Steps for the NSWC/CD Virtual Library Project

The proposed initial research for the Virtual Library project at NSWC/CD will involve developing two intelligent agents. The first agent will search multiple database sites to retrieve relevant documents per the user's keyword requests. The second agent will develop a user's profile dynamically to better tailor the user's search.

Specifically, an intelligent agent is needed to query multiple site databases (for example, the Carderock TIC, the Dahlgren Library and the Indian Head Library) simultaneously from a proxied Web browser interface at either site and deliver the results back to the end-user's browser. It must know a definable query language (SQL) and be able to communicate using the ANSI standard Z39.50 protocol (Web-based protocol for querying databases). The agent must be able to authenticate itself in order to access databases. The agent must also be able to accept and return binary, as well as ASCII text data.

The second intelligent agent is needed to act as a proxy "virtual agent" for TIC online users. Each user will be able to define their own information profile which will be used to set an intelligent agent's criteria to periodically search the Web and deliver search results back to the end-user, by e-mail or some other user-defined way. The agent must also build a user's profile on the fly. It must be able to discern duplicate information and filter out redundant results. The agent must have a definable scope for querying (i.e., the level of links to follow, etc.). The agent must be able to avoid sites/files where bots are not authorized (i.e., recognize robots.txt files). The research steps proposed for this effort are:

- *Web Development*: Develop the appropriate Web sites that will support user querying, access, and search modifications. In particular, emphasis must be given to the mode of presentation of query results. The Web site must be able to support display in various forms such as html and pdf among others. Appropriate support must also be provided for display of images and sound.
- *Testbed Development*: Identify and develop a testbed for testing the effectiveness of the proposed solution. We propose that the research team in collaboration with appropriate authorities at NSWC identify:

a) the volume of documents stored at various databases

b) the types of documents and their quantities stored at each location

c) the volume and urgency of requests from users for each of the locations, and

d) the rate at which these requests are satisfied from each location.

These measures will allow the research team to sample appropriate documents from each location to form a part of the testbed. This will also facilitate development of an objective measure of success of the proposed solution versus the traditional approach. If successful on the testbed, the proposed solution can eventually be phased in over the entire database.

- *Tool Exploration*: Research and demo available commercial agent tools (e.g. Verity's Search '97/Agent Server and Open Sesame/ Browne and Company's Learn Sesame), as well as public domain agent tools.
- *Tool Integration*: Develop the design for integrating the two proposed agents within the Virtual Library project.
- *Agent Testing*: Encode and test these intelligent agents on the testbed described above.
- *System Refinement-1*: Refine the agents based upon results from the initial tests.
- *User Evaluation*: Once the system has been refined by the research team, we propose the release of the system to a select set of users. These may be obtained from the usual sample of users as well a group from the library team. It is then recommended that the research team obtain feedback from the test user community. We propose an online feedback mechanism that may be offered after

each search or after every few searches performed by the end user. In addition, a more detailed survey can be requested from the user at the end of the test period.

- *SYSTEM REFINEMENT-2*: Refine the Web sites and the agents based on results from user evaluations.

Since several of these activities such as testbed development, tool testing and integration can be conducted in parallel, we anticipate that this would be a six to nine-month effort whose deliverable would include: the software code for the two intelligent agents and a brief user's guide on how to use them.

FUTURE RESEARCH

Several issues will need to be examined in the future of this and other intelligent agent projects in this domain. To accommodate the increasing volume of information retrieval and cataloging over the next few years, developers must examine the need for high speed access to document databases. With the advances in telecommunications technology, such high speed access is increasingly becoming possible. Furthermore, state-of-the-art storage devices will be required to support documents, images and possibly sound.

One of the important benefits of digital libraries is the long-term maintenance of digital documents. Careful thought must go into acquiring the appropriate infrastructure to ensure this. Furthermore, with the increasing use of Internet for accessing digital documents, the incorporation of security modules both on the Web site and the catalog and document databases will require significant energies.

CONCLUSIONS

In the past decade, computer technology has become increasingly powerful and easy to use. With the advent of the World Wide Web, the production and exchange of digital information has increased exponentially. Consequently, the development of digital libraries is gaining increasing significance. The large volume of documents in digital libraries, the myriad forms of these documents and the dynamic nature of digital documents call for automated mechanisms that expedite the function of library cataloging while maintaining the efficacy of human catalogers. Expert systems have been proposed as a possible solution for this cataloging need. However, 15 years of evidence indicates that expert systems are not suited for the task of digital cataloging, primarily because of the cost constraints. In this chapter we have proposed the use of intelligent agents for library cataloging. Although the technology is still in its infancy, it is potentially viable for digital libraries. The increasing use of intelligent agent technology in ongoing library projects confirms and corroborates our conclusions.

ENDNOTES

[1] This research was made possible by sponsorship from Dave Glenn, Director of the Virtual Library Project, U.S. Naval Surface Warfare Center-Carderock Division, West Bethesda, Maryland.

[2] http://purl.oclc.org/scorpion

[3] Discussion of this is available at http://mydl.soe.umich.edu.

[4] Details of the Digital Library Initiative are available at www.nsf.gov.

[5] Details of the Aristotle project are available at (www.public.iastate.edu/~CYBERSTACKS/Aristotle.htm)

REFERENCES

Anderson, B. (1990). Expert Systems for Cataloging: Will They Accomplish Tomorrow the Cataloging of Today?. *Cataloging & Classification Quarterly,* 11 (2).

Beerud, S. (1994). A Learning Approach to Personalized Information Filtering. *Learning and Common Sense Section T. R. 94-01,* MIT Media Laboratory. [On-line]. Available: http://agents.www.media. mit.edu/groups/agents/papers.html.

CIG. (n.d.). [On-line]. Available: http://dis.cs.umass.edu/research/searchbots.html

Chander, P., Shinghal, R., Desai, B., & Radhakrishnan, T. (1997). An Expert System to Aid Cataloging and Searching Electronic Documents on Digital Libraries. *Expert Systems With Applications Journal, 12,* (4).

Clarke, A. & Cronin, B. (1983). Expert Systems and Library/Information Work. *Journal of Librarianship, 15.*

Eichman, D. (1995). Ethical Web Agents. *Computer Networks and ISDN Systems, 28.*

Gaynor, E. (1994). Cataloging Electronic Texts: The University of Virginia Library Experience. *Library Resources and Technical Services, 38,* (4).

Gilbert, D. (n.d.). *Intelligent Agents: The Right Information at the Right Time.* [On-line]. Available: http://www.networking.ibm.com/iag/iaghome.html.

Information Interchange Report. (n.d.). *Intelligent agents and information retrieval.* [Online]. Available: http://www.techapps.co.uk/iiartagt.html

Lancaster, F.W. & Smith, L. C. (1998). "Intelligent Technologies in Library and Information Service Applications. *Report for the Special Libraries Association,* University of Illinois at Urbana-Champaign, Graduate School of Library and Information Science.

Liebowitz, J. (Ed.). (1998). *The Handbook on Applied Expert Systems,* CRC Press, Boca Raton, FL.

Liebowitz, J. & Beckman, T. (1998). *Knowledge Organizations: What Every Manager Should Know,* CRC/St. Lucie Press, Boca Raton, FL.

Michelson, A. (1991). Expert Systems Technology and Its Implications for Archives. *National Archives Technical Information Paper No. 9,* March 1991.

Ordille, J.A. & Travis, L. (1996). When Agents Roam, Who Can You Trust? *Proceedings of the First Annual Conference on Emerging Technologies and Applications in Communications.* Los Alamitos, CA, IEEE Computer Society Press. 188 - 191.

Palmer, M. (1990). *Expert Systems and Related Topics: Selected Bibliography and Guide to Information Sources,* Idea Group Publishing, Hershey, PA.

Poulter, A. (1994). LIS Professionals as Knowledge Engineers. *Annual Review of Information Science and Technology, 29,* 1994.

Rapoza, J. (1996). Service Filters News for Intranets *PC Week 13* (21)

Richardson, J.V. (1996). Add an Engine, *Internet World, 7* (5).

Ruschoff, C. (1995). Cataloging's Prospects: Responding to Austerity with Innovation. *The Journal of Academic Librarianship, January.*

Russell, S. & Norvig, P. (1995) *Artificial Intelligence: A Modern Approach,* Prentice Hall, NJ.

Tillett, B. (1995). Keynote: Cataloging Rules and Conceptual Models. *National Cataloguing Conference,* New South Wales, Australia, October 19, 1995.

University of Texas Report. (1998) "AI/Expert Systems in the Library—Cataloging," University of Texas—Graduate School of Library and Information Science, http://fiat.gslis.utexas.edu/~palmquis/courses/project/

Valauskas, E.J. (1994). AppleSearch: How smart is Apple's intelligent agent? *Online. 18,* (4), 52-64.

Weibel, S. (1987). Automated Title Page Cataloging. *The Annual Review of OCLC Research,* July 1986-June 1987.

Chapter XII

Librarians as Info Architects: New Roles for Archivists and Reference Librarians in the Digital Environment

Paula J. Wolfe
University of Arizona, USA

Lori A. Olson
University of Wyoming, USA

INTRODUCTION

Many Internet users believe that archival collections should and will be digitized and placed on the World Wide Web for all to use. This belief derives from several unrealistic ideas about what the Web can do, what archival collections are, and that technology, including processing, storage and display, is free. Attempts have been made by small and large libraries to meet expectations only to find that staff requirements, as well as financial and technological issues, present too many difficulties to overcome (Nelson, 1996). Archivists are now reevaluating the Web and the benefits it offers to their repositories.

In view of these issues, we are suggesting an alternative of digitizing representative samples of holdings and providing a teaching guide for primary source interpretation for student use. The Library of Congress is currently developing primary source resources with teaching units on the Web. Unlike most repositories, the Library of Congress has a tremendous amount of collection material to draw upon as well as the financial support and staff that can be devoted to such large-scale projects (http://www.lc.org). For most archives we advocate a similar product but on a much smaller scale that still provides the same advantages to users.

This chapter will outline a Web resource design that focuses on displaying primary resources for new and potential users. The design we suggest fits archive collections with a limited budget and a small staff. The resource comprises documents or artifacts that are digitized for Web display. They are organized into a file that is separately linked from the Web page. These items are chosen from collections within the holdings and are associated historically or by general topic. The goal is to choose items that support and aid a teaching curriculum and direct users to larger pertinent high demand subject documents while offering a representative sample of the holdings.

THE NATURE AND PATRON USE OF MANUSCRIPT COLLECTIONS

Manuscript repositories and archives are responsible for collecting the records and manuscripts of a variety of organizations, families and individuals. These historical records are viewed as having continuing historical value (Ellis, 1993). Archives are often associated with a larger parent organization, such as corporations, or they may be associated with special collection departments within larger library organizations. Some manuscript repositories may also be separate entities or departments based on their collecting focus and size of their holdings.

Many diverse users utilize archives. The main constituents are historians and scholars who seek information about the past. This information is often found in primary source documents such as photographs, letters, diaries, records, journals and artifacts. Historians conduct research using these documents to formulate questions, to determine time and context, to estimate credibility and to construct historical narratives or arguments (National Standards for United States History, 1994). Historians generally view history as a process of movement and causality, not something that is discovered only in a textbook. They uncover facts and interpret them by giving them meaning and a relationship with the past (Leinhardt, Stainton and Virji, 1994).

Curriculum Use

Traditionally, the methodology of teaching history to young students has not mirrored the historical methodology of historians. Today, many educators recognize the importance of implementing a more constructivist approach to teaching history rather than the traditional, expository method of teaching (Hohmann, 1993). This approach involves a curriculum that may include a textbook as a secondary source, but it also allows students to engage in more fulfilling research by exposing them to primary source documents.

This shift in curriculum may prove challenging to the school or academic librarian in providing appropriate materials that can be categorized as primary in nature, especially since most educators and students do not always have direct access to archives or special collections. Many librarians meet this challenge by focusing their efforts on on-line and electronic information retrieval systems (Neuman, 1997). Archivists, despite their direct access to many valuable primary source documents, are also challenged with the task of providing students physical access to the documents. One of the main differences between archivists and librarians is that archivists provide very supervised or mediated access to their holdings (Gilliland-Swetland, 1998). In most archival repositories, access requires in-house use only. Because of their uniqueness and historical value, archival materials are non-circulating. In many larger repositories, on-line access to bibliographic databases and finding aids are available; however, these are only references to items located in collections. A researcher may still have to contact the archive or manuscript repository to obtain a copy of the appropriate items within a collection. Traditional means of providing copies include photocopying, a relatively inexpensive means of duplication. Photographic reproductions of visual images are also an alternative, but are often costly and not within the budget of a public school educator or student. Even though many archives are very accommodating to students and educators, using a photocopy of an original primary source may not be aesthetically acceptable. Scanning and digitization may prove to be an effective method of providing students and teachers with useful primary source material.

SELECTING APPROPRIATE MATERIAL TO DIGITIZE

The archive or library that has made the decision to digitize portions of collections should have an objective they would like to meet. Many repositories use digitization as a means for providing a broad overview of what is available in their holdings. Digitizing selected items from a collection allows researchers to view the potential of what can be found on their selected topic.

A mission statement for the library should lead any Web development. The library must define the mission of the Web site and goals for resources held within the site. From this statement goals for Web resource development will be derived. The importance of a mission statement cannot be overstated. The library presents itself to a global audience on the Internet. This audience has expectations and many have limited knowledge of archives. The Web is an ideal format for expanding public awareness, widening patron and donor base, while promoting the archival holdings. Keeping the library's mission in mind when designing Web-based resources will help maintain a library-centered Internet site meeting the goals of the library.

The benefits of Web resources that reflect the archival holdings are many. The vast amount of archived information has increased with the number of researchers remaining the same (Murphy, 1996). Introducing students to primary sources will help increase the number of users, justify the large expense of storing information and verify the type of information to be archived. Increasing public awareness of primary sources in archival libraries and the benefits for student learning are important long-term issues.

Benefits to Digitizing

Preservation needs could be addressed through digitization as well. Original primary source documents that see frequent use are a concern for long-term conservation needs. Digitizing and making these items available electronically could save further wear and tear on originals. Many photographic collections need to be handled with extreme care. Digitizing prints may be a less expensive alternative than creating photographic prints. Heavily used photographs related to a topic could be identified for digitization. This doesn't mean that an archivist must digitize an entire collection. Selecting heavily used or requested items is a more realistic means of digitizing. The goal is to create a representational sample of the holdings that give an historical overview of a topic using primary source materials. Adding a teaching unit to a selected group of topic-specific digitized documents increases the Web resource value, in addition to exposing patrons and students the opportunity to view multiple perspectives on a historical event and develop critical thinking skills (http://www.lc.gov). An added benefit, the Web resources created from the holdings will expand patron knowledge of archival holdings.

Document Choice

While it is not practical or financially possible to digitize every item in an institution's holdings, there are ways to determine which items may be valuable or in demand by researchers. One way is to keep accurate statistics on users and their research topics. Because of current trends in K-12 curricular movement toward the integration of primary sources in the classroom, archives and manuscript repositories could realize an increase in this user population. User statistics could assist archivists and librarians in selecting materials from collections that are frequently requested by K-12 users. If a topic is frequently requested, selected documents could be scanned and represented as highlights of larger collections to give students a sample from which to draw. Many repositories develop teaching guides to accompany selected documents related to a topic. Topics may be selected according to current curriculum requirements that are subject driven locally or nationally.

The American Heritage Center, the archives at the University of Wyoming, developed an on-line teaching guide to accommodate the frequent requests from students interested in the Heart Mountain Relocation Center records housed in the repository. The guide includes scanned images from collections related to Japanese relocation during World War II, as well as suggestions and lessons for using the documents in the classroom (www.uwyo.edu/ahc/).

The educational branch of the National Archives and Records Administration in Washington, DC has been working with educators and librarians to develop extensive on-line teaching guides that conform to the guidelines suggested by the National Standards for United States History (www.nara.gov).

Organizational Process

Several steps are useful in creating subject-oriented Web resources from archival holdings. The steps are not mutually exclusive and require knowledge of holdings and interest of patrons. There are two groups of professionals that should be consulted for ideas on what topics could be developed for primary resource Web collections. The two groups are professional information specialists (reference librarians and archivists) and educators (local teachers and professors). These groups have intimate knowledge of patron interests, local school curricula, course assignments and research interests. Reference librarians, public and university, help a large number of patrons and are very familiar with subject requests. They interact with a diverse clientele with varied subject or research interests. Many of these interests remain constant over time and some new areas of interest always occur. Maintaining contact with these professionals by interviews or surveys can help expand the archivist's knowledge of research and define the interests of local patrons. It can also be used to promote the archival holdings through the reference librarian and their contacts with local constituents. Contact also assures that reference librarians will maintain familiarity with archival holdings.

Role of the Archivist

However helpful local professionals can be, the archivist, familiar with the holdings or individual collections, often can guide and expand subject interests of patrons. Therefore, all archivists in the institution should be consulted on topic and material options within the library. The holdings within archival libraries are often a disparate group of collections, all items of which are not usually catalogued. Each archival library possesses expertise within the institution that should be drawn upon. Individual archivists may be intimately familiar with specific collections or important materials that patrons may or may not request. Familiarity with all the documents in a collection can be very difficult. Letters, diaries, photographs, maps, etc., may complement other documents within the repository, either as a historical foundation or direct association. These complementary primary source materials are ideal for the type of Web resource we are suggesting.

Summary of Organizational Process

1. Review primary source materials frequently requested by patrons.

2. Contact local teachers and professors about their teaching curriculum that may be aided by materials within the archived holdings.
3. Maintain contact with area reference librarians for topics of continual interest to patrons.
4. Maintain use statistics or record of topic and collection usage by patrons.
5. Review materials in diverse collections that may complement the theme of the Web resource.
6. Work with the teacher to develop a curriculum for the resource.

EXAMPLES OF PRIMARY SOURCE MATERIALS IDEAL FOR WEB RESOURCE USE

The exact nature and type of material that a library chooses for a Web resource will be individualized by the selection criteria discussed in the previous section. Due to the tremendous number of materials in archive holdings some types of documents can be joined together more appropriately. The sources chosen for the Heart Mountain Web Collection (http://www.uwyo.edu/ahc/classroom/hm/index.htm) are of interest to Wyoming citizens and World War II scholars. The topic was chosen to aid local teachers in creating a curriculum for further study by high school students in Wyoming. The topic of Japanese-Americans interned during the Second World War is of interest to historians worldwide. A Web resource such as Heart Mountain is ideal because it serves multiple interest groups, locally and globally.

TECHNICAL CONSIDERATIONS

Web Page Creation

The HTML coding (hypertext markup language) required for the type of Web resource we are suggesting is minimal. The sophistication and knowledge required to create a Web resource need not be extensive to achieve our goal. The size of the resource, number of pages, number of images, scale of images and organization of the material is of prime importance. A resource of only a few pages of documents or images can be created with minimum HTML coding and storage requirements.

Graphics

Graphic size, meaning how much memory is used per image, is the key in Web display. Download time, the time it takes for an image to appear on the screen, is directly related to the image format standard one chooses. Scanned images require compression which saves computer memory and decreases download time for users. Compression is "the reduction of the amount of data required to recreate an original file, graphic or movie. Compression is used to reduce the transmission time of media and application files across the Web" (Weinman, 1996).

Two file format standards that are commonly used on the Web are GIF, Graphics Interchange File and JPEG, Joint Photographic Experts Group. Both compress files to a small usable size and decrease download time for the user. File size is reduced while image quality is retained for viewing on a computer screen. Image type is the most important consideration when choosing a file format standard.

JPEG works with 24-bit or 16.7+ million colors. It uses lossy compression, meaning that it will discard some data to reduce the image file size as much as 100:1 (Weinman, 1996). With computer display of images, however, one does not necessarily lose quality. With JPEG one can change compression settings and control image quality. JPEG work best with photographic style images rather than graphic style images. One would use JPEG file format for images with small color changes that have soft edges such as photographs, grayscale files, scanned paintings and computer graphics. Colors can be large in number but subtle changes in edging and lighting. Sharp edge colors will become blurred with JPEG.

GIF file format standard can contain only 256 colors or less. Rather than the 24-bit lossy JPEG files, GIF files have to be only 8-bit. Unlike JPEG, they have a compression scheme that suggests higher quality of image. However, the 8-bit file requirement does not insure a higher quality of image. Choosing the correct format for the image can insure a high quality image on screen. GIF file format works well with graphics that have blocks of color and sharp lines, such as cartoons, line-art, and flat illustrations.

Scanning

Scanning a printed single page document is the easiest and

requires little extra thought on display or storage. With a little HTML coding, the single image can be easily viewed on the Web. Multiple page documents require prior decision on display, order, image continuity and storage, prior to scanning. A useful technology is OCR, Optical Character Recognition. This can be easily used to convert documents to machine readable format, edited in Word or another text editor, and then converted to an Adobe Acrobat file for easy retrieval. OCR technology allows the original format and graphics to be maintained. Any documents that are better viewed in the original format and have a large number of pages work best in a single downloadable file. This technology allows this and is easy to use and transfer from scanner to computer.

Styles of Scanners

The ability to scan black-and-white or color images has become easier and less expensive. Today a scanner can cost from as little as two hundred to as much as thousands of dollars, all dependent upon size and resolution. Scanners have not only become cheaper but more sophisticated, offering high resolution and high speed with large flatbeds for oversized objects.

There are two "styles" of scanners, flatbeds that push the paper scanner past the image, or one that pushes the paper past the scanner. Flatbeds are recommended to protect the document from being damaged. Archived material may also be in book form, diaries, sketchbooks and other formats that will only work with a flatbed scanner.

Scanners vary in size. The most popular office scanner is 8 x 14 inches. These will scan gray-scale colors with resolutions of 400 to 600 dots per inch. The higher the dots per square inch, the greater the resolution and the higher the cost for the scanner. A 600 dpi or higher is recommended to maintain a high quality of image.

Software

In addition to a scanner, computer interface software is needed and usually is included with the purchase of a scanner. One may upgrade software to Adobe PhotoShop or other image software. This software is essential for the manipulation of the image, alterations of size, color, shape, etc. The image can then be rescaled and compressed into one of the standards such as GIF or JPEG. Adobe PhotoShop is the software package most commonly used. There are many commercial or shareware products available.

DISCUSSION AND CONCLUSION

The World Wide Web offers archivists outreach opportunities. Services, holdings description, donor information and digital facsimile of material can be offered as representations of the archives. Access to archival holdings have revolutionized collections on the Internet. Archivists have an ideal opportunity for patron communication and expansion to a global audience. Archivists can also utilize the Web for new opportunities in scholarship. This can be a mixed blessing. The Web offers opportunities but also a new responsibility to a global audience. An archival Web presence brings decisions about intended audience and a repository information and services on the Internet (Landis, 1995).

There are numerous Web sites from archival libraries. They vary from stagnant, unchanging homepages that provide the barest information on the collections to dramatic, ever changing sites with facsimile materials, such as the Library of Congress site. Most fall somewhere between, depending upon sophistication of the staff in working with the Internet and the financial backing for Web development. Many, however, are moving to blend descriptive with digitized artifacts; images that represent the varied special collections and thus provide patrons with a representation of the archives. Many archivists have come to realize that the majority of users are unfamiliar with archival terminology, organization, relationships, hierarchies and principles (Landis, 1995). The Web, thus, provides a forum for educating new potential users to archival libraries and to primary sources. It has the potential to expand the understanding and the importance of primary sources and to educate these new users in the potential of these resources in research and general study.

One of the future implications for utilizing the Web to present digitized documents is the potential for attracting more non-traditional researchers to the archival user group. One objective of the archive should be to attract more students and teachers from the K-12 constituency. In addition to making these materials available in lesson format, it will be essential for archives to start implementing various assessment tools as part of the Web-based lessons to determine the effectiveness or popularity of the digitized lesson. For example, adding a simple counter to the lesson may give the archives an indication of how often the site is accessed. In addition, providing opportunities for on-line feedback to the sources would provide archivists a valuable tool for assessment. For example, encouraging students and teachers to provide descriptive contributions to the value of selective sources or soliciting suggestions for additional materials to be digitized would ultimately assist the archives in developing productive relationships with their users (Gilliand-Swetland, 1998).

Providing access to selected scanned images would also be helpful to students in different cultures around the world. A student in China studying the Vietnam War in an American History course would have an opportunity to access primary source documents related to their topic. Many of these materials were only available to scholars who were able to visit the repositories until a short time ago (Chen, Fales and Thompson, 1997). In the future, as more materials and Internet access become available around the world, archivists and librarians should realize an increase in international user populations.

While many research libraries are considering the possibility of applying digital technology to preserve their archival materials, this preservation technique will most likely not be implemented to permanently replace original documents. Due to the uncertainty of the longevity of digital storage methods, and the intrinsic or artifactual value of original documents, librarians remain skeptical of digital technology for long-term preservation (Kenney, 1993). In the meantime, scanning of archival materials will continue to increase due to the short-term benefits of giving original documents a remission from being physically handled by researchers, scholars, educators and students.

REFERENCES

Brophy, Jere. (1990). Teaching social studies for understanding and higher-order applications. *The Elementary School Journal, 90,* 351-417.

Bruce, B.C. and Leander, K.M. (1997). Searching for Digital Libraries in Education: Why Computers Cannot Tell the Story. *Library*

Trends, Spring, 747-770.

Chen, E., Fales, C., and Thompson, J. (1997). Digitized Primary Source Documents from the Library of Congress in History and Social Studies Curriculum. *Library Trends*, Spring, 664-675.

Ellis, Judith. (1993). *Keeping Archives*. Port Melbourne, Victoria, Australia: D.W. Thorpe.

Gilliland-Swetland, Anne J. (1998). An exploration of K-12 user needs for digital primary source materials. *The American Archivist, 61*, 136-157.

Graves, J.K. (1997). Design Considerations for the Library of Congress Learning Page: Providing Learners Context and Access to the Collections. Library Trends, Spring, 677-686.

Hohmann, Judy P. (1993). Discovering documents: The power of primary source materials in the classroom. *History News, 48(5)*, 13-17.

Kenney, Anne R. (1993). Preserving Archival Material Through Digital Technology: Final Report of the New York State Program for the Conservation and Preservation of Library and Research Materials. Cornell University.

Landis, W. (1995). Archival Outreach on the World Wide Web. *Archival Issues, 20*. 127-147.

Leinhardt, Gael; Stainton, Catherine; and Virji, Salim M. (1994). A sense of history. *Educational Psychologist, 29*, 79-88.

Lesk, M. (1997). Practical Digital Libraries: Books, Bytes and Bucks. San Francisco: Morgan Kaufman Publishers.

Library of Congress. Using Primary Sources in the Classroom. [Online] Available: http://lcweb2.loc.gov/ammem/ndlpedu/primary.html. [1999, March 15].

Lynch, Clifford A. (1997). The uncertain future for digital visual collections in the university. *Archives and Museum Informatics, 11*, 5-13.

Nelson, P. (1996). Digitizing Archival Photographs for Access and Preservation at Thomas Jefferson University: The JEDI Project. *Microform and Imaging Review, 25*, 99-106.

Murphy, C. (1996, May) Backlog of history. The Atlantic Monthly, 277, 20-25.

National Standards for United States History: Exploring the American Experience. (1995). National Center for History in the Schools,

University of California, Los Angeles.

Neuman, Delia (1997). Learning and the digital library. *Library Trends, 45,* 687-707.

Olson, Lori A. (1999). Heart Mountain Web Collection. [Online] Available: http://www.uwyo.edu/ahc/classroom/hm/index.htm. [1999, March 15].

Tibbo, H.R. (1996). Advocating Archives: An Introduction to Public Relations for Archivists. *Library Quarterly, 66,* 92-94.

Wallace, D.A. (1996). Archives and the Information Superhighway: Current Status and Future Challenges. *International Information and Library Review, 28,* 79-91.

Wallace, David A. (1995). Museums and archives on the World Wide Web: Resource guides and the emerging state of the practice. *Archives and Museum Informatics, 9,* 5-30.

Weinman, L. (1996). *Designing Web Graphics: How to Prepare Images and Media for the Web.* Indianapolis, IN: New Riders Publishers.

Chapter XIII

Subject Access to Quality-Assured World Wide Web Resources: Strategies for Information Professionals

Robert Newton and David Dixon
Robert Gordon University, Scotland

The development of the Internet, and in particular the World Wide Web, has offered students, teachers and researchers a rich new scholarly resource, allowing unprecedented ease of access to local, national and international information. However, the World Wide Web is badly organized, much of the information found there does not meet the rigor normally expected by academic discourse, and the technologies developed to cope with the vast explosion of online information have proven to be inadequate in a number of ways. Subject catalogues of Internet resources, compiled by information professionals expert in the information retrieval systems which have proven successful in libraries over the last hundred years, are increasingly important in ensuring easy access to high quality WWW resources. After a brief general discussion which expands on the need for well-organized subject gateways to Internet resources and outline some of the problems their development and coordination present, the chapter will examine in some detail three examples of subject gateways, two of which were developed to support teach-

ing and learning by the School of Information and Media at the Robert Gordon University, Aberdeen, Scotland. A final section will deal with the implications for information professionals of developing effective Internet subject gateways.

INTRODUCTION

Over little more than this last half decade the Internet, and in particular its rapidly developing graphical interface the World Wide Web, have developed to become a major resource for teaching and learning within the higher education sector. Students as well as teaching staff and researchers are now able to access tailored learning materials, bibliographic and other datasets, OPACs, reports and official publications, scholarly articles, conference papers and on-line reference works with unprecedented ease from their desktops almost regardless of their geographical position.

The rise of the Internet as an educational resource has taken place within the context of its general explosion in terms of the extent of the network, the speed of its technological development, the quantity of information found there and the numbers and diversity of the network's users. The same few years has also seen the rapid expansion of home use of the Internet and the commercialization of the World Wide Web, so it is now no longer mainly the preserve of the academic community but a burgeoning and largely uncontrolled information economy. The huge increase in the number and diversity of Internet resources, and the opportunities for publication presented by the Web, has come with a price: much of what is found there is of poor quality, is ill designed, lacks reliability or is offensive to the point of illegality. For academics and academic librarians, seeking both to exploit the possibilities of new information and communications technologies and to maintain the traditional rigor of scholarly discourse, the Internet presents a perplexing challenge: how can the wheat of reliable and original on-line information be separated from the worthless chaff?

BACKGROUND

This challenge is made more daunting by the inadequacies of the information retrieval tools, notably search engines, which have developed alongside the rapidly exploding WWW. Novice users of search engines regularly find hundreds, thousands or even tens of thousands of citations to Web pages returned in response to a seemingly narrow search query. More sophisticated search techniques, which limit the findings to a particular portion of the Internet (for example, to the UK Joint Academic Network) or to particular parts of the HTML document (for example, the title of a document), can greatly add precision to searches. However, the price of this gain in precision is that highly relevant sites which fall outside the limits of the search will be missed.

As the ranking techniques of a new generation of search engines become more sophisticated, so that the relevancy of WWW resources are increasingly judged on a new range of criteria including popularity (how well-used a site is), authority (how many other sites link to a site) and importance (how many 'significant' sites such as Yahoo link to a site), we can expect the search engines results to improve (Berst 1998). However, the fundamental problems created by search engine's dependence on natural language querying and automatic compilation of their huge inverted files are unlikely to change even with the maturing of search engine technologies (Taylor and Glemson, 1998).

An alternative approach to information retrieval – compiling catalogues of documents through a process of considered intellection – has existed for centuries. For example, Roger Chartier's *The Order of Books: Readers, Authors and Libraries in Europe Between the Fourteenth and Eighteenth Centuries* (1996) relates early European cataloguing practice to the emergence of modern notions of authorship. Since the first appearance of Melvil Dewey's cataloguing scheme and Charles Cutter's rules for cataloguing, both published in 1876, librarians have developed modern expertise in maximizing precision, relevance and usability of information retrieval systems. In contrast to earlier schemes which often catalogued books according to their physical features such as size and format, modern information professionals have placed an emphasis on providing access to documents according to subject.

Developing the tradition of subject cataloguing within an on-line environment will be crucial for academic librarians as well as a whole range of other information managers hoping to organize access to WWW resources in ways that maximize the ease and effectiveness of information retrieval for their end-users. By creating catalogues of on-line resources with links only to documents which meet an agreed set of quality criteria, it will be possible for librarians to continue to encourage scholarly rigor even within the uncontrolled information environment of the WWW.

Catalogues arranged by subject ranging from personal pages of 'favorite links' to the huge Yahoo directory and its more recently developed imitators already have a strong presence on the WWW. Sites such as The Mining Company (http://www.miningco.com/) and the Argus Clearinghouse (http://www.clearinghouse.net) are generally slicker, less extensive but almost identical in principle to Yahoo, while many search engines including AltaVista (http://www.altavista.com/), Lycos (http://www.lycos.co.uk/) and Excite (http://www.excite.com/) have incorporated subject guides and directories into their service. Within the academic sectors there are already examples of both general and subject-specific gateways to quality-assured information.

The development of subject gateways can be set against the background of library cooperative activities and in particular the efforts made by libraries in cooperative cataloguing which have sought to attain the goal of universal bibliographic control. It is argued that they provide librarians with the opportunity to make an impact on the organization of access to digital resources. This can be effected both at a local level through initiatives aimed at meeting the subject needs of particular groups of library users, and at a national and international level by encompassing digital resources into the strategies of national libraries for organizing comprehensive access to information irrespective of the medium in which the information is published.

However, there are several problems with subject gateways which require a strategic response from the information and library community if their full potential is to be reached.

- Particularly outside the academic sector, the development of large-scale Internet directories has tended to be led by computer sciences without much input from information professionals and without the benefit of the key cataloguing concepts and insights developed over the last hundred years. Indeed computer scientists have tended to discover, reinvent or stumble across, in a rather unfocused and underdeveloped manner, concepts well-known to librarians. (For an excellent discussion on the contribution of library science to the organization of the Web, from the perspective of a non-librarian, see Levy, 1996).

- Apart from the many ad hoc classification schemes now being used to organized the WWW, the *Beyond Bookmarks: Schemes for Organizing the Web* page reports a wide variety of national and international, general and subject-specific schemes being deployed (Scout Report Selection 1998a). While the Dewey Decimal Classification System (DDC) is the most popular, it is not necessarily the best – advances in faceted classification during this past century have the potential to come to fruition within an on-line environment where shelf order is irrelevant, but the attractive familiarity of DDC may cause these opportunities to be lost.

- Subject catalogues compiled by the intellection of information professionals can never be the whole answer to on-line information retrieval but one within a range of strategies. The rapid explosion of ever-changing on-line information simply makes the traditional cataloguer's objective of universal bibliographic control impossible. Search engines must not be dismissed for their inadequacies but continually improved. Automated classification programs such as the pioneering Pharos project should be developed further (Scout Report Selection 1998b).

- Given that no library – or even large corporate organization – has the resources to develop and maintain a thorough subject catalogue of the WWW, the intervention of libraries is necessarily pragmatic, focused on resources or sections of the Web of particular relevance to their end-users. However, this library-specific approach has the danger that many libraries will duplicate their efforts in maintaining Internet resources, or that users will find the Internet subject catalogues of various libraries frustratingly diverse in their use of classification schemes, bibliographic standards and layout.

YAHOO

The example of Yahoo will be used to illustrate, in some concrete and pragmatic detail, some of the issues outlined above. Yahoo illustrates the popularity of a subject approach to on-line information retrieval, but by critically evaluating the service from the perspective of academic users it also illustrates why much thought is needed in designing and organizing effective subject gateways for academic use.

It is a testament to the speedy development of the WWW that Yahoo, despite only being founded in 1994, is among the very earliest of the major Internet search tools. It is also a testament to its success and the validity of its original vision that, despite the somewhat workaday design of its core service which has changed little over the pass half decade, it remains by far the most popular Internet resource. According to figures for October 1998 from the independent Media Matrix company, almost half of Internet users (48.9%) access Yahoo from work and 39.4% from home (Search Engine Watch, 1998a). This compares to 25.3% using Excite from work, 22.4% Lycos, 23.7% Infoseek and 20.7% AltaVista. In each case the figures for home access are between 5 and 9% lower. Among the major Internet search tools only Yahoo and Lycos generated a net income last quarter, but Lycos' income was marginal while Yahoo generated a healthy $4 million (Search Engine Watch, 1998b). Of course, a wide range of factors from effective off-line advertising to successful partnerships with other key Internet players contribute to Yahoo's success in terms of audience reach and income generation. However, what is clear is that Internet users find its subject catalogue of WWW resources a useful route to the information they seek.

Given the success of Yahoo, it might be objected that there is no need for librarians to worry about subject access to the Internet: we already have a centralized subject catalogue for the Internet, which many companies, including the leading search engine companies, are attempting to imitate. However, such objections can be clearly over-ruled on at least three grounds.

Coverage

Yahoo is by no means complete in its coverage of Internet resources. Its estimated fifty-strong cataloguing team can not hope to keep abreast of all that is published on the WWW, and, as the development of various international versions of Yahoo suggests, the service is regionally bias. In the face of criticism from Web authors about longed delays between the submission of URLs and their inclusion in the catalogue (Search Engine Watch, 1998c), Yahoo's editor-in-chief described the company's objective as something other than compiling an exhaustive subject catalogue of the Web. Yahoo is a 'media company,' she claimed, 'aggregating information that we think is useful' (Oakes, 1998). Implicit in this is a selection policy, although the detail of this policy has not been made public and perhaps has not even been fully articulated within Yahoo itself.

Organization

Like other subject catalogues, Yahoo depends on a classification scheme. However, it is not one of the established schemes developed by librarians over the last hundred years. Rather Yahoo's classification scheme is home-grown and designed for general popular Internet users. Among its main classes are categories which could be subject headings in the established schemes ('Arts and humanities' and 'Social science,' for example), but also much narrower categories which would be found much further down the hierarchy in conventional schemes ('Computers and Internet'), categories which relate to the type rather than the subject of information ('News and media,' 'Government' and 'Reference'), and categories which seem to range across a number of subjects and overlap with other categories ('health' and 'society').

While it could be argued that Yahoo's scheme successfully meets the needs of most of its users, it does create ambiguities particularly at lower levels of the hierarchy. Also, the uniqueness of Yahoo's organization makes it impossible to integrate with any other service or systems of knowledge organization. Recent years have seen vast developments in the theoretical knowledge and practical application of multifaceted approaches to classification, but these have been largely ignored by commercial ventures such as Yahoo. To a limited extent Yahoo does allow multiple approaches to accessing a subject: for example, Yahoo classes geography as a science, but there is a link to the subject from the social sciences directory also. However this does not compare to the radical possibilities opened up for WWW information retrieval by SCORPION (http://orc.rsch.oclc.org:6109) and other research projects.

Bibliographic record

Yahoo gives very little information about the sites it links to. Basic bibliographic information such as author, publisher, date of publication, edition, format and so on is almost invariably missing. The briefest of descriptions is sometimes offered, but often only a title.

While only the biggest of library networks will be able to approach the classification of the Web on anything like Yahoo's scale, the experience of Yahoo does hold lessons for even the small-scale development of subject gateways. The popularity of the service does testify to the utility of a subject approach to online information. However, information professionals working to provide their users ease of access to the most relevant and reliable WWW resources should also learn:

- selection criteria should be tailored to the needs of their end users and explicitly stated.
- the classification task undertaken should be manageable and sustainable, so that the gateway does not become dated and incomplete in its coverage.
- the choice of classification scheme should be informed by an understanding of the relative values of the various schemes available.
- ease of integration with other relevant services (for example, an institution's printed collection) should be among the key factors considered in choosing a classification scheme.
- the bibliographic record for each Internet resource catalogued should be comparable in quality to traditional catalogue entries, and should be rich enough to allow the end-user to make an informed choice about the relevance of a resource without having to visit it.

NATIONAL INITIATIVES

As has already been noted, the cooperative tradition which has been a feature of the professional work undertaken in library and information science led to the development of a number of very important subject gateway initiatives. This is evident in the United Kingdom in the very successful gateways which have been established as part of the eLib program which arose out of the Follet Report on library infrastructure (Joint Funding Councils' Libraries Review Group, 1993). These are exemplified by BUBL (http://www.bubl.ac.uk), OMNI (http://www.omni.ac.uk), SOSIG (http://www.sosig.ac.uk), EEVL (http://www.eevl.ac.uk) and a range of others. A useful summary of the process involved in establishing such a gateway is provided in the EEVL background paper (Moffat, 1996) which describes this as "a process of identification, filtering, classification and indexing of networked resources before they are added to a database" and goes on to note that:

> [...] the end result is an organized database of resource descriptions which users can browse or search to identify items of potential interest. Resource descriptions are the most obvious benefit since users can make an assessment as to whether it is worth connecting to a resource before actually connecting to it.

Further examples of large scale information gateways can readily be instantiated from other countries, for example, the Gateway to Educational Materials (http://www.geminfo.org) project in the United States, the DutchESS (www.konbib.nl/dutchess/index.html) gateway in the Netherlands and the pan-European project DESIRE (www.desire.org.uk). Collectively such projects have now contributed a considerable body practical expertise and research on the tools (e.g. MetaWEB and ROADS) and methods for building large scale Internet information gateways. The main issues which have become apparent from this work can be summarized as follows:

- There is a need for an explicit statement, or collection development policy, to define the scope and coverage of information gateways.
- Library and subject-specialist involvement is critical to the success of developments which need to have institutional rather than individual commitment.
- More attention needs to be paid to the classification of metadata and in particular the development of transnational standards for describing Internet resources.
- Clear and substantive information needs to be provided on the context, scope, authority and provenance of resources referenced by the gateway and also on the accessibility and restrictions on use of such resources.

A further critical issue which has yet to be fully addressed is related to the economics of funding subject gateways. Currently funding is dependant on central support, and many gateways have been the direct result of large government-funded initiatives. The monies for such funding cannot be guaranteed and the issue of sustaining the gateways will depend on securing recurrent funding or developing a commercial model in order to permit revenue to meet costs. Much more research is needed on the costs and economic models on which such gateways can be maintained. This inevitably will have to be tied to the development of a model for managing such gateways which will provide an infrastructure in which the 'big players' in the field can collaborate effectively to ensure that such resources as become available can be optimized and a central strategy for content coverage and standards can be developed and adhered to.

Within the context of large scale developments such as those described above, there is considerable scope to investigate the provision of local initiatives which target the collection of subject resources for very specific audiences and aim to integrate the use of such material with existing print-based materials. The following sections look at two such initiatives which have been undertaken at the School of Information and Media at the Robert Gordon University in Scotland.

NETLEARN

The impact of the Internet on teaching and learning has been a subject of concern to a group of researchers at the Robert Gordon University over the past two years or so. The approach taken to the question of how librarians can prepare themselves for their new role in electronic networked environments has been essentially practical, and the team have sought to develop projects which provide practical evidence of the manner in which the information professional can operate effectively rather than simply to speculate on the potential benefits or threats to established working practices. At the outset of the first of these projects (NetLearn), it was obvious that the technology was in a state of flux, but it was decided that there was much to be gained from experimenting with use of systems in order to establish procedures and expertise in developing Web resources even if (as proved to be the case) the actual systems might require considerable modification in the light of possibilities offered by new hardware and software.

The NetLearn project was a SHEFC (Scottish Higher Education Funding Council) initiative which involved the development of a Web site at the Robert Gordon University, which provides a directory of resources to support academics and students who wish to retrieve relevant information on Web-based materials to support teaching and learning Internet skills. The project was initiated in 1996 , and development and maintenance of the site is ongoing.

The initiative was developed largely as a response to meeting the challenge of providing an easy means for educators to access the growing range of teaching materials which were available directly or promoted via the Internet. Shotsberger (1996) surveyed existing efforts at using the Internet for instructional purposes, but any attempt to provide a comprehensive survey today would be doomed to failure. Keeping pace with the growing number of Web-based resources and quickly determining their relevance for specific teaching applications was becoming a gargantuan task. It had become apparent to many commentators that the rapid growth of such resources was creating considerable difficulties because of a range of familiar problems: inadequate organization of the Web; deficiencies in search engines; and the lack of a standard description of Web-based materials.

For librarians these problems might be translated into the more familiar problems of classification and cataloguing; however, the traditional approaches offered by librarians to provide solutions to these problems for large print-based collections of resources were obviously inappropriate for providing a practical solution to the very real need to develop a support mechanism for academics working in this field. The proliferation of a large number of Web sites with very similar content both exacerbated the problem and indicated the need to raise awareness of existing materials in order to stem the tendency towards duplication of effort. Despite the much heralded development of more sophisticated search engines to increase the relevance and precision of the material provided in response to user queries,

Figure 1: Example of link and abstract

Beginners Central - Excellent online tutorials covering the basics of Web surfing. Manageable size, stays practical and therefore easily absorbed. Includes FAQ list and the facility to e-mail your own questions. Beginners' Central has been rated a 4 Star site by NetGuide Magazine and I-Way magazine has chosen Beginners Central as one of the top 500 Web sites in the world.

MEDIUM: WWW (with e-mail question service available)
STYLE: Page turning
COMMENTS: Good coverage of practical usage issues. Well designed, highly recommended by others.
CURRENCY: Updated monthly

those who have experience of searching the Web would generally concur that search tools remain inadequate with respect to providing precise, detailed and exhaustive indexing of the vast 'hyper-structure' of the Internet, subject as it is to continual extension and revision. In order to examine the practical problems that information workers would face when attempting to subject part of the Web to 'bibliographic control, the project sought:

- to identify educational and Internet training-resources presently available via the World Wide Web.
- to create a directory of Web-based educational resources which would allow others to identify these resources, locate them and evaluate their relevance and utility.
- to make the NetLearn directory available via a Web site which would provide for users critical and descriptive information about the educational sites and allow users to connect directly to the sites themselves.

Newton et al. (1998) provide a description of the methodology by which the site was developed. Essentially, directory entries were created for identified resources and these were collated into an HTML (HyperText Markup Language) document which was placed on the Robert Gordon University's WWW server. Entries for all selected sites include an abstract, consisting of an overview of the available materials, together with a number of fields indicating the nature of the site in terms of, for example, the medium of delivery, the presentation style of the site, the site's currency and additional evaluative comments. The 'catalogue' entries were created using a format illustrated in the following example:

A variety of feedback mechanisms were used both to monitor use of the site and attitudes toward it. The result of such evaluation showed conclusively that the NetLearn project provided a successful model for facilitating access to Internet resources which emphasizes the importance of the expertise of individuals (in particular information professionals) rather then relying on technology based solutions for managing information retrieval from the Web. The site can be accessed on the Robert Gordon University Web Server at: http:// www.rgu.ac.uk/~sim/research/netlearn/callist.htm.

Figure 2: The NetLearn home page

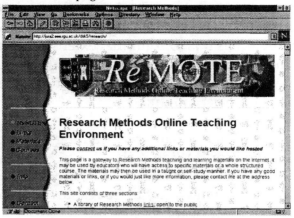

REMOTE

The ReMOTE project was an internally funded initiative at the Robert Gordon University which involved the development of a Web site which aimed to:

- provide an organized directory of external links to other WWW-based teaching and learning materials on research methods
- integrate this with a 'library' of materials which had been produced in-house and were to made available via the Web and
- provide an interface to allow incorporation of these materials on a variety of taught undergraduate and postgraduate programs.

Virtually all UK Higher Education Institutions teach research methods, either at the latter stages of undergraduate study or in postgraduate programs, where research methods is seen as a key component in preparing students to undertake study leading to an MA or MSc qualification. Typically the topic is taught as a program of lectures and seminars.

The key features of research methods which makes it an appropriate area to develop as an Internet resource are that:

1. It is generic and transferable. The end product will be applicable throughout the Robert Gordon University and all Higher Educa-

tion Institutions across a wide range of courses.

2. Because of the wide range of potential topics which it is designed to support, students find that they may have to concentrate their efforts unevenly on different components within research methods: some may, for example, require more detail on quantitative analysis, whilst others do not need to study this topic in such depth because it will not be applicable to the type of dissertations or projects in which they are engaged. It is envisaged that the basic units will be extensible to allow students to explore in greater depth areas of the subject which are of interest to them whilst clearly making them aware of the knowledge and procedural requirements for achieving credits on the course, by exploring Web links to more specialist sources. As such, the system will be particularly useful on postgraduate programs of study, where students may require simply to upgrade some specific skills or techniques and can do so on an Open Learning basis.

The aim of ReMOTE was not only to provide a direct link to such specialist sources but also to integrate this with easy access to teaching materials which had already been developed within the University and which the project team converted from paper based to Web documents. Both categories of material were to be used as 'plug ins' when developing Research Methods courses tailored for specific taught programs. It was envisaged that staff would create pathways through the 'electronic library' which was being built up by making links from online program descriptors to appropriate 'readings'— using links to online materials in the same way as references to the sources would normally be given in paper based documents. This resource library might therefore contain, for example, interactive Computer Assisted Learning packages, which are available freely via the WWW and which could be conveniently downloaded and used in teaching or self-study, online texts or journal articles or sources of statistical data. The project, therefore, sought to extend on the experience gained in creating the NetLearn directory to cover additionally the problems posed by integrating an in-house library of materials to which there were necessarily limitations of access for nonregistered students. In addition to developing research methods teaching materials the project team have also experimented with using the same interface to develop and deliver materials on Communications Skills

Figure 3: The ReMOTE home page

and is currently involved in a project to deliver parts of a tertiary level teaching program via the Web.

The ReMOTE site is available at: http://jura2.eee.rgu.ac.uk/dsk5/research.

IMPLICATIONS

Both the NetLearn and ReMOTE projects aimed to show how information professionals could use their traditional skills in classification and cataloguing of resources to provide a service with added value and which went beyond the bounds of single institutional catalogues of resources. It is suggested that the extension of the methodology employed in this subject area to others would provide considerable benefit to those who wish to identify relevant Web-based materials. The feedback from the NetLearn project certainly seems to indicate an enthusiasm for providing a directory to assist ease of access to educational resources within a narrow subject range. The challenges for the future are:

- how to expand on this approach and develop a strategy which may prove to be more generally applicable to a more extensive organization of the Internet and
- how to implement a strategy for systematically maintaining such initiatives.

There is a role for a range of participants via some form of collaboration amongst those that have traditionally been involved in the production of bibliographic tools, such as publishers, interest groups, academics and libraries. There is also, it is argued, a need for an overarching vision that would determine how those developing such tools might together work towards a form of 'universal bibliographic control' of the Internet, avoiding unnecessary duplication and gaps. It is suggested that, as indicated by some user feedback from academic and educational support services staff, this is an area in which libraries could play a central role. This echoes the sentiments of Schneiderman (1996) that, because of their skills, librarians potentially have a key role in 'organizing the Internet.'

The task of creating and maintaining Internet directories to cover a large range of subject areas is obviously too daunting for any single library. However, it is suggested that by developing a suitable strategy to develop a collaborative approach by the library community, a significant impact could be made by providing a range of well maintained Web directories. Indeed the creation and integration of such directories with the print-based collections of a particular library provides an opportunity for the library to enhance its service significantly by organizing and providing access to a much wider range of information sources. Furthermore, in what has been termed the Hammond Initiative project, EARL is currently investigating the potential for development of a large range of subject specialist Internet sites to facilitate access to and use of a range of topics (from a public library reference service perspective) and to "index them and keep them available for public library staff to use as reliable and authenticated sources of information" (Copeman, H. E-mail correspondence. 11 December 1997). The project team suggests that NetLearn may provide a useful framework for developing such an initiative.

It also became apparent from these local initiatives that there were other areas of expertise which library professionals need to develop in order to maintain and develop subject gateways. Issues related to copyright of material, rights for downloading or mirroring material from other Internet sites and provision of advice to staff on legal and ethical issues in the use of online sources are areas which should fall directly within the domain of the librarian.

Another important issue which was identified was the need to be very clear about access to materials included in the subject gateway. Because of the fact that education is increasingly conducted in a competitive environment, it is difficult to maintain a fully integrated environment for all teaching materials. The separation of 'publicly available' resources from those which were for use only within the university posed some problems. It was also felt that to compensate for the relatively small amount of material available in comparison with the print-based materials held in the University library that students should have been provided with a transparent interface to the library catalogue to see a wider range of relevant published material in very specific disciplines. They would then have been able to check its availability at the point at which they were making use of the online materials. Indeed students should ideally have been able to access to some of these published materials in electronic form. Such considerations were beyond the remit of the project which only examined the use of freely available electronic resources on the Web and the materials specifically written by academic staff of the University to support their teaching and which could be made available via the Web. Again, however, it provided evidence of the important role which the information professional could potentially fulfill in integrating bibliographic data and digitized texts within tailored learning environments. Certainly some of these issues are being examined and the development of 'virtual library' collections. Projects such as SCOPE and e-LIB are significant developments in this respect, and there are a host of projects concerned with the development of electronic journals (The homepages of SCOPE, the Scottish Collaborative On-demand Publishing Enterprise, are available at http://www.stir.ac.uk/infoserv/scope/. The homepages of eLib, the Electronic Libraries Programme of the UK Higher Education Sector, is available at http://www.ukoln.ac.uk/services/elib/.) But it was felt that the current mode of access to electronic materials was too fragmented and administratively restrictive when attempting to create a learning environment in which the student has access to the material without necessarily having to be unduly concerned about the mechanics of getting it.

CONCLUSIONS

Given the scale of the task of cataloguing the Internet, developing subject gateways to quality-assured Web resources cannot be the only method of bringing bibliographic control to the WWW. Other strategies, such as automatic classification and improving the effectiveness of search engines, must be explored and developed. Also renewing cataloguing and classification skills within an online environment is not the only area of professional changed required by the rapid emergence of new information and communication technologies. Instead, librarians need to reassess all their roles in order to fulfill the demand for professional expertise within a changed information environment.

However, developing subject gateways tailored to the information needs of a particular group of end-users is a vital way in which librarians can continue in their traditional role of facilitating easy access to relevant, high quality resources. In the context of academic libraries, ordering online learning materials into subject gateways requires librarians to develop, by working closely with course designers and teachers, a rich understanding of students' educational needs. Classification and cataloguing within an online environment merges into rather than is distinct from the design and creation of original learning materials, demanding new as well as renewed skills from librarians.

Two areas for further research and development can be identified. The first is the question of classification schemes: how can the advances in classification theory be best applied and developed in the context of the Internet's unmanaged information environment? The second is the question of cross-organizational cooperation: how can the disperse efforts to bring orders to parts of the Internet through the maintenance of subject gateways be coordinated and linked, so that end-users can easily move between and cross-search the specialist subject gateways developed by various libraries?

REFERENCES

Berst, J. (1998). Smarter Searches: Why Search Engines Are Again the Web's Next Big Thing. ZDNet AnchorDesk, 23 December. Available online at http://www.zdnet.com/anchordesk/story/story_2913.html. Last viewed 18 July 1999.

Chartier, R. (1994). The Order of Books: Readers, Authors, and Libraries in Europe Between the Fourteenth and Eighteenth Centuries. Cambridge: Polity.

Joint Funding Council Library Review Group (1993). *Report (The Follet Report)*. Bristol: Higher Education Funding Council.

Levy, D. (1996). Cataloging in the Digital Order. Paper presented at Digital Libraries '95: The Second Annual Conference on the Theory and Practice of Digital Libraries. Available online at http://csdl.tamu.edu/DL95/papers/levy/levy.html. Last viewed 18 July 1999.

Moffat, M. (1996). An EEVL Solution to Engineering Information on the Internet. Aslib Electronics Group 38th Annual Conference. Available online at http://www.eevl.ac.uk/paper1.html. Last viewed 18 July 1999.

Newton, R., Marcella, R., and Middleton, I. (1998). Netlearning: creation of an online directory of Internet learning resources. *British Journal of Education*, 29(2), 173-176.

Oakes, C (1998). Does Yahoo Still Yahoo? *Wired News*. 11 February. Available online at http://www.wired.com/news/news/technology/story/10236.html. Last viewed 18 July 1999.

Schneiderman, R.A. (1996) Why librarians should rule the Net. Enode, 1(4), 5 September. Available online at http://www.igc.org/e-node/1996/enode0104a.htm. Last viewed 18 July 1999.

Schotsberger, P.G. (1996). Instructional uses of the World Wide Web: exemplars and precautions. *Educational Technology*, 36(2): 47-50.

Scout Report Selection (1998a). Beyond Bookmarks: Schemes for Organizing the Web. Available online at http://www.public.iastate.edu/~CYBERSTACKS/CTW.htm. Last viewed 18 July 1999.

Scout Report Selection (1998b). Project Aristotle(sm): Automated Categorization of Web Resources. Available online at http://www.public.iastate.edu/~CYBERSTACKS/Aristotle.htm. Last viewed 18 July 1999.

Search Engine Watch (1998a). Media Metrix Search Engine Ratings. Available online at http://www.SearchEngineWatch.com/reports/mediametrix.html. Last viewed 18 July 1999.

Search Engine Watch (1998b). Search Engine Profits and Losses. Available online at http://www.SearchEngineWatch.com/reports/profits.html. Last viewed 18 July 1999.

Search Engine Watch (1998c). Yahoo: Delays Expected. Available online at http://www.SearchEngineWatch.com/reports/mediametrix.html. Last viewed 18 July 1999.

Taylor, A. G., and Clemson P. (1996) Access to Networked Documents: Catalogs? Search Engines? Both? OCLC Internet Cataloging Project Colloquium Position Paper. Available online at http://www.oclc.org/oclc/man/colloq/taylor.htm. Last viewed 18 July 1999.

Chapter XIV

Progress and Prospects for Esonian Libraries

Sirje Virkus
Tallinn Pedagogical University, Estonia

INTRODUCTION

The rapid development of information and communication technology (ICT) over the past decades has created new challenges and opportunities for libraries and librarians. As a result of ICT, library services to users have changed, the management of libraries has evolved and the roles of librarians have multiplied. The new millennium presents new opportunities to exploit an ever-growing array of information and communication technologies in the provision of library services. As one millennium draws to a close and a new one begins, there are a lot of questions to answer:

- What will the opportunities be for the expanded use of ICT in libraries?
- How will ICT be used or misused?
- What will be the impact of ICT on libraries, librarians and library users?
- How will the library organization change?
- What is the future of librarianship?
- How will ICT change the role of libraries and librarians?
- How will education and training for librarianship change as a result of emerging technologies?
- Will instruction of patrons differ in the new millennium?
- Will new ICT challenge the existence of libraries?

INFORMATION AND LIBRARY INFRASTRUCTURE

Estonia is a small country situated on the Baltic Sea with the population of 1.46 million and a land area of 45,215 km. Estonian librarianship emerged in the first quarter of the twentieth century, influenced by German and Anglo-American librarianship. After the Second World War it conformed to Soviet librarianship of that time. Already before the Estonian Republic reestablished its independence in 1990, the library specialists started to create the conception of the development of the Estonian libraries in the conditions of the independent democratic state. A row of conflicts and obstacles in the realization of the main functions of the libraries were pointed out (Valm, 1996). In the former Soviet Bloc countries of Central and Eastern Europe, most information technology was unavailable, unaffordable or discouraged for a long period. The improvement of the internal infrastructure was needed to become an integral part of the global information infrastructure.

The rapid development within ICT is in process of changing everyday lives in Estonia now. The changes in the library network in Estonia have taken place mainly in connection with the transformation of the economic structure, changes in territorial and administrative situation and with optimizing the library service. As the institution that provides printed matter and information free of charge, the library has acquired new functions and heavier responsibility in today's Estonia. The libraries are trying to maintain a central, intermediate function as providers of all published information for all citizens and in helping to navigate through an increasing flood of information also in an electronic environment.

The advanced national library network with sufficient financial resources guarantees the development of unified national information system and information infrastructure. A national library information system that consists of research, special, public and school libraries is an inseparable part of the Estonian information infrastructure, and libraries have an increasingly important role in making reading matter accessible to the Estonian public now.

There are about 1,290 libraries of different type in Estonia. Estonian research libraries have had coordinated development for about three decades. The publication of the union catalogue of foreign periodicals was initialized in the 1960s and the publication of the union catalogue of foreign books in 1974. In the 1990s the activities were continued by the working group of collections at Estonian Librarians' Association. The list of central research libraries and their operation principles, the fundamentals of collection development and the acquisition plan for research and special libraries have been confirmed by the regulations of the Minister of Culture and Education.

The creating of the suitable research library network started at the beginning of the 1990s. The systematic transition to the modern information technology in Estonian libraries started in 1992 when the plan for establishing an information system for libraries was developed. According to the plan basic technology will be transferred to modern information technology during the period 1996-2005. As a result of that project 1,500 workplaces with modern information technology will be established in 591 different Estonian libraries (Virkus, 1998).

The cooperation between Estonian research libraries became more intensive in the process of creating an information system and forming ELNET Consortium, in order to coordinate the division of resources and integration of technological solutions, in 1995. The primary task of the Consortium was to select, obtain and implement integrated library software. After lengthy discussions the software for the integrated system of research libraries, INNOPAC, was selected. The implementation of a common integrated system presupposes cooperation between libraries at the highest level and creates possibilities for coordinated collections development. The implementation of a new library system will inevitably bring together many changes in people's everyday work—there will be new tasks and different responsibilities for staff, there will be changes in working routines and there will be a need for reorganizing all of the library's workflow. Since 1997 research libraries are learning, testing, adapting and implementing the INNOPAC system.

The information system of research libraries, which is based on INNOPAC software and is located on two servers, will be simultaneously:

- Estonian national bibliography,
- union catalogue of participating libraries,
- tool for storing and managing local data (online catalogue, acqui-

sition, patrons, circulation) of each member library,
* center for distributing (downloading) bibliographic records, and
* database for coordinated collection development (Järs 1998).

The system is based on resource sharing through a wide area network. Employment of such a centralized cataloguing system assumes that the cooperation between participants is realized on the highest level. This model cannot be used in public libraries, because each public library has its own system, which is accessible through local area network. The systems of research and public libraries are different as to several essential parameters (operating system, network protocols, user interface, exchange format, character sets, authority files, classification, subject indexing, etc.), which makes cooperation more complicated, and demands additional means and expenses (Järs, 1998).

PUBLIC LIBRARIES

The network of the public libraries is relatively stable and has stayed capable for development. Libraries have become more popular and the need for public library services has grown. In the period 1990-1995 it has been considered to be necessary to open 11 new libraries, 10 of them in countryside (Valm, 1996). In a society on the way to market economy, a public library is often the only institution that offers services free of charge for everybody. At present, the public library is primarily a place for storing and accessing freely available information and serves as a refuge for people with low incomes, but it is not really providing for people's contemporary reading interests and needs. Many positive changes have taken place in the development of the public libraries as a regional information centers, the services of which can help individuals and groups in self-development, hobbies, entertaining, satisfy one's information and cultural needs and self-managing. Poor financing of public libraries by central and local authorities has still created a situation where libraries do not meet the expectations of society while they are at the same time an integral part of its social and economic structure. The majority of public libraries have chosen the system Kirjasto 3000 to create their own electronic catalogues and provide information services to their readers and for which substantial support was allocated by the Open Estonia Foundation.

The number of special, institution and trade union libraries has decreased by nearly a hundred because many of these enterprises and institutions have ceased to exist. Many unions, societies, churches, prisons and other organizations are considered to be motivated to start or legalize their libraries.

The changes in the information environment are not only of technological character. The range of external influence on the libraries covers political influences (the European Union, languages, users); economic influences (competition, sponsors, state share, etc.); juridical influences (Legal Deposit Copy Act, copyright, licenses, standards); influences on the changes in the educational and cultural sphere (professional knowledge, training, the role of libraries, structural changes), etc. How to cope with these transformations? Whether to be on the front line— a precursor and experimenter or to wait for training support from outside about trends in developed countries? The same question arises comparing other information technology systems in Estonia (e.g. The Tiger Leap). The watchword of Estonian libraries, so far, has been a balanced development. The state has declared in the basic principles of its information policy that, first and foremost, it will concentrate on:

- updating legislation;
- developing of private sector;
- designing relations between the state and its citizens;
- raising awareness of the problems of an information society.

The real contribution of the state is, first and foremost, the development of the information structure and the provision of technical access to information. The responsibility of the libraries is to make society aware of the information to which the access has been created, of the essence of the information systems and how to find easily, acquire and make use of this information (Reial, 1998).

In 1994 the "Programme of Estonian Informatics Development up to 2000: Estonia in the way to the information society" was worked out. Unfortunately, we must say that the development of information and communication technology has been more rapid than the program took into account, and the document is quite outdated today.

The decree "The Main Conceptions of Cultural Policy of the Estonian Republic," passed by the Parliament on September 16, 1998, states: *Libraries act as integrated state information system, striving to provide the population with exhaustible, exact and easily accessible information and access to the information resources of the world. The state library information system, containing research, public, school and other libraries, is an inseparable component of Estonian national information infrastructure* (Valm, 1998).

The decree "Principles of Estonian Information Policy," passed by the Parliament on May 13 1998, expresses the same idea, but in a different context: *The State constitutionally guarantees the principle of the openness of information. The direct responsibility of the Government is to guarantee the free movement of information, implying that public organizations must without delay disseminate information about their daily operations. Provision of such information must be compatible with the following requirements:*

- *Every applicant must be guaranteed equal opportunity to access information;*
- *Information must be provided actively and systematically and, as a whole, be easy to comprehend.*

Responsibilities for the correctness of public information must be determined in order to increase its reliability. The Government promotes the establishment of information access points to guarantee the availability of information (Eesti, 1998).

Today when more than 50% of the population of Estonia visits all kinds of libraries and the demand for various information services is rising, it's obvious that the attitude towards the libraries must radically change, because only stable legislative and financial basis can guarantee the development of national information system. Libraries urgently need a state program, which could connect them with other information programs in Estonia (Valm, 1998). It must still be acknowledged on the state level that establishing the common, integrated, user-friendly and all Estonian library system is also a strategic question and otherwise it will have negative effect on the development of economy and foreign policy.

THE INTERNET

In Estonia the link to the Internet was created in 1991, but real Internet access did not become available until 1992 when several institutes of the Estonian Academy of Science were connected to the Nordic Internet networks. As a result, the Estonian Academy of Sciences Library was the first library in the former Soviet Union with a dedicated connection to the Internet. Other major Estonian research libraries (i.e., the National Library of Estonia (1992), the Tartu University Library (1993) were connected later.

After the starting period when the users were only network specialists, new non-computer users and even nontechnical users appeared. In less than three years since the Internet was made available to Estonia the Internet doors opened for many Estonian users: governmental institutions, universities and scientific and research institutions, libraries, secondary and vocational schools, commercial institutions, nonprofit organizations and individuals.

Academic networking in three Baltic States began largely thanks to the individual initiative of Baltic scholars and to the support from abroad (UNESCO, EC, Soros Foundation, etc.). There wasn't enough support on the state level. The first official Internet course in Estonia was held in the Tallinn University of Educational Sciences (TUES) in November 1993 by Dawn Mann (Radio Free Europe - Radio Liberty) under an IREX Special Project Grant. At that time TUES was the only place in Estonia where it was possible to use the Internet through public terminals so widely. As Dawn Mann's course was organized in order to help all Estonian librarians better use the Internet, the number of participants from each library was limited. After that course participating persons started to spread the knowledge and skills of using the Internet in Estonia. Several courses were organized at the Library of TUES for the librarians of Estonian academic libraries. The Internet course was added to the curriculum of the Department of Information Studies of TUES in 1993 as well and the Center of Information Work within the Department of Information Studies started to deliver Internet courses in the framework of continuing professional education (Virkus, 1995).

The national telecommunications network is one of the key areas of development in Estonia. Rapid development in this particular field has enabled the connection of the libraries, schools, universities, research institutions, various communities and business organizations to a joint data network and further, to establish connections with international networks. The Internet has become an essential communication medium for academic and research institutions as well as businesses in Estonia, and the amount of Internet users is growing very rapidly. In 1992 there were 23 Internet hosts in Estonia; in July 1998 the number of hosts was 20,063. In July 1998 Internet hosts per 10,000 inhabitants in Europe were: Finland 859, Iceland 797, Norway 687, Sweden 411, Liechtenstein 396, Denmark 380, Netherlands 341, Switzerland 300, United Kingdom 226, Austria 189, Belgium 177, Israel 174, Luxembourg 159, Germany 156, Estonia 139, Slovenia 110, Hungary 86, France 76, Latvia 39, Poland 29, Lithuania 22 (Interneti, 1998).

The concept of a virtual library is spreading rapidly in Estonia. Library patrons are searching in online public access catalogues, requesting interlibrary loan services, receiving digitized documents from electronic archives without ever stepping into a library. The expectations of the library patrons have changed. More and more remote services are expected, and at the same time, the functions and tasks of information specialists in libraries have changed. The information services librarians have become involved in user education programs to provide information literacy training to library patrons, teaching them to manage independently in electronic information environment.

Still, the majority of academic libraries have policies to answer only to those questions that are submitted by their own users, with the exception of questions that have a concern in this university itself. Most of the e-mail and Web form services state that they would only answer brief factual or short answer questions. Responses are generally sent within 24-48 hours. Tartu University (TU) Library has offered the electronic service by its WWW homepage since December 1997. The service has not been limited to the Tartu University community. The Web form of the electronic information service was designed as short, simple and user-friendly as possible. Limits on this service are defined by the length and nature of the query (Meltsas 1998).

Significant changes have taken place in interlibrary loan of Tartu University Library as well. They can be defined as following:

- the creation of new interlibrary loan and document delivery system, oriented to Western countries; and
- the implementation of new library technologies.

The rebirth of ILL and the creation of document delivery (DD) were mostly due to the help of Scandinavian colleagues. The growing popularity of ILL/DD services can be explained by:

- changes in the methods of teaching at the university;
- high level of the users' computer skills;
- skyrocketing prices for printed materials that caused the decrease in acquisition volume;
- free access to databases; and
- availability of electronic communication at the library.

At present ILL/DD service at the TU library is based on the use of new technologies (80%) of the requests are processed electronically and fixed prices for services. They had to reconsider their work from the marketing point of view as well. The range of services offered by separate libraries, library consortiums and information centers is very wide. A number of factors should be considered while making the choice, such as thematic expediency, the efficiency of turnaround time, the simplicity of searching and ordering and, the most important —reasonable prices. Future ILL/DD development should be carried out in two directions: the expansion of ILL/DD services within Estonia and performing international ILL/DD on general grounds.

The implementation of coordinated acquisition among libraries on the republican level can be provided only by well-organized ILL/DD service in all leading libraries; that means adequate staffing and at least moderate technical equipment. Interlibrary loans and document delivery gives access to the resources of all libraries (Lustsik, 1998). There is a still an urgent need in many libraries to develop completely new services and to integrate them into appropriate traditional ones.

DISTANCE EDUCATION AND LIBRARIES

Higher education is in crisis in much of the world (Daniel, 1996). Distance education (DE) is one among the many possible solutions that have been proposed to deal with these problems. The question still remains how remote students access the information they need to support their learning and what kinds of services libraries can provide.

The ideas of modern DE started to spread in Estonia in 1993 and all Estonian universities have recently realized that distance education is very important in the strategy of the university to give adults lifelong learning opportunities. In 1999, a Distance Education working group was also established within the Estonian Librarians' Association. There are a lot of questions for the Estonian librarians and information professionals and for the Working Group at the moment:

- how to establish a service for distance learners
- how to maintain and expand a distance learners services
- what services are reasonable to provide and what services are not
- how to provide the best services that we can, and
- what do we have to do to become a major partner in the DE system, etc.

Several libraries have started activities in assisting the course writers in identifying appropriate literature and network resources to support the preparation of the course, providing advice about networked resources, negotiating cost-effective online access for students and providing physical learning facilities for students. Representatives of Estonia are also participating in the activities of Library and Learning Support Working Group that was established within the European Association of Distance Teaching Universities (EADTU) in June 1998.

The Group is committed to the development of library and learning support services as an essential element in innovative and cost-effective approaches to learning. The Group provides a forum and a focus for those responsible for library and learning support services within member institutions. It aims to address strategic issues as well as seek to identify, disseminate and encourage good practice in supporting both on campus and distance learners. By these means the Group will seek to promote equal access to library and learning support for citizens throughout Europe.

Still, in Estonia, the drafts for decisions concerning educational policy do not define a learning environment as a space of information flow, and where, consequently, the efficiency of the space is higher the more information it contains. Resulting from this, both the library as a learning center and the library as an obligatory element of the educational space are left out of the education strategy (Olesk, 1998).

PROFESSIONAL TRAINING OF ESTONIAN LIBRARIANS

Changes in society demand changes in education, its content and management and training systems. Education is in the midst of a monumental paradigm shift, and the way that all instructors teach and the way all students learn is also changing. There is a shift from a teacher-centered to a learner-centered process, from a pedagogic approach to a facilitative one. Essential are the learning process and the quality of education. The growth in responsibility of librarians under a country's changed conditions also requires high-quality professional education, flexible continuing education and professional development in all levels. The Department of Information Studies of Tallinn University of Educational Sciences, the only institution in Estonia offering an academic-level education for librarians and information professionals, therefore places particular emphasis on reshaping its education and training system so that they can meet the demands of lifelong learning in the information society. Education on college level has been organized in Viljandi College of Culture.

The history of professional library training in Estonia is 70 years long. Librarians' training became a regular issue for the Estonian Librarians Association in the 1920s; in 1927 librarianship became an optional subject in the curriculum of Tartu University; 1944 saw the opening of the Department of Bibliography, and 1954 that of the faculty of librarianship. Two-hundred-and-six graduates majored in librarianship or in philology and librarianship from 1945 to 1968 (Noodla, 1969).

From 1944 to 1965 librarians with a university degree were educated at Tartu State University. The degree of success varied from year to year, the shortage of academically qualified teaching staff was strongly felt. Since 1965 it has been possible to get a degree in librarianship at Tallinn Pedagogical University (TPU), which was, until 1992 Tallinn Teacher Training Institute. The Department of Librarianship and Bibliography was founded in September 1966. In September 1991 it was turned into the Faculty of Library and Information Science, made up of the Department of Librarianship, that of Scientific Information and the Chair of Book Science. Since 1993 the Faculty of Social Sciences at the Tallinn Pedagogical University has housed the Department of Information Studies that has chairs of Library Science, Information Science and Book Science.

Unified curricula, compulsory in the whole Soviet Union, did not allow librarians to prepare for the peculiarities of the information environment in which they had to work later on. The all-Union curricula could be adapted only up to 5 percent, and the content of education and its four-year duration were rigidly prescribed for all the 130 secondary and 29 higher special-education institutions (institute of culture, universities, pedagogical institutes, etc.) located in the territory of the Soviet Union (Lesokhina, 1985).

Systematic modernization of the curricula of library and information science in TUES started in 1988. Beginning in the autumn term of 1994, the TUES offers full-time university credit courses. The undergraduates of the Department of Information Science study major, general and additional subjects. The basic degree course provided by the department is the bachelor's degree (160 credits), with information studies as the major component. The allocation of credits to components is as follows:

1. Information Studies 105 credits comprising:
   Approbatur: (lower level) 15 credits
   Cum laude approbatur : (intermediate level) 40 credits
   Laudatur : (higher level) 95 credits
   Bachelor thesis on information science 10 credits
   Moving to each following level presumes that the previous level has been achieved.
2. Additional subjects 30 credits
3. Optional subjects 5 credits
4. General subjects 20 credits

This flexible structure of studies allows the students to complete their own curricula according to their interests and goals, and gives them better opportunities to compete in the employment market (Lepik, 1997).

The department educates professionals for service, administrative planning and research tasks in the whole sector of information management, including library and information services.

Since 1991 it has been possible to take advanced degree courses at the Department of Information Studies of TUES. These postgraduate studies lead to two degrees: Master of Information Sciences (MA) and Doctor of Philosophy in humanities (PhD). The master's and doctoral studies provide an opportunity to develop the professional knowl-edge obtained during the first level of studies and to deepen the researcher's qualities in a narrower field in librarianship, information and book science.

The amount of information technology courses has increased from 5 to 51% during the period 1988-1999. Information technology courses in the Department of Information Studies of the TUES have enabled it to offer technological knowledge and skills to many gradu-ates and tried to help them to integrate into modern technological and virtual environments. At present it is characteristic that information technology has been used in many different courses: cataloguing, collec-tion development, information sources and retrieval, etc. The content of information technology courses has been changed a lot as well.

The modernization of library and information science education has happened also in implementing modern teaching methods in education. One possibility to improve university education and con-tinuing education is distance education. Distance education enables them to widen education possibilities, to change stereotypic teaching and learning models, to facilitate self-consciousness and open the university to every person. The study process of modern distance education started in the Department of Information Studies in 1994. Two distance education projects have been designed for distance learn-ers: the distance education pilot project for school librarians and the long-term project "Information Technology in Libraries" (Virkus, 1997).

Library education on the college level is organized at the Viljandi College of Culture, founded in 1952, and initially located in Tallinn as the School of Cultural Education. Continuing professional education is organized on following levels:

State-wide: The Center for Continuing Education of Cultural Work-ers (established in 1985), the National Library of Estonia and the Center of Information Work of the Department of Information Studies of TUES organize various courses and workshops for the staff of different types of library. The Estonian Children's Library takes care of children's and school librarians' continuing education.

Local: The research and special libraries arrange courses for their own similar library staff (e.g., by Tallinn Technical University Library for the other technical libraries, and by the Estonian Medical Library for hospital libraries, etc.), and the central city and county libraries do the same for other librarians in their regions.

During recent years academic libraries have provided various types of formal training for their users. Now libraries also play an important role in the development of networked distance education. In spring 1997, Chalmers Technical University Library made a proposal to TTU Library to participate in the project DEDICATE— Distance Education Information Courses with Access Through Networks, at EU program "Telematics for Libraries." This project involves 9 university libraries, which all are members of IATUL. The aim of the DEDICATE project is to develop cost-effective DE courses in information literacy.

Continuing education is varied and flexible, catering for the needs of those librarians who have an LIS degree and for those without it. The system has been devised so that it embraces qualification improvement, in-house training, continuing education and retraining. Short- and long-term courses should facilitate ongoing continuing education.

INTERNATIONAL COOPERATION

In order to make the international professional community aware of Estonian libraries, our librarians should keep track of the worldwide developments and keep in mind the need to promote Estonian librarianship (Lepik, 1997).

In cooperation and coordination between libraries the Estonian Librarians Association (ELA) plays an essential role. Estonian Librarians' Association was founded in 1923 and re-founded in 1988. Its main goals are to solve professional problems, to organize interlibrary cooperation, to work out different forms of cooperation and to conclude the cooperation agreements in librarianship (acquisition, bibliographic describing, classifying and indexing, union catalogues, librarianship specialty information, library automation, advanced training, professional requirements for librarians, librarianship terminology, problems of salaries and financing, etc.). All these problems are discussed by ELA working groups, and their aims are to bring library process up to international standards.

At ELA's instigation, Estonian librarians reestablished their relations with International Federation of Library Associations and Institutions (IFLA). Until 1989 Estonia used to be represented by high-level Soviet library officials. Since 1989, however, when ELA restored its status in IFLA (ELA was an IFLA member from 1928 to 1940), ELA has started to participate in the activities of various IFLA sections and round tables. Estonian librarians are standing committee members in the following sections:

- parliamentary libraries;
- education and training;
- classification and indexing;
- public libraries.

IFLA membership facilitates Estonian librarians' international professional cooperation and participation in joint projects and helps to develop and initiate research projects. The NLE became an IFLA institutional member in 1993 (sections of parliamentary libraries, information technology, interlending and document delivery) and the Library of Academy of Sciences joined IFLA in 1994 (sections of science and technology libraries, rare books and manuscripts) (Lepik 1997).

International associations of research and special libraries have an essential role in dealing with librarians' professional problems and their development. The NLE and Tartu University Library are Ligue des Bibliotheques Europeénnes Rechereche (LIBER) members, and Tallinn Technical University Library joined the International Association of Technological University Libraries (IATUL) in 1990.

Participation in international professional organizations became more active in 1993 (the International Association of Music Libraries (IAML); the CDS/ISIS User Association and UNESCO's Network of Associated Libraries (UNAL); the International Association of School Librarianship (IASL), etc. TUES Department of Information Studies is a founding member of the European Association for Library and Information Education and Research (EUCLID, 1991); students belong to BOBCATSSS (Organization of European Library and Information Science Education School Students). Several professional organizations, IFLA, IATUL and ABDOS, have lately arranged their regular meetings in Estonia, thus enabling our librarians to participate in the international library scene without much cost.

Estonian librarians participate also in the work of Bibliotheca Baltica, founded in 1994 in Tartu, with the aim of uniting library institutions of the Baltic Sea region countries, and of Arbeirgemeinschaft der Bibliotheken und Dokumentationsstellen der Ost-, Ostmittel- und Südeuropaforschung (ABDOS) (Lepik, 1997).

Estonian librarians have tried to make as much use as possible of the opportunities offered for professional development by foundations, libraries and training programs in Europe and America. The Congressional Research Service (CRS) of the Library of Congress has been active in training parliamentary librarians since 1992, including a workshop in Tallinn in 1993. Estonian parliamentary librarians have also been trained in the parliamentary libraries of Finland and Sweden. Good training opportunities have been offered by the Library of Congress - Soros Foundation librarian international programme for the Washington metropolitan area. So far four Estonian librarians have qualified. Since 1991, more than 10 Estonian librarians have been on study tours or attended training sessions in Germany organized by Deutsches Bibliotheksinstitut, Bibliothekarische Auslandstelle (Lepik 1997).

CONCLUSIONS

The Estonian library and information world is trying to take the best possible advantages of changes in the world, adapt themselves to new technologies, new demands and new customers. In the changing information environment, an accelerated move from collection-based to access-based services, resource sharing, skilful use of ICT and the opportunities of network environment will be expected from the libraries and librarians in Estonia.

REFERENCES

Daniel, J. (1996). *Mega-universities and knowledge media: technology strategies for higher education.* London, Kogan Page.

Eesti (1998). Eesti Infopoliitika põhialised = Principles of Estonian Information Policy. Tallinn, 1998.

Interneti 'tihedus' Euroopas = Internet Density in Europe (http://www.ciesin.ee/ESTONIA/europe9807.html)

Järs, J. (1998). Koostöö võimalikkusest rahva- ja teadusraamatukogude vahel. Ettekanne Eesti Raamatukoguhoidjate VII Kongressil "Raamatukogud avatud ühiskonnas, 22.-23.oktoobril Tartus. (In print).

Lepik, A. (1997). Training of trainers and professional development: Estonian prospective. In: *Human Development: Competencies for the Twenty-First Century: Papers of the IFLA CPERT Third International Conference on Continuing Professional Education for the Library and*

Information Professions, (IFLA Publications 80/81), 105-113. München: K. G. Saur.

Lesokhina, V.S. (1985). Problems of training library personnel in the USSR. *Journal of Education for Library and Information Science*, 25(3), 1985, 200-6.

Lustsik, M. (1998). Raamatukoguvahelise laenutuse ja dokumentide levi töökorralduse põhimõtted. Ettekanne Eesti Raamatukoguhoidjate VII Kongressil "Raamatukogud avatud ühiskonnas, 22.-23.oktoobril Tartus. (In print).

Meltsas, M. (1998). Infoteenindusest virtuaalses raamatukogus. Ettekanne Eesti Raamatukoguhoidjate VII Kongressil "Raamatukogud avatud ühiskonnas, 22.-23.oktoobril Tartus. (In print).

Noodla, K.(1969). Raamatukogunduse õpetamisest Tartu Ülikoolis 1927-1967. In: Education in librarianship at Tartu University 1927-1967, Teadusliku Raamatukogu töid, Vol. 2, 1969, 3-24.

Olesk, P. M. (1998). Miks õppiv Eesti ei mõista raamatukogusid?. Ettekanne Eesti Raamatukoguhoidjate VII Kongressil "Raamatukogud avatud ühiskonnas, 22.-23.oktoobril Tartus. (In print).

Reial, M. (1998).Eesti raamatukogud uuenevas infokeskkonnas. Ettekanne Eesti Raamatukoguhoidjate VII Kongressil "Raamatukogud avatud ühiskonnas, 22.-23.oktoobril Tartus. (In print).

Valm, T. (1996).The Development of library activities in Estonia in 1990-1995: *Papers of the 5th Congress of Baltic Librarians*, 7-12. Tallinn: Estonian Librarians Association.

Virkus, S. (1997). Distance education as a new possibility for library and information science education in Estonia. In: *Human Development: Competencies for the Twenty-First Century: Papers of the IFLA CPERT Third International Conference on Continuing Professional Education for the Library and Information Professions*, (IFLA Publications 80/81), 249-255. München: K. G. Saur.

Virkus, S. (1998). Cooperation in the Field of Distance Education in Library and Information Science in Estonia. In *Advances in Librarianship*, 22, 141-155. New York: Academic Press.

Chapter XV

The Growing Support Crisis in Federal STI

R. David Lankes
Syracuse University, USA

Federal agencies in the United States federal government that provide Scientific and Technical Information (STI) face a growing support crisis brought on by the Internet. As these organizations use the Internet to provide increased access to databases and automated resources they are finding more users from the general public are asking more questions. These organizations need to be prepared to support an increasingly diverse user group via the Internet. Projects of the National Library of Education (AskERIC and Virtual Reference Desk) are reviewed and used to raise and discuss issues in supporting STI applications in a government setting. Finally a set of recommendations is presented to help plan digital reference services in this context.

INTRODUCTION

Federal Scientific and Technical Information (STI) providers such as the National Library of Medicine, National Library of Education, National Agricultural Library and the Defense Technical Information Center face new challenges as use of the Internet grows. Organizations that specialize in the production of databases and collections of materials (including images and texts) now find themselves in an unfamiliar support territory. Collections once meant for small specialized audiences are now being used by increasingly naïve and diverse

Figure 1: As user access of STI products increases, the support burden also increases

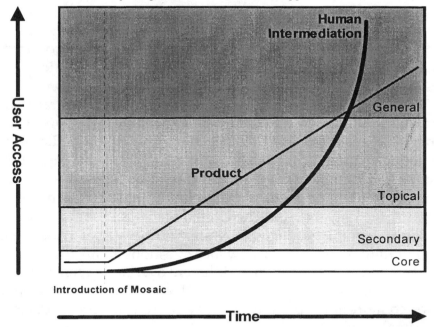

audiences. Where once STI agencies could assume a level of sophisti-cation and self-support by their intended audiences, they now find themselves overwhelmed with questions from the general public.

Only recently have STI agencies begun to realize the impacts of the Internet, which was originally seen as a cost effective dissemination alternative to print. Alternate formats, new media capabilities and new means of inter-agency linkages are now possible and their impacts increasingly understood. Evaluation of Web sites and prod-uct design in a client/server environment are rapidly developing in sophistication and use. In addition agencies have realized larger audiences and claimed this increased user access as a sign of success in information dissemination. However, as shown in Figure 1, in-creased user access comes not only from reaching more of an agency's core audience, but crossing into new audiences and users. Now those accessing the product include:

- *Core* - users who are familiar with a specific STI product,
- *Secondary* - audiences with great knowledge of an agency's scope, but are unfamiliar with a given product,
- *Topical* - those familiar with an agency's topic on a broad scale, •

General - the general public with minimal understanding of the agency or its products.

So while dissemination in terms of users accessing a product may be increasingly successful, the sophistication of that audience now varies widely.

The unintended consequences of this "Internet embrace" have affected traditionally low-funded, low-staffed help and support desks. As new audiences come to STI collections, the nature of the support interaction changes dramatically. New audiences have caught these agencies unaware, and the agencies must now scramble to understand new policy, budgetary and technological approaches—often inventing them as they go. The United States National Aeronautics and Space Administration (NASA) support personnel, used to interacting with rocket scientists, now face questions about alien life from school children. Further, with the inherent overlap of agency missions and topics, questions may be submitted to one agency that would be answered more appropriately by other information providers within the federal government.

There are several issues that further complicate the support question including:

- *Policy* - The issues of increased support are complicated by a diverse policy environment. For example, are Web logs and user questions private, or should they be seen as part of the public record[1]? Is a federal agency responsible for archiving all user access data including e-mail questions and Web logs? How can a government agency institute tiered levels of service while remaining true to its mission?
- *Technology* - Traditional help desk software to date has been telephony oriented and unable to deal with the increasing use of the Internet for user support. Help desk software to this point has been designed as closed systems. How can these services better interoperate in a network of support?
- *Budget* - How does an STI agency budget for an expanding support function when the number of users is unknown and the character of those users constantly changes? How do these agencies build cost and fee structures to allow them to interoperate on a greater scale?

This chapter examines these issues by first examining the state of user support in the CENDI (CENDI, 1999) STI agencies and looking for parallels in library based digital reference research. Digital reference is defined as the provision of human intermediation (often experts) in electronic networks such as the Internet. Finally, a case study from the National Library of Education (National Library of Education, 1997) will be used to clarify the current situation in customer support, and future research will be discussed.

CENDI Agencies

CENDI is an interagency working group that represents senior Scientific and Technical Information (STI) managers from nine programs in eight U.S. Federal Agencies (see Table 1). Its name is drawn from the federal agencies that compose the group. According to the organization's Web site, the mission of the organization is as follows:

"CENDI's mission is to help improve the productivity of Federal science and technology-based programs through the development and management of effective scientific and technical information support systems. In fulfilling its mission, CENDI member agencies play an important role in helping to strengthen U.S. competitiveness and address science- and technology-based national priorities" (Hodge, 1997, p. 1).

In 1997 CENDI released a report from a series of meetings regard-

Table 1: CENDI Agencies and Contributing Units

Agency	Contributing Unit
Commerce	National Technical Information Service (NTIS)
Education	National Library of Education (NLE)
Energy	Office of Scientific and Technical Information (OSTI)
National Aeronautics and Space Administration	Scientific and Technical Information Program (NASA STI)
Agriculture	National Agricultural Library (NAL)
Department of Health and Human Services	National Library of Medicine (NLM)
Defense	Defense Technical Information Center (DTIC)
	National Air Intelligence Center (NAIC)
Interior	USGS/Biological Resources Division (USGS/BRD)

ing activities related to the impacts of the Internet on customer service and product development (Hodge, 1997). This report outlined current use of internal and public support help desks within these STI agencies.

The report concluded "agencies are finding a new user community for their products and services, but resources originally intended for the agencies' more traditional audiences are being stressed to provide services to the new communities" (Hodge, 1997, p. 1). Further "the increase in inquiries from nonregistered users and nontraditional customer groups leads to more questions that are out-of-scope for the particular agency. This leads to referrals to other agencies and organizations" (Hodge, 1997, p.7).

These issues of change in audience and the tools used to support those audiences are not unique to STI. In fact, libraries internationally are dealing with the impact of the Internet on customer support. In the following section, the author will explore the changes in library customer support through the reference function.

IMPACTS OF THE INTERNET ON REFERENCE SERVICES

The literature shows significant impacts on reference services prompted by greater access to the Internet and Internet tools. These impacts include new skills needed by information specialists and reference librarians (Bobp, Kratzert & Richey, 1993). The Internet is also expanding traditional library collections and improving location and access to reference resources (e.g., ready reference materials and pathfinders through World Wide Web sites, access to catalogs and electronic reference sources through telnet, etc.). Most significant to this chapter, the Internet affords reference services the ability to conduct entire reference transactions (from specifying users' needs to delivering information from the collection) via the Internet (Still & Campbell, 1993).

A great deal of literature has focused on augmenting traditional reference services with Internet resources and capabilities. This literature ranges from evaluation criteria for on-line reference sources (Balas, 1995) to discussions of technology used to locate and access Internet resources (examples include Feeney, 1993; Bobp, Katzert & Richey, 1993; Gainor & Foster, 1993; Arms, 1990; Branse, 1993; Machovec, 1993). In these discussions, the interface to the user remains the same, but the collection is expanded to include Internet resources. These new resources change the reference environment. Mardikian and Kesselman (1995, p. 22-3) presented five "rationales for changing reference:"

- Increasing access to resources beyond the library (networked resources including the Internet).
- Lack of geographic constraints for users ("users may no longer need to come to the library to obtain information").
- The need to differentiate services to different populations of users (i.e., inside an organization and outside an organization) in the face of shrinking budgets.
- Increases in complexity of information resources and the need for specialized knowledge.
- New options (primarily in staffing) for answering reference questions.

These rationales highlight the redefinition of librarians' roles within a traditional geographically defined library setting. However, the same issues are directly relevant to supplying scientific and technical information support in a government context. The Internet is shattering traditional boundaries for information centers, libraries and government agencies alike.

CHANGING ROLES OF REFERENCE LIBRARIANS

Reference librarians and customer support specialists face new responsibilities, training requirements, tasks and role in response to the "increasingly automated [library] over the past three decades" (He & Knee, 1995 p.7). He and Knee presented the idea of an electronic services librarian. In regards to reference services, they stated, "It is important for electronic services librarians to be familiar with traditional as well as electronic reference sources. By learning traditional sources, they will be able to recognize which Internet resources may also be valuable" (p. 9). He and Knee called for librarians to update their skills in response to perceived changes to the reference environment. This need for updated skills is the same in the context of STI agencies and their staff.

The burden of learning and applying the application and evaluation skills of the Internet falls upon the information professional. In the case of a library, the reference librarian must master the new Internet tools for his or her users. The reference librarian acts as "a bridge which has technology at one end and the user at the other" (Callahan, 1991). Learning, however, is not limited to just applications and technology. It also applies to learning to deal with change. McClure et al. stated "library staff . . . must learn from their colleagues in the computing services how to become more comfortable with the type and rate of change that will accompany the networked environment" (McClure, Moen & Ryan, 1994). This notion of change and the need for technical proficiency is echoed throughout most of the literature concerning reference services and the Internet.

Accompanying the changes in reference librarians' skills are changes in the reference librarians' roles, particularly in regards to staffing. Oberg states "paraprofessionals can and do perform well at a reference desk, freeing librarians to concentrate on higher-level tasks" (Mardikian & Kesselman, 1995, p.21). Mardikian and Kesselman presented a three-level staffing model to reflect the changing role of the reference librarian (see Table 2).

Accompanying this shift in responsibilities for reference librarians (to higher-level tasks) is a call for greater collaboration with other types of professionals. Lewis (1995) believed the infusion of new tools for location and access into libraries means "a significant upgrading of skills of most librarians and will mean professionals who are not librarians will have to be offered positions along side of, or in place of, librarians." McClure, et al. (1994, p.67) listed partnering with computing services, faculty and other "external organizations and companies" as critical success factors in building the virtual library. Indeed, STI services have already formed strong relationships with computing centers and technical organizations as discussed by McClure et al. (1994).

The changes for librarians just outlined also pertain to information professionals in STI agencies. Whether their title is librarian, customer service representative or analyst, these information professionals must expect to change their roles and skill sets in reaction to the increased use of the Internet for customer support.

Digital Libraries

The Internet is also used to provide better access to a library's collection. The Internet is used to organize materials for reference patrons (Jensen & Sih, 1995) and allow patrons[2] access to reference sources such as online public access catalogs (He & Knee, 1995). This literature includes discussions of standards for information interchange (Moen, 1992). The literature seems to present a continuum for reference services and access in relation to the Internet. There has been a general belief that libraries and reference services are headed "towards a virtual future" (Strong, 1996). However, this future has not been widely explored.

Sutton's (1996) four-part typology of libraries anticipated the expansion of reference collections to include the Internet, as well as the use of the Internet to access an individual library's collec-

Table 2: Mardikian and Kesselman's Staffing Levels (From Building and Maintaining Internet Information Services: K-12 Digital Reference Services)

Level 1: Minimum Human Intervention
Self-guided building tours
Automated telephone answering machines
Better signage
Better floor maps
Library quick guides
Step-by-step guides
Computer-assisted instruction for self-service instruction
Computerized information kiosks

Level 2: Library Interns/Trained Paraprofessional Staff
General library orientation and general bibliographic instruction
Directional inquiries
Ready reference searching
Bibliographic verification on OCLC, RLIN, and the online catalog
Assist with search strategy formulation
Technical assistance with machine problems
Basic informational services with referrals as needed

Level 3: Librarians, Subject Specialists
Individual research consultations
Specialized reference services
Office hours in departments
Member of a research team with teaching faculty
Liaison activities with departments
Specialized instructional services
Integrate information literacy into the curriculum
Research and development efforts
Mediated online searching
Create CAI programs and expert systems for users
Ongoing evaluation and needs assessment

tion. This four-part typology created a continuum from a paper-based ("traditional") library to a fully "digital" library without walls (Sutton, 1996, p.129). It consists of:

- *Traditional*: "a specific place with a finite collection of tangible information bearing primary entities like books and journals . . . [denoted as] paper" (Sutton, 1996, p. 131).
- *Automated*: a mix of paper and digital reference resources and meta-information that "point to non-digital media" (Sutton, 1996,

p. 135).

- *Hybrid*: typified by the use of both print and digital meta-information sources (increasingly digital) and the coexistence of both digital and paper primary resources. This type of library allows for the first time remote access to "some subset of the library's digital collection or to digital resources"(Sutton, 1996, p. 136).
- *Digital*: ". . . the library as a logical entity. It is the library without walls—the library does not collect tangible information-bearing entities but instead provides mediated, geographically unconstrained access to distributed, networked digital information" (Sutton, 1996, p. 138).

From this typology, Internet information systems, specifically digital reference services, can be seen as "digital" libraries. Since such services transact all information delivery via the Internet, they are fully digital.

Sutton (1996) stated that in a digital library the primary task of the librarian is to provide "context" (Sutton refers to Saffo's [1994] concept of context). That is to say, the collection becomes so large (it could be considered to consist of the entire Internet) that patrons no longer desire the full range of information available on a given topic, but the "best" information. The librarian's role shifts from advocate to a collection to a filter for the user. Since the patron is no longer bound by geography (or technology), the user will select services based on how well they create a context useful to that user.

This would indicate that the role of STI customer service shifts from the simple provision of materials and/or technical assistance (software help for example) to one of context provision. The STI customer support specialist will need to provide high-level synthesis and be able to adapt scientific and technical information to a user's context. This also calls for STI agencies to tier service levels. Providing in-depth analysis for the entire public would be impossible. Perhaps these synthesis services should be reserved for core audiences (see Figure 1).

The shift in STI provision to a truly digital environment raises a number of legal, ethical and operational issues as discussed in the following section.

ISSUES IN DIGITAL STI PROVISION

Internet-based STI services and other digital reference services can vary in many aspects including number of staff, number of questions answered, technology used, and subject areas covered. However, they do experience many common issues. For instance, many services are familiar with the experience of starting what they had planned to be a small, controlled question-answer service for a specific population (possibly as an outgrowth of another Web resource or initiative) only to very quickly become overwhelmed by hundreds of questions from the general Internet public. In addition, many services struggle with legal issues regarding liability for information provided and confidentiality of user information posted on services' Web sites. Common issues are summarized on the following pages.

Legal and Ethical Issues

User Confidentiality. STI customer services that plan to make user correspondence public through a question-answer archive, etc., should consider how they will ensure confidentiality of any information that can be used to identify a user (e.g., name, e-mail address, postal address, phone number, etc.). This is especially important when dealing with students since educators and parents may discourage children from providing personal information that will be accessible to all Internet users worldwide. This concept is consistent with the American Library Association's Policy on Confidentiality of Library Records (American Library Association, 1986) and the American Library Association Code of Ethics, which states "We protect each library user's right to privacy and confidentiality with respect to information sought or received and resources consulted, borrowed, acquired or transmitted" (American Library Association, 1995 Online). STI customer services would benefit from adopting core policies and philosophies of established library associations.

Service Liability. Services rely on their information specialists to provide information based on expertise and knowledge. Services should make sure that users are aware of the limits on information provided. This is especially important for services whose expert information can be interpreted as professional advice (e.g., medical, legal, etc.) but is a valid concern for all types of digital reference services.

Operational Issues

Lack of Software. Currently, there is a lack of software available to assist Internet customer support services in managing the question-answer process. Some services have attempted to automate the question-answer process by developing original software packages (many based on PERL scripts). Other services manage the process using an e-mail program and a pencil and paper to record question routing activities. Traditional help desk software has been created with several assumptions that make applying them to Internet customer support difficult, namely:

- Telephony support - existing help desk software was developed around call centers and an assumption that customers would get support over the phone. Even as these organizations begin including Internet options they are being built around modern Web technologies such as Java. Basic functions such as importing e-mail into these systems can be challenging.
- Finite question domains - many software packages assume support of a limited product and therefore a finite domain of answers. Synthesis functions and high-level open ended domains have a difficult time adapting to the limited tiers of software functions available. As an example, many default options assume that all customer support specialists are the same (not specialists in different areas).
- Scale - the current support options tend to be expensive and require large computing infrastructures. These systems are built around teams of 20 or more, and do not match well to teams of two or a set of part time support specialists (see cost and pricing models below).
- Cost and pricing models - pricing for help desk packages is based around a "per seat" licensing system. The more people involved in supporting users, the higher the cost. Further these packages carry high installation and maintenance costs.
- High customization - few (if any) help desk packages work off-the-shelf. Most require intensive customization and installation

(especially for linking to the Internet and existing databases). This process of installation can be lengthy, expensive and require additional staff to support the customized application.

These limitations are not insurmountable, and are being addressed by today's vendors. However, STI agencies are warned to spend a great deal of time at the beginning of a process shopping vendors and looking at the customer support services that will use the applications developed.

Marketing and Publicity. While some services openly embrace the opportunity to attract users, others are more hesitant for fear that they may receive more questions than they can handle. Different techniques for advertising a service include registering the service with a Web search engine, placing notices on other organizations' Web sites and posting messages on related electronic discussion groups, etc.

Question-Answer Policy. Answering user questions is not always as straightforward as it may sound. Decisions must be made early on regarding the following questions: What types of questions will and will not be answered? What are the necessary components to include in a response? How will vague user queries be handled? What is the turnaround time for a response? Decisions on these issues will aid staff in conducting day-to-day tasks and will help services focus on intended goals.

Supplemental Resources. Most services offer some type of Web-based resource to supplement their question-answer service; in some cases, it is the service that supplements the preexisting resources. The most popular types of resources are question-answer archives and collections of frequently asked questions, or FAQs. Other resources may include supplemental information about a popular topic and lists of links to other resources. Services often encourage users to review the collections first before submitting an original question. Issues related to supplemental resources include type of user interface, number of question-answer sets included, frequency with which resources are updated and staff member(s) responsible for resource maintenance.

This is only a short list of issues that STI services will encounter as they move their customer support to the Internet. Others include:

- Liability - what is the legal exposure of STI services in the scientific and technical fields including medicine?
- Cost recovery - can a government agency charge for customer support when it already charges for products being supported either through direct fees or taxes?
- Service tiers - can there be different levels of services for the core, secondary, topical and general audiences?
- Establishing a per unit cost for customer support - how can customer support be priced either for outsourcing or establishing base-line budgets?
- International Support - can a federal agency utilize taxpayer money to support international users? This is particularly problematic on the Internet where it is nearly impossible to establish the geographical origin of an inquiry?

The following sections examine some of these issues in a as addressed by one CENDI member, the National Library of Education (NLE). NLE is currently dealing with these issues through the AskERIC service which it offers to the general public.

ASKERIC: A CASE STUDY IN FEDERAL STI DIGITAL REFERENCE

The United States federal government formed the Educational Resources Information Center (ERIC) in 1966. The government envisioned ERIC as a national information system designed to provide users with ready access to an extensive body of education-related literature. Today, National Library of Education within the U.S. Department of Education supports ERIC. One of ERIC's primary products is the ERIC database. This database is the world's largest source of education information. It contains over 800,000 abstracts of documents and journal articles on education research and practice (Abdal Haqq, 1995) and is available in approximately 3,000 locations worldwide as of January 1995 (Stonehill & Brandhorst, 1992). AskERIC went online as an Internet-based question answering service in November of 1992 (ERIC, 1992) as a special project of the ERIC Clearinghouse on Information & Technology. The service had a dedicated staff of one with assistance from the ERIC Clearinghouse on Information & Technology and a doctoral student from Syracuse University's School of Information Studies. Within a year, the service had added automated services (FTP, Gopher, WAIS) and increased its staff by three.

As the number of incoming questions doubled, AskERIC's staff increased. When the automated services (primarily Gopher) grew beyond the existing time and effort of the doctoral student, a second coordinator level position was added. AskERIC then expanded from a pilot project of three states (Texas, New York and North Dakota) to the entire United States. The system needed to become available 24 hours a day, seven days a week. A Research and Development (R&D) team was created with separate resources for experimentation. The goal of R&D was to keep AskERIC current in the constantly changing Internet environment. Also created with the expansion was a separate set of resources for interfacing with state and regional networks originally known as the Virtual Communities group. AskERIC also increased its systems infrastructure with the help of Sun Microsystems. The increase in the technical infrastructure led to the creation of a systems component to AskERIC that operates as a SunSITE[3].

Currently AskERIC is in its seventh year of operation. It provides many types of Internet services (e.g., World Wide Web, e-mail, phone support). AskERIC is also one of a handful of global SunSITEs. The project has increased its staff and computing power by an order of magnitude. The project has gone from one person in a back room with a NeXT workstation, to over 30 staff around the country working on high-end workstations to meet the needs of educators around the country. Throughout that time, the growth has been user-directed: educators and other users have determined the types of services offered and the level of resources allocated.

AskERIC Today

Today AskERIC serves over 70,000 educators a week through its services. It constantly seeks out new partners from education, industry, and government to provide its clients with the best information. As shown in Table 3 AskERIC has five components.

AskERIC will continue to change in the future as educators' needs change and as the network matures. Already several AskERIC initiatives have begun incorporating challenges outlined in the National

Table 3: Functional Components of the AskERIC Service

AskERIC's Question/Answering Service (Q&A)	A set of trained information specialists around the country take educators' questions via e-mail and use a variety of networked and traditional resources (ERIC database, Internet sites, mailing lists, etc.) to answer these questions.
AskERIC's Virtual Library (AEVL)	A set of coordinated automated Internet information systems that provide documents on the process of education (including more than 900 lesson plans, subject-oriented InfoGuides, and archives of educator discussion groups such as MIDDLE-L, LM_NET [(Eisenberg & Milbury, 1994] and EDTECH).
AskERIC's Partnerships (originally Virtual Communities)	AskERIC's outreach services to acquire resources for AskERIC's user services (Q&A and AEVL).
AskERIC Research & Development (R&D)	An effort to investigate the networking tools of today and tomorrow. This group also advocates the position of education in today's high-performance computing and networking effort.
AskERIC Systems (Systems)	Support group that maintains systems (hardware and software), purchases technology and acts as a technical liaison with technology partners such as Sun Microsystems and Personal Library Software.

Figure 2: AskERIC's User Services: AskERIC uses e-mail to inform (formally and informally) and direct its primary services. The user receives feedback in the form of either an e-mail response or the requested file.

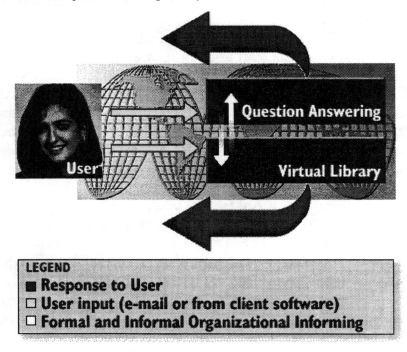

Information Infrastructure (Executive Office of the President, 1993).

The AskERIC Organization

All five of AskERIC's areas guide the management of AskERIC's Internet information services. Each area, however, does this in a different manner, and to a different degree. While AskERIC concentrates on user input, it must deal with other forces that seek to create policy. AskERIC Research & Development, for example, stresses new technology in vision setting activities. AskERIC Partnerships (see below) concentrate on exterior interests in policy setting.

User Services

AskERIC's user services provide the primary method of guiding AskERIC's Internet information services. Of AskERIC's five units, only two are directly accessible to end-users; the Question Answering Service (McKee, 1995), and the *Virtual Library* (Morgan, 1994). These services (described above) represent the main user input, and therefore, the primary means of directing the organization. Figure 2 represents this input.

In the question answering service, user questions and comments are the major source of information. At the date of this writing the *Question/Answering Service* receives over 1,200 questions a week at peak periods. Trends in questions and comments represent users' situations and information needs. These trends are communicated to the rest of AskERIC particularly to the Virtual Library. An example of this communication is the development of the InfoGuides — pathfinders to Internet and ERIC resources on given topics. The topics are derived from incoming questions to the Q&A service.

The *Virtual Library*, to a great degree, represents repeated trends in *Question Answering Service*. The Virtual Library also "informs" the *Question Answering Service*. It does this by informing question answerers (Network Information Specialists) what resources are available in the AskERIC Virtual Library and how to access them. It also informs the larger AskERIC organization of "hot" areas on the automated services. This is determined by often-accessed Web pages. Currently the AskERIC Virtual Library averages over 2 million hits per week.

In combination, then, the *Question/Answering Service* and *Virtual Library* represent not only the interfaces of AskERIC to the user community, but also the primary means or gathering data on what users want and how the service is satisfying those needs. This data forms the direction of the project. The user input forms the primary influence in building and maintaining AskERIC's Internet information services.

Technology Services (Research & Development and Systems/ SunSITE)

AskERIC also considers technology in determining the strategy of the service. However, the technological input is considered secondary to user input. The Research & Development effort exists both within the AskERIC organization, and outside it. Not all of the researchers in *Research & Development* are employees of AskERIC. Many researchers are students from Syracuse University. One could view *Research & Development* either as a part of AskERIC, or as a separate research effort working on AskERIC material. Figure 3 below depicts this relationship.

The main purpose of *Research & Development* is to look for future technologies that may be useful to AskERIC and K-12 educators. However, AskERIC does not implement these technologies until the user services (*Question/Answer Service or the Virtual Library*) feel there is broad enough acceptance from the end-user population. AskERIC could not use the World Wide Web, for example, until the user services felt there was enough access for their users. So while *Research & Development* does help to manage and direct the service, it is always constrained by the needs of the user services.

The Systems group of

Figure 3 AskERIC R&D's Relationship to Other AskERIC Components: The figure represents the use of Research and Development efforts to scan the Internet technology environment. Rather than setting direction, Research & Development informs other sections of AskERIC.

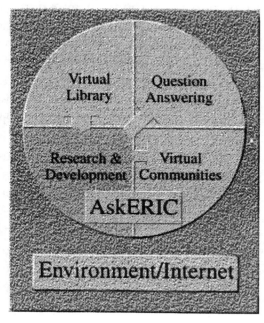

AskERIC serves a different technical purpose. Whereas *Research & Development* seeks innovation, *Systems* seeks stability. It is the responsibility of the *Systems* group to ensure all computing and network platforms are available to the other AskERIC components (except for *Research & Development* which is mostly self-supporting). *Systems* also overlaps in responsibility with the *Partnership* group (described below). Once a relationship is established with a technical organization (such as Sun Microsystems or Personal Library Software), *Systems* forms a relationship with a technical contact within the partnering organization. This relationship is used to support the technical infrastructure provided by the partner as well as solicit opportunities and feedback from this partner.

Partnerships

Another component of the project that contributes to AskERIC's ongoing activities is the *Partnerships* group. The *Partnerships* group is responsible for soliciting funds, resources and projects from organizations external to AskERIC. *Partnerships* also acts as a liaison to external partner organizations (such as state networks, The Federal Department of Education and various organizations). The *Partnerships* team acts as a liaison between external organizations and AskERIC. This branch of AskERIC, however, does not determine policy or direction. The *Virtual Library* group assists and directs most efforts of the *Partnerships*. If the Library does not see a fit between the external organization and AskERIC, then contact is not continued.

The *Partnerships* team also works with the *Systems* group and the *Research & Development* group on a project-by-project basis. The technology services act as a sort of contractor to provide specifications and technical expertise to the project. These relationships can be seen in Figure 4.

AskERIC Summary

AskERIC can serve as a case study for how STI agencies can provide user-centric services to a core constituency and the general public. It represents one way to learn from the shifting field of digital reference and one example of combining product (the ERIC database and the Web sites) with service. This blending of service and product is discussed by Davis and Meyer (1998) in their book, *Blur*. It is applied directly to federal information by Lippencott and Cheverie (1998) in

Figure 4 Relationship of AskERIC Partnerships Group to AskERIC and Other Organizations: The Partnerships area takes input, resources, and projects from outside of AskERIC and coordinates with internal AskERIC sections to determine the usefulness and feasibility of new projects, and new resources.

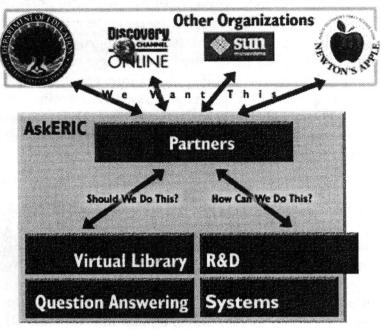

The 'Blur' of Federal Information Services: Implications for University Libraries.

However, AskERIC also must contend with increased demands on its customer service and the constant evolution of the Internet environment. AskERIC, through the contracts used to support it, has created a linear cost relationship with demand. The United States government pays per question answered, thereby creating a situation where the more questions asked, the more it costs the government. So as the government succeeds in providing more users with better information, it creates a greater strain on its resources.

In response, this year the government made provisions to allow private funds to support the AskERIC project. Third party corporate and non-NLE sources can be used to augment NLE funds. This use of non-federal resources raises interesting questions. It will be interesting to watch as STI agencies diversify their funding of customer support. How will the government maintain a non-bias perspective in the face of corporate money? How will the agency retain identity amongst multiple sponsors?

In an attempt to find alternatives to sole-source government support of the education community, the NLE with the White House Office of Science & Technology Policy created the Virtual Reference Desk Project.

VIRTUAL REFERENCE DESK

The primary purpose of the Virtual Reference Desk (VRD) is to build a cooperative digital reference network for the United States' primary and secondary education community. Such a network would link students, teachers and parents to experts from multiple communities (e.g., federal agencies, libraries, professional organizations and corporations). Such a network would allow services like AskERIC to off-load out of scope questions and benefit from a community of innovation.

Work of the first three years of the project have led to a series of tools that can be of use to digital reference services, including STI agencies. These tools include:

- Descriptions - exemplary digital reference services are studied and described. These descriptions provide a blueprint of services and their workflows. A "meta-description" of digital reference services has been created to serve as an exemplar and basis of software tool development (Lankes, 1998).
- Planning methods - a planning system has been created based on theory, literature and experience. This methodology allows organizations to either plan for a new AskA service or examine an existing service (Lankes and Kasowitz, 1998).
- Training programs - A series of self-guided training materials (Lankes and Kasowitz, 1998) and courses has been developed to train information professionals on how to build and maintain digital reference services in K-12, library and STI settings.
- Standards - the Virtual Reference Desk team is developing a metadata standard to allow questions to be exchanged from digital reference service to digital reference service. The Question Internet Profile (QuIP) outlines a basic XML application that can allow rich interoperation within a given digital reference community, and basic interoperation amongst all digital reference communities (Lankes 1998).

This method of creating an extended community of interest to provide a distributed network of support is an option that should be explored in other STI domains.

CONCLUSION AND RECOMMENDATIONS

The Internet is indeed a great development in the distribution and coordination of federal scientific and technical information. If indeed STI is "an essential ingredient of the innovation process — from education and research to product development and manufacturing" (United States Congress Office of Technology Assessment, 1990, p.1). and people are increasingly looking to the Internet for this information, then the way in which we support this information on the Internet is just as vital.

As the number of users accessing Internet STI sites grows, policy makers and managers must be aware that the populations they serve are also growing more diverse and needy. Simply building self-service interfaces for highly specialized, often highly educated staff no longer works. Today users at all levels must be involved and considered in the creation of tools and the building of support systems. In essence, increased Internet product access equals increased need for customer support.

Increased customer support on the Internet should also be tiered. As Mardikian & Kesselman (1995) pointed out, an organization must know when to use human resources for customer support and when to automate. The expensive human resources should be used for high-level synthesis and the creation of tools for users. Web pages and on-line help can work well for simple factual answers and basic directions. All too often organizations (including libraries) switch these two tasks.

It is important for STI agencies to think of service and product as linked. A database with no support is of limited use. Further, in some cases, agencies need to think of service as a product. It is very conceivable that the resources supporting the population of a database may be matched or exceeded by the amount spent applying and supporting it with high-level analysis and synthesis. After all, with increasing sophistication of Web harvesters and search engines, the problem is not finding information, but rather finding too much information. The day will indeed come when users will pay more to filter out information than access it.

There is a need for continued software and standards development in federal STI support. Much work has been done in getting databases on the Internet and metadata standards for data interchange, but little has been done to connect support agencies. Questions should regularly (and effortlessly) change hands about STI providers to balance load (the number of questions) and scope (the topic of questions).

Finally, STI agencies should seek to create a community of support. Look outside traditional agency and contractor resources to provide expertise and synthesis. In the education community, volunteer and barter systems can be established to link experts to users. However, in other areas such as medicine or science, there may be need for transaction systems where monies are exchanged for expertise.

Federal STI agencies face a great challenge. As they succeed in organizing and distributing information, they may well be spelling their own doom. With increased awareness and access come increased support demands. The Internet presents both opportunities and headaches to customer support. The promise of 24-hour-a-day, 365-day-a-year support is a titillating (and real) opportunity, but many policy, economic and technological barriers remain. Agencies must first recognize the need to provide high-level human support on the Internet, then they must determine the level of support they can provide and then they can take advantage of the distributed real-time resources they have available to them.

If agencies continue to believe that Web pages and databases are sufficient to serve a general public, they will come to find a public confused and very unsupportive.

ENDNOTES

[1] For example via the Freedom of Information Act in the United States.

[2] Patron is a library term synonymous with user or customer.

[3] SunSITEs are university-based projects that use donated equipment from Sun Microsystems.

REFERENCES

Abdal Haqq, I. (1995). *ERIC as a resource for the teacher researcher* (ERIC Digest). Washington, DC: ERIC Clearinghouse on Teaching and Teacher Education. (ERIC Document Reproduction Service No. ED 381 530).

American Library Association. (1971/1986). Policy on confidentiality of library records [Online]. Available: http://www.ala.org/alaorg/oif/pol_conf.html [1998, August 5].

American Library Association. (1995). American Library Association Code of Ethics [Online]. Available: http://www.ala.org/alaorg/oif/ethics.html [1998, August 5].

Arms, C. (1990). Using the national networks: BITNET and the Internet. *Online, 14* (5), 24-29.

Balas, J. (1995). The Internet and reference services. *Computers in Libraries, 15* (6), 39-41.

Bobp, M. E., Kratzert, M., & Richey, D. (1993). The Emergence of systemwide electronic access to information sources: The Experience of two California State University libraries. *The Reference Librarian, 39*, 111-130.

Branse, Y. (1993). Internet resources: How not to get tangled up in the net. *Bulletin of the Israel Society of Special Libraries and Information Centers, 19* (2), 21-25.

Callahan, D. R. (1991). The librarian as change agent in the diffusion of technological innovation. *The Electronic Library, 9* (1), 13-16.

CENDI (1999). Welcome to CENDI: Federal STI managers group. [Online]. Available: http://www.dtic.mil/cendi/index.html [1999, March 15].

Davis, S. M. & Meyer, C. (1998). *Blur: The Speed of change in the connected economy*. New York: Addison-Wesley.

Eisenberg, M. B., & Berkowitz, R. E. (1990). *Information problem solving: The Big Six Skills approach to library and information skills instruction*. Norwood, NJ: Ablex.

Eisenberg, M. B., & Milbury, P. (1994). LM-NET: Helping school library media specialists to shape the networking revolution in the schools. *School Library Media Annual, 12*, 33-53.

Executive Office of the President. (1993). The national information infrastructure: Agenda for action. [Online]. Available: http://gopher.cni.org:70/0/cniftp/pub/nii/niiagenda.txt [1997, April 1].

Feeney, A. (1993). Internet applications: STUMPERS-L. *Computers in*

Libraries, 13 (5), 40-42.

Gainor, L. & Foster, E. (1993). Usenet and the library. *Reference Services Review, 21* (3), 7-22.

He, P. W., & Knee, M. (1995). The challenge of electronic services librarianship. *Reference Services Review, 23* (4), 7-12.

Hodge, Gail (1997). Impact of the Internet on customer service and product development among the CENDI [Online]. Available: http://www.dtic.mil/cendi/publications/inet97_2.html [1997, August].

Jensen, A., & Sih, J. (1995). Using e-mail and the Internet to teach users at their desktops. *Online 19* (5), 82-86.

Lankes, R. D. (1998). *Building and Maintaining Internet Information Services: K-12 digital reference services.* Syracuse, NY: ERIC Clearinghouse on Information & Technology.

Lankes, R. D. (1998). The Virtual Reference Desk: Building a Network of Expertise for America's Schools. [Online]. Available: http://www.vrd.org/Workshop/WhitePaper.PDF [1998, April]

Lankes, R. D. & Kasowitz, A. (1998). *AskA starter kit: How to build and maintain digital reference services.* Syracuse, NY: ERIC Clearinghouse on Information & Technology.

Lewis, D. W. (1995). Traditional reference is dead, now let's move on to important questions. *The Journal of Academic Librarianship, 21* (1), 10-12.

Lippencott, J. K. & Cheverie, J. F. (1998). The "Blur" of federal information and services: Implications for university libraries. *Journal of Government Information, 26* (1), 25-31.

Machovec, G. (1993). VERONICA: A Gopher navigational tool on the Internet. Online *Libraries and Microcomputers, 11* (10), 1-4.

Mardikian, J., & Kesselman, M. (1995). Beyond the desk: Enhanced reference staffing for the electronic library. *Reference Services Review, 23* (1), 21-28.

McClure, C. R. (1994). User-based data collection techniques and strategies for evaluating networked information services. *Library Trends, 42,* 591-607.

McClure, C., Moen, W., & Ryan, J. (1994). *Libraries and the Internet/ NREN: Perspectives, issues, and challenges.* Westport, CT: Mecklermedia.

McKee, M. (1995). A day in the life of a virtual librarian: Helping you zip around the Internet. *School Library Journal, 41* (4), 30-33.

Moen, W. (1992). Organizing networked resources for effective use:

Classification and other issues in developing navigational tools. *Proceedings of the American Society for Information Science Mid-year Meeting*, 10-21.

Morgan, N. A. (1994). *An Introduction to Internet resources for K-12 educators. Part I: Information resources*. (ERIC Digest). Syracuse, NY:ERIC Clearinghouse on Information and Technology. (ERIC Document Reproduction Service No. ED 372 757).

National Library of Education (1997). Access for all: A new national library for tomorrow's learners. The report of the National Library of Education Advisory Task Force. (WWW Document). Available: http://www.ed.gov/pubs/AccessforAll/title.html [1997, April 1].

Saffo, P. (1994). It's the context, stupid. *Wired*, 2 (3), 563-567.

Still, J., & Campbell, F. (1993). Librarian in a box: The use of electronic mail for reference. *Reference Services Review*, 21 (1), 15-18.

Strong, G. E. (1996). Toward a virtual future. In K. Low (Ed.), *The roles of reference librarians: Today and tomorrow* (pp. 153-161). New York: Hawthorn Press.

Stonehill, R., & Brandhorst, T. (1992). The three phases of ERIC. *Educational Researcher*, 21 (3), 18-21.

Sutton, S. (1996). Future service models and the convergence of functions: The reference librarian as technician, author and consult-ant. In K. Low (Ed.), *The roles of reference librarians: Today and tomorrow* (pp. 125-143). New York: Hawthorn Press.

U.S. Congress, Office of Technology Assessment (July 1990). *Helping America compete: The role of federal scientific and technical information*. Washington, DC: U.S. Government Printing Office (OTA-CIT-454)

Chapter XVI

Remote Access: The Development of Information Services and Technology in the Global South

Lucinda R. Zoe
Baruch College, New York, USA

When the development of equitable worldwide telecommunications became recognized as a critical component for global competition and economic growth, the technological status of economically developing countries appeared on the international agenda. The primary problem was one of infrastructure, with two thirds of the world population without access to telephone services. As multinational corporations pushed for a global restructuring of the telecommunications sector issues regarding control of worldwide telecommunications networks by the industrialized nations, and the imbalance in the flow of information, left the economically developing nations of the global south reticent to fully cooperate. This chapter examines the development of information technology and services in the global south and provides an historical overview of significant events and factors that influenced the introduction and growth of communications and information technology globally from the 1960s to the 1990s. The technological foundations that are discussed in this chapter provide a contextual framework for understanding the burst of activity that followed in international Internet-based library services in the 1990s.

INTRODUCTION

The emergence of the post-industrial information age brought with it a number of complex issues related to global information policies and access to information and communication technologies. The politics of information during the 1970s focused primarily on issues related to human rights, and governments struggled with the necessities of trying to protect the rights of privacy while allowing business and government to collect and process information about their citizenry (Spero, 1982). Economically developing countries rallied for greater control of news and access to communications media while the United States continued to demand a free flow of information, claiming it to be a basic human right and necessary for approaching any sort of international information issue or policy. However, information quickly became the economic commodity it was predicted to be and quite suddenly policy-makers the world over were faced with a whole new set of difficult issues. As governments fought to secure a share of the global information market, they began to protect their interests by throwing up barriers against transborder data flows. As an economic commodity, governments want to control and tax the information that crosses their borders. This view of the handling of information is, of course, in sharp contrast to the United States democratic idea of free flow of information.

UNESCO, the United Nations Education Science and Cultural Organization, assumed a leadership position for economically developing countries, recognizing the need to develop communications capabilities throughout the economically developing nations. In response to increasing international tension due to the emergence of the information sector in the global arena, UNESCO, along with other international and regional organizations, proposed what was called the 'New World Information and Communication Order' (NWICO). This proposal attempted to address the emergence of the new technologies in developing countries and called for a more equitable distribution of information resources. Although the proposal was controversial, it was also seen as an opportunity to promote global dialogue on critical communication and information issues. The United States government, along with other U.S. interest groups, attacked it on the grounds that it would weaken democracy by posing a threat to the free flow of information and hinder freedom of expression and speech. As a result, the United States government announced its withdrawal from UNESCO in December 1983. It was viewed by some communication scholars to be a threat to United States economic and political hegemony (Roach, 1987).

The issues surrounding the emergence of communication and information technologies in economically developing countries and the ability of all nations to participate in the information society are complex and varied, going far beyond the recognition of information as an economic and political commodity. Indeed, issues regarding health care, education, agriculture and human rights were all driving forces behind the emergence of the new technologies worldwide. While library scientists and information specialists praised the abilities of the new technologies developed for information management —computerized online catalogs, commercial online database services, CD-ROMs, laser printers, fax machines and electronic networking and e-mail to name a few — the small information centers and libraries in the developing nations of Asia, Africa and Latin America struggled with fugitive materials that do not fit neatly into traditional classification schemes and basic issues of access. However impressive the new information technologies and communication systems appeared, use was difficult, if not often impossible in areas where the infrastructure was not solid; the telephone system was unreliable or erratic; power supplies were often interrupted, or nonexistent for days, if not weeks; equipment, maintenance costs and access to continued materials (disks, paper, ribbons, etc.) were beyond the financial resources of the organizations; privacy, confidentiality and protection of information was difficult; and traditional information sources available from Western databases were suspect and often viewed as promoting the Western capitalist system of development, which was thought to be both unsustainable and unjust (Menon, 1990).

This chapter examines the development of information technology and services in economically developing countries by exploring the major initiatives of the United Nations, Intergovernmental Organizations, rural libraries and information services and the grassroots efforts that were underway in the 1970s and the 1980s. The chapter provides an historical overview of significant events, political factors and grassroots activities that influenced the introduction and growth of international communications and information technology from the 1960s to the 1990s. Developments in the 1990s, particularly regarding the introduction of the World Wide Web and the increased use of Internet-based library services, are addressed in more depth in other chapters in this book.

A brief note on the language used to discuss what is now often referred to in international discourse as the global south is necessary. While problematic, the use of the phrase "developing countries" is used in this chapter. It should be noted that the notion of "developing nations" or the "Third World" is essentially a Western one, and is used to describe the developing nations of Asia and the Pacific, Africa, the Middle East and Latin America and the Caribbean. This characterization is thought to be ethnocentric by most outside the Western world and is generally not adhered to by those not from the West when talking about the world (Vogeler & De Souza, 1980). However, in the context of the literature to be discussed, the terms will be used as they are in the literature.

BACKGROUND

The world's leaders and decision-makers recognized the development of equitable worldwide telecommunications as a critical component for global competition and economic growth in the late 1970s and early 1980s. The primary problem facing many nations was one of infrastructure, where in the majority of economically developing countries the provision of basic services, such as access to telephone services, were not routinely in place. However, the development of such infrastructures was not a high priority for the developing nations, who often viewed such services as luxury items that benefited the urban elite. Their concerns were focused on more immediate issues that had a direct impact on their existence such as health care, food and educational services. There was a fear the resources spent on developing telecommunications systems would mean less funding for these more pressing life and death priorities (Hills, 1993). It took quite a number of years for the economically developing nations to acknowledge and accept the positive connections between the provision of telecommunication services and sustainable economic growth and development. Given a basic mistrust of the multinational corporations that were pushing for such developments, along with the issues outlined in the NWICO, the developing nations were reticent to fully cooperate. In particular, there was concern regarding control of the worldwide telecommunications network by industrialized nations, the imbalance in the flow of information and the confrontational nature of the United States position on negotiations surrounding any global restructuring of the telecommunications sector. What resulted was an impasse and stalemate on the development of international information policies. This impasse, and the impact it had on the development of international cooperation and policies, was the subject of numerous articles in the development communication and information literature in the mid-late 1980s (Greenberg, 1985; Williams, 1988; Neelameghan & Tocatlian, 1985). The impasse, according to Senior Foreign Service Officer Allen Greenberg in a 1985 article, lie with the United States' "inability to organize, within the government and with the private-sector, effective responses to international challenges in the arena where trade, technology and foreign policy concerns intersect" (Greenberg, 1985, p.42).

In 1984 the Independent Commission for World Wide Telecommunications Development issued a report, known as the Maitland Commission, that examined the availability of telecommunication services between the developed and developing nations. Specifically, it reported on the inequities of telephone services and determined that "more than half the worlds' population live in countries with fewer than 10 million telephones between them and most of these are in main cities; and two thirds of the world population has no access to telephone services" (International Telecommunications Union (ITU), 1984). Further, it reported that the majority of telecommunications facilities in developing countries were government-owned monopolies put in place to serve the needs of government and as a result were confined to urban areas to be used by government officials and for commerce. The Maitland Commission also found that in less developed countries where there were telephone services, it was unsatisfactory and did not meet the demands of the public, with poor quality equipment, inadequate maintenance, repeated failures to make connections and quite often a black market. Finally, the Maitland Commission made the case that failures in the quality and extent of adequate telephone networks in developing countries had a direct impact on local economies and had resulted in a decrease in economic growth. The report also found that developing countries had consistently underinvested in telecommunications. Thus began the first steps in making a case for telecommunications as an independent development issue and priority. Additional studies were being done to support the notion that development of the telecommunications sector within developing nations was a profitable investment with positive long-term economic effects (Hudson, 1984; Gilles, 1986; Saunders, Warford &Wellenius, 1983). If developing countries were to install the appropriate infrastructures and catch up with the developed nations in the telecommunications sector, the Maitland Commission determined that it would cost around $12 billion per year (ITU, 1984, p.14).

Regardless of the importance of such networks to the global economy and the increased growth of economies in the developing nations, funding for these projects was scarce. The World Bank considered support to the telecommunications sector to be beyond the scope of their mandate. Further, the United Nations Development Program (UNDP), which provides funding for the ITU's technical programs, actually decreased its annual support for telecommunications projects in the mid-1980s from over $24 million (US$) per year from 1980-1982, down to $20 million per year from 1982-1985 (Hills, 1990, p. 79-80). And even though the development of a stronger international telecommunications infrastructure was clearly to the advantage of the United States, real financial support was not forthcoming even though promises had been made following the United States withdrawal from UNESCO. When the United States withdrew in 1984, the Reagan administration publicly committed $47 million (US$) per year in support of alternative bi-lateral programs that would fund projects that adhered to UNESCO's original mandate that were proposed by United States government agencies working in conjunction with the private sector. A joint proposal of the United States Telecommunications Suppliers Association and the United States State Department was submitted that involved a multimillion dollar package of communications projects to aid the less developed countries in developing their telecommunications infrastructure. This package would have provided the foundation for the development of a mechanism for coordinating these efforts on a global scale. However, none of the proposals were to come to fruition because the Reagan Administration vetoed the whole project and zeroed out the $47 million annual promise of support in its 1986 budget (Greenberg, 1985, p. 46). In addition to the fiscal problems that plagued the development of much-needed telecommunications infrastructures, there were other restraints that stunted growth. Lack of trained staff and personnel, insufficient environmentally suited equipment that could operate in adverse climates, deficiencies in spare parts and maintenance expertise as well as government interference regarding the management of the networks all contributed to the ability of the developing countries to improve their telecommunications sectors. All of these factors contributed to a continued imbalance of power, resources and access to information, putting the developing nations at a distinct disadvantage particularly with regard to the development and success of their libraries and information centers that needed to take advantage of the new technologies.

Even though telecommunications was directly linked to development, and electronic information and communication networks were exploding on the international stage and transforming societies, the global communications revolution was still highly suspect. While developing countries recognized the advantages of having effective telecommunications networks, they were keenly aware of the increasing control of multinational corporations. Enrique Gonzalez-Manet in his 1988 book, *The Hidden War of Information*, pointed out that less than 10 gigantic corporations held global control over telecommunications—each earning over $10 billion in annual sales and operating with virtually no regulation. The interests and power of these multinationals over those of the "public good" continued to dominate the debate, and the development communication literature of the 1980s and the perceived gap between the information rich and the information poor widened. The primary issues for the developing nations were dependence and autonomy, and the fear of cultural conquest by Western ideologies was very real. The continued failure of the United States to develop coherence communications policies of its own, as detailed in William Dizard's book on *The Coming Information Age: An Overview of Technology, Economics and Politics* (1982) contributed to the failure of the international community to develop adequate global communications policies. It was not, however, for lack of trying.

Prior to and following the NWICO debates within UNESCO, there continued to be initiatives within UNESCO to foster greater international cooperation. In October of 1986 UNESCO established the Intergovernmental Informatics Programme (IIP) to stimulate greater cooperation between nations and to bridge the gap between the information rich and poor (Danzin, 1987). In addition to being a catalyst of cooperation, the IIP's first priority addressed the teaching and training of instructors followed by the development of a curriculum on the use of computers and the processing, storage and retrieval of information. The second priority had three objectives: the creation of centers to develop software applications that were appropriate and specific to regional needs; the development of networks to enable these computer centers to exchange information and files and foster a sense of cooperation between the human resources by linking specialists together for joint problem solving; and the provision of assistance to governments and other national machineries in the development of information policies. There was hope that this new initiative would encourage greater resolve at a national level and propel leaders and social reformers to recognize the enormous potential of the emerging information technologies to transform society at every level.

DEVELOPMENT OF INFORMATION SERVICES

United Nations Initiatives

In spite of the complex political issues that had grown out of the NWICO debate, UNESCO continued to work programmatically in the area of information technology because they have a long history of involvement in the support of library and documentation programs. Since their inception in 1945, they have had a libraries program that had a significant impact on international activities. UNESCO provided leadership in the development of cooperative international library programs that included training for librarians and information workers and stressed the need for national library planning (Williams, 1988). From 1945-1980 UNESCO focused their efforts on the development of national libraries and the information infrastructure on a national level—with a greater attention to the developing nations. Working with a few well-known international library associations, the International Federation of Library Association (IFLA) and the International Federation for Documentation, they made progress in developing an international library community. The hope was to create a unified system that when linked together would form a worldwide bibliographic system where information could be shared and exchanged. This national library program, called the National Information System (NATIS), was created in the 1960s and focused on the development of national libraries, archives and documentation centers that would all be integrated into the worldwide bibliographic system. Each country would create its own standards, bibliographic control plans and a national information policy. All the plans would be shared with other nations and coordinated on a regional, then a national level and would lead eventually to the ultimate achievement: Universal Bibliographic Control (UBC). An impressive effort to be sure; however, a number of obstacles stood in the way of success and the full implementation of the program. The first being structural ones within the United Nations organization itself. The library program was initially set up within the Department of Cultural Affairs, which meant that issues dealing with scientific and technical information and mass media were not part of the library program, but instead were located in the Science Sector of UNESCO. This put the two units, scientific documentation and library planing, in competition with one another for the same financial resources. The two programs dealing with information were merged in 1977 when the General Information Program (PGI) was established. Advocates of scientific information had begun to work towards the construction of an international information system in order to build a worldwide system of scientific and technical information to assist in development efforts. However, the biggest obstacle to the success of the PGI was UNESCO's involvement in the NWICO debate and the attempt to develop national and international information and communication policies. The controversy surrounding this issue had a dramatic impact on plans for creating a coherent international information system and reaching the goal of Universal Bibliographic Control. The PGI continued to promote the development of libraries, archives and documentation services and established programs to encourage the applications of information technology in the developing countries. They provided support in setting up local databases, helped provide access to remote online databases and tried to strengthen national and international telecommunications networks (Tocatlian and Abid, 1986). They also continued to work in close collaboration with IFLA in helping nations gain access to international bibliographic standards in order to contribute to the UBC efforts. Further, the PGI was quite active in the provision of educational services and support. They were organizing training sessions, seminars and courses on the use of new technologies, preparing and disseminating teaching materials and textbooks on information storage and retrieval techniques and facilitating consultant missions to advise governments on how to plan and implement library and information services. Major programs were launched to foster cooperation and information exchange on regional levels, often working in conjunction with other UN agencies such as UNDP. In the 1986-1987 budget allocation, a high priority was placed on training activities, the establishment of regional networks and the development of information infrastructures (Tocatlian and Abid, 1986).

Intergovernmental Organization Information Systems

The result of this effort was the eventual rise of a number of international information systems, mainly systems created by intergovernmental organizations (IGOs). IGOs are defined as organizations that are founded on a formal agreement between the governments of nations' states which must include three or more nations and have a permanent secretariat, or executive mechanism, for performing the ongoing work of the organization (Williams, 1989). Legally, IGOs are created from treaties or similar international agreements between nations. IGOs play a significant role in most areas of international relations and focus their efforts on all areas of society from social and economic to educational, scientific and cultural affairs. They often perform a range of services and contribute to the world's overall standard of living. A few examples of IGOs include the Food and Agriculture Organization (FAO), the International Labour Office (ILO), the International Monetary Fund (IMF), the World Bank, the World Intellectual Property Organization (WIPO) and the Organization for Economic Cooperation and Development (OECD). As a result of their extensive work, they produce a plethora of information in the form of studies, reports, research, conferences proceedings, books, journals, etc. They are quite diverse in their mission and their approach to documentation, and most all of them maintain some sort of library or documentation center. They have developed a number of sophisticated bibliographic information systems and networks that collect, index and store information for retrieval and dissemination. However, each IGO uses their own system for cataloging and classifying materials, and there have been very little collaborative efforts to improve the bibliographic control process although it has been the subject of much discussion. Although the goal of UNESCO efforts was to encourage IGOs to use international standards for cataloging and bibliographic description from their inception, a 1985 study reported that the majority of them had not made any progress in this area (Jacque, 1985). Given the early efforts of UNESCO to coordinate these types of activities on an international scale and its focus on regional and international cooperation, it is somewhat surprising that the majority of these international networks and information systems were developed without adhering to international standards or that there wasn't a greater effort to migrate to a common system as bibliographic activities became automated.

Although the IGOs produce a lot of information and have built automated information systems, access to these materials and systems are quite difficult and problematic. Approaches to the distribution and dissemination of information products vary with each IGO but generally take the form of sales, depository libraries and subscriptions. Many issue catalogs of materials available upon request, and a number of the larger IGOs have established official sales outlets or use commercial dealers to sell their products. Gaining access to the data files of these organizations is even more difficult, as only a few of the catalogs provide information on these services and they are not made readily available to the depository libraries. So even though the IGOs have developed a wide range of impressive databases and information systems, they are not that accessible to users. Or as stated in one article on the information systems of IGOs, even the trained professional special librarian, who is known for being able to locate obscure materials, will have difficulty penetrating these systems and even finding out what, exactly, is available. "IGO information daunts the best of us, but is not impossible. It simply takes knowing the potential that awaits us in these information resources, as well as persistence" (Williams, 1989, p.7). In general, users of these systems are intended to be researchers and policy makers and not the average citizen. Given the access issues and the inconsistency of the information systems, a great deal of the information systems created by the IGOs is underutilized. Fortunately, working parallel to the efforts of UNESCO and the IGOs, alternative information and documentation centers around the world were organizing themselves to address the issues brought on by the information revolution.

Non-Governmental and Grassroots Initiatives

In 1982 in Lisbon, Portugal, a meeting of Documentation Centers on Third World Issues was organized by the FAO, the Non-Governmental Liaison Service (NGLS) of the UN and the International Documentation and Communication Center (IDOC) in Rome. The six-day meeting, titled "Documentation for Change," grew out of issues related to the NWICO debates and brought together documentation centers from all over the world to formulate a response to NWICO and develop strategies for action. Forty-six people representing 37 organizations from Asia, Africa, North and Latin America and Western Europe spent six days discussing the role of documentation in development. This was a very important event in the grand scheme of things as the meeting's main purpose was "to contribute to the study of linkages among documentation, development and the people's participation and to promote cooperation among documentation centers in the various geographical regions in order to support the activities of NGOs and other groups involved in social change" (IDOC, 1982).

Many of the grassroots documentation centers were linked to social movements with an explicit purpose to effect change. Their goals were not to compete with the emerging databases and information networks, but to create an alternative form of communication and dissemination of information that allows grassroots participation. As documentalist Stafford Beer stated in a 1970 report to the House of Representatives, "We can generate data indefinitely; we can exchange data forever; we can store data, retrieve data and file them away. But we have to ask why. The purpose is regulation. And this means translating data into information. Information is what changes us. My purpose is to effect change—to impart information, not data" (Beer, 1970, p. 223). Documentation work, as understood by those who do it, is a dynamic process created to provide specific information at the time it is needed in a changing environment. The documentation centers themselves must be organized and designed to serve the needs of its users—whoever they may be (Viera-Gallo, 1981).

The centers came together in Lisbon to discuss emerging communication technologies and what could be considered "appropriate technologies" in different parts of the world and to examine the priorities and focus of one another. Four themes emerged that were each addressed by working groups: 1) rural development and food systems; 2) communication processes and new technologies; 3) people's rights and development; and 4) communication dynamics. They reviewed who was working to implement rights already established in law and who was working to change or create new laws. They discussed documentation at the service of social and liberation movements around the world and how important it was to the work of each of them to set up a continuous exchange of information and experiences. Participants clarified their roles as documentation centers and worked towards methods of continuous support and cooperation. All the centers at the Lisbon meeting saw themselves as part of a social movement, and there was a great deal of emphasis on direct action at a grassroots level and full participation of the constituents they intended to serve. Of particular interest was their approach to documentation techniques and new technologies. In this regard, they felt a need to put these issues in proper perspective—that rather than being at the center of discussions, it was critical to recognize that techniques and technologies were not an end in themselves, but rather an instrument at the service of their objectives. A good deal of attention was given to the new technologies and an attempt was made to acknowledge the specific needs of different types of documentation centers and the communities they served. Not all centers needed or wanted to be on the cutting edge of what the new technologies offered. In some cases, it was inappropriate technology. Preserving and defining means of retrieving oral traditions on a village level was, for instance, identified as an important component to keep in mind when examining the needs of each centre and their users. While it was generally agreed that it was important to stay on top of the new technologies in order to improve information processing and retrieval where appropriate, it was also recognized that use of these technologies often produced negative social side effects. Select participants agreed to study the use of electronic systems and share results among others in order to integrate the use of technology successfully where it would be beneficial to users. There was much discussion about the imbalance in information flows and the line between the "data rich" and "data poor" countries. It was determined that some of the larger NGOs and centers could use their maneuverability within their own regions and connections to reverse the dominant trends and work towards a "new documentation order." It was hoped that this would lead to a democratization of data and greater access to information in the data rich countries. To this end, they agreed to develop communication networks among themselves to facilitate the exchange of information. This was discussed at length, particularly within the context of the four themes of the working groups. A commitment was made to build and strengthen this network using personal contacts, establishing directories of centers and using the new communication technologies.

By the end of the meeting a recommendation was made to establish a network of groups who were exploring the use of the new information technologies in order to exchange ideas and feasibility studies, share resources and experiences. Given their view that documentation centers see themselves as part of a social movement to increase participation and individual rights, they defined themselves not as databanks, but as effective channels for change. This meeting marked the beginnings of an international initiative to define and coordinate the work of documentation centers, and it would prove to have a profound impact on the continued emergence of documentation centers the world over.

Two years later, in October of 1984, a second international meeting of documentation centers took place outside of Rome that included participation from 35 grassroots community documentation centers from all over the world to discuss the impact and use of computer technology on their work. By 1984 the use of computer technologies in development organizations had grown and there was a need to explore better ways to make use of the technology. The participants determined that information was critical in the development process and the livelihood of the communities they served depended on the ability to access and use information. The participants recognized that in many cases the people most deprived of basic human rights were also those who were denied the power to communicate and receive information. By working together as a network they could tackle problems together by agreeing on compatible electronic mail systems to enhance communication between them and work towards avoiding a duplication of efforts or the creation of mutually exclusive systems. The meeting culminated in the creation of what was called the "Velletri Agreement" which laid the framework for the establishment of a network which they named Interdoc (Sayer, 1987). Interdoc would become an active network of information sharing and cooperation among grassroots NGOs who were committed to structural global change. It was built on the principle that it would be successful only if it were created by and would serve local grassroots activities. The Velletri Agreement proposed that it was not the management of information that was the critical issue; it was the use and provision of the right kind of information to make concrete and sustainable improvements in the lives of people. Following the meeting and the establishment of Interdoc, the first action was to select a suitable electronic mail service. After investigating numerous companies and services, they chose Geonet, a system run out of Germany and used by a number of environmental groups, and a London cooperative called Poptel that had been created to serve labor and social action organizations. By 1987 the majority of Interdoc members were connected to the network and in regular communication with one another.

Almost immediately groups working on various issues, such as labor, human rights, peace initiatives, consumer advocacy and health care began to use the new network to exchange articles, follow the movements of multinational corporations and plan meetings and conferences. It was through this network—getting connected to Geonet or Poptel and gaining access to e-mail— that women's groups began to get involved and participate. Interdoc members were conscious of the exclusive nature of this new technology, recognizing that many organizations still did not have the necessary computer equipment and local infrastructures to fully participate. As a result, they took on the role of identifying what was available electronically either within their own network or on commercial databases, and developed initiatives to make the information available in other formats to organizations working without access to computers and information technology. Further, Interdoc also took on the task of organizing training sessions and seminars and providing assistance to new members with connectivity and instructions on how to use the network and operate within the system. The produced a bimonthly magazine in English and Spanish and prepared guides to computer communication and technical issues. Their goal was to improve the global exchange of ideas among organizations and encourage the development of a global perspective on the role of information in social change and the development process.

As commercial databases from the West became more prevalent and widely used for research purposes, it became clear that unless efforts were made to collect and store information coming out of local and regional communities, policy makers would rely more and more on the flow of information coming from the West. Again the imbalance in the flow of information from the developed to the developing nations was an issue. It became a priority to develop decentralized NGO databases and to provide means of access and sharing among groups. It was reasoned that many NGOs collect a similar type of information and if they could develop means of exchange it would save time and money in scarce resources. Generally, information gathered at the local and regional levels is collected from within the context of social action such as, for instance, reporting human rights violations or missing persons and news of political prisoners to international organizations. Access to these technologies was viewed as a significant instrument for social change by organized groups and NGOs.

Although there continued to be infrastructure and access problems that impeded the flow of information, the wheels were set in motion to develop regional connectivity. There also continued to be some resistance to the spread and use of the new technologies that dealt with issues related to cultural values, technological dependence and a very real fear of losing jobs to computers. However sophisticated the new networks, the lack of appropriate telecommunications infrastructures and problems with maintenance, service, supplies and trained personnel remained substantial obstacles to the success of many developing countries in taking advantage of the new technologies. In some cases, countries were being subjected to massive marketing schemes and the hard-sell tactics of telecommunications transnational corporations and rushing too quickly into the information age without adequate planning. China, for instance, imported $300 million worth of computer components in 1984 for over 120,000 units, and by mid-1985 half of them remained in warehouses and unused due to a lack of skills and programmers (Hurtado, 1987). Unfortunately, training is often an afterthought when new technology is introduced. Moreover, the uses and potential of the technology needs to be clearly and carefully disseminated to the people so that workers view the new technologies as resources that can make their work easier rather than a threat that may replace their job. When this does not occur, the introduction of new technologies are often perceived with suspicion and uncertainty, which can further hinder productive use and successful integration.

Resistance also came from governments who sought to restrict the flow of information in or out of their countries. Where national telecommunications services were state-operated, governments could use their control to prevent the use of technologies that allowed the rapid transfer of reports and documents to thousands of people around the world. By the late 1980s transborder data flow, security, censorship and the characterization of access to information as a human right took its place on the international stage. The primary issue for the grassroots movement was that the powerful new information and communication technologies not remain exclusively in the hands of government and business, but that they be used by and for the people of the world.

Rural Libraries and Information Services

If the people of the world were to make use of the technological and scientific resources that were available and be successful in sustainable development initiatives that improved their daily lives, then efforts had to be made to devise means by which information could reach those who need it—farmers, small businesses, community planners. Thus it was necessary to support the development of micro-information environments at a village level where there could be fuller participation in the whole information gathering and dissemination process. Farmers need information about weather conditions and crops, women need information about reproductive health care and nutrition and community leaders need information about environmental conservation and microenterprise development. With or without telecommunications technologies, rural communities need information services developed to suit their needs. Running parallel to the activities and initiatives regarding the introduction and use of information technologies in the economically developing countries throughout the 1980s was increased attention and discussion regarding rural libraries and community information services. A body of literature emerged in the library and information science field on the inappropriateness of library services in developing countries modeled on those of Europe and North America (Igbinosa,1986; Kempson, 1986; Kotei,1977; Mchombu,1984; Tsebe,1985). Many of the library services that grew out of NATIS, UNESCO's library program initiatives of the late 1960s and 1970s, were proving to have little relevance to the rural communities they were designed to serve. Services that had been set up through foreign assistance and based on traditions of foreign information practices were not effective. African librarian Shiraz Durrani made this point quite clear in a 1980 article on "Libraries and Rural Development":

> "The colonial-established library services which survived in the post-colonial period were (and often are) the opposite of what a national library and information service should be. The intended users of such services were the minority of colonial settlers, administrators and the local elite, leaving out the majority of the population. Services were thus urban and ruling class oriented. Most of the material was in a language foreign to the people of the country (i.e., English)...the emphasis was more on buildings than on services. Foreign advisors came to tell us how to run our libraries, how to import the Library of Congress System, how to build library buildings and services to impress a few rather than inform the many."

In this analysis of rural library services, Durrani posits that as long as community library services are dominated by influences from the outside, they will not be capable of developing services for local people. Further, the adoption of foreign library practices creates a dependency on foreign libraries. For instance, rather than learning how to catalog their own materials, they are taught to search the American National Union Catalog to find entries, which leaves them incapable of cataloging locally published materials and making them available to their users. This approach to library services is no different than the "development" many of these communities had seen which provides roads that serve the transportation needs of plantations owned by multinationals, or urban structures built to house offices of foreign firms. This type of "development," Duranni claims, benefits only foreign interests and the urban and rural elites. If a library service is to be relevant, then the first step is to determine if the current service objectively serves the needs of all the people or not—without the assistance of foreign library "experts" and "consultants." This can be done only by going directly to the people, to their homes, and factories and fields and taking an active role in their lives and struggles. What librarians and information workers should be doing, rather than cataloging foreign books, keeping their structures tidy and quiet and striving to attain Universal Bibliographic Control, is learning how to extract appropriate and relevant information from materials received from around the world, translate it into local languages and dialects and disseminate it in usable forms such as oral presentations, radio broadcasts, handbills, pamphlets, posters, photographs and audio or video tapes. This type of service doesn't require learning sophisticated telecommunications technologies. The technical skills of the librarian or information worker should strive to complement the needs of the communities in which they work.

A University librarian from Botswana, H.Kay Raseroka, echoed a similar theme in a 1986 article published in *IFLA Journal* on "Relevant Library Services in Developing Countries." She reported that library services in developing countries were still too focused on collecting and processing information from abroad rather than on locally produced materials. There remained a lack of commitment to any systematic collection of grey literature and documents that are produced by local governments and NGOs which is often produced in the form of plans, gazettes, documents on civic entitlements and duties, citizen rights, pamphlets, reports, posters and numerous other types of materials that are often photocopied and stapled together rather than neatly bound books with clear author and title data. Problems associated with systematically collecting such materials such as lack of classification schemes, fragility of documents and procurement have made it difficult to build good local collections. Moreover, she submits that an even more serious obstacle is that librarians have been trained to undervalue the importance of such materials. If these materials were valued and viewed as being of primary importance, then the true task of librarians in developing countries would be to collect, process and make provisions for easy access and dissemination of all locally produced materials.

While information sources from developed countries are necessary to some extent to serve a relatively small group of academic and government researchers, they should not be the focus of community library services and be handled instead by a few select institutions. However needed locally produced information is, it remains elusive—yet it is produced to inform and assist in the self-development efforts of the nation. The agencies responsible for collecting and disseminating this critical information, she reports, have failed to provide access to relevant information. And libraries and librarians are in the forefront of this failure.

Libraries in economically developing countries should be the well-organized facilitators of bringing locally generated information to the citizens and policy-makers that need it. This, Raseroka claims, cannot be overstated. Collection development policies need to be overhauled and redirected towards a systematic collection development of locally produced materials, and processing procedures should be reoriented to accommodate such a collection. Given the illiteracy rates in many developing countries, librarians and information workers must aim to actively support extension workers and become more involved in dissemination and outreach efforts. This will require active participation within communities, rather than the passive provision of space and materials. "Participation can only be effective if librarians move out of the protective walls of traditional librarianship and do not wait for the user to register and then base deduction of reader needs on the information provided on registration forms. Conducting reader surveys will not suffice. Librarians must have a clear community profile from which accurate information needs can be measured" (Raseroka, 1986, p. 290).

Given the critical analyses that were emerging in the literature on the subject of rural and communities' library services, in 1987 the IFLA Section on Public Libraries developed a program to address the issue of the provision of appropriate library services to rural communities. A working group met at the 1987 IFLA conference in England and planned a four-stage program that included: a literature review to establish current practices and provide guidelines; a research project to evaluate the nature and extent of the need for community information services; the establishment and monitoring of a small number of experimental community services that would include testing a new manual on developing rural community resource centers in developing countries; and finally, dissemination of results. Financial support from UNESCO provided the necessary funds to hire consultant Elaine Kempson, who had considerable experience in both developing community information services and in working in developing countries.

Kempson made use of another guide in the field written by Shirley Giggey, *Rural Community Resource Centres: A Guide for Developing Countries* (Giggey, 1988) in preparing her report. The final report drew from the literature of communication, community development and librarianship and was designed to provide a blueprint for those interested in developing relevant community information services. The information was presented in three sections, each with an overview of the literature, followed by clear and specific practical guidelines. The overarching philosophy was based on a participatory approach whereby local communities must be closely involved and play a significant role in the development of the centers. The three sections included analyzing community needs, which included guidelines on how to profile a community employing various research techniques to analyze community needs; establishing appropriate services, which focused on the community development approach and how to set up a two-way information service and employ active information workers; and monitoring and evaluating performance, which provided specific means for conducting such activities. The report was commissioned because it was clear that traditional approaches to developing library services had not been successful. It is important to note that both UNESCO and IFLA, the premier international library association, recognized the failure of traditional approaches to the provision of library services and supported such an effort. Although there continued to be major efforts on the international front to attain the goal of Universal Bibliographic Control, by the beginning of the 1990s it was no longer a primary focus of international library initiatives.

Amidst the organizing being done on an international scale in the field of documentation, as evidenced by Interdoc and the initiatives that grew out of the Lisbon conference, as well as the increased awareness of information as a critical component in both the development process and in social change movements, information and documentation centers emerged in every region of the world throughout the 1980s. This was the climate that fertilized their growth and fostered the development of information services around the world over the next decade. While the development of international communications and information policies continued to remain elusive and problematic throughout the 1990s with little progress made in coordinating efforts on an international scale, individual information services and centres, driven by a grassroots movement, continue to emerge and find their way into the information age.

CONCLUDING REMARKS

The information revolution was clearly underway throughout the 1970s and 1980s on an international scale. As the presentation of international initiatives regarding information technology and the delivery of services above details, it was an active period that involved players from the highest levels of national governments to the smallest rural libraries and grassroots organizations. The integration of information and communication technologies into the social, cultural and political arenas of the world stage demanded attention from policy makers, governmental leaders, women's organizations, grassroots activists and information workers the world over. It became clear that however remote the area, access to timely and relevant information was critical for sustained development and progress. This climate of intense attention and discussion on information and the delivery of services further motivated an already robust and politically engaged international community of documentalists, librarians and grassroots activists.

In her critical analysis of library services, African librarian Raseroka suggested that when libraries and librarians try to force Western methods and priorities, such as Universal Bibliographic Control or creating national library programs that adhere to Library of Congress standards, onto the rest of the world, they have been at the forefront of the failure to provide responsible and relevant collection and dissemination of information. That, in effect, what has been seen in the ideological foundations of international librarianship, is a 'modernization' approach to information services reminiscent of the old development paradigm. This chapter suggests that a number of the documentation center initiatives operating within and serving the international grassroots community were operating outside of the standard paradigm by developing their own unique systems for classification and retrieval and embracing the tools of technology as needed for their own agendas. The implications of this historical overview and discussion suggests that documentation and resource centers that serve an active community of users, like the rural libraries, should be supported by the international library community and encouraged to create their own unique method of providing appropriate information services. Given the growth of the World Wide Web and the trend toward increased Web use internationally, the technological foundations are in place for continued innovation in the delivery of relevant information services throughout the world.

REFERENCES

Beer, S. (1970). An Argument of Change: Managing Modern Complexity, in *The Management of Information and Knowledge*, presentation to the Committee on Science and Astronautics of the U.S. House of Representatives, January 27, 1970, p. 223.

Danzin, A. (1987). Unesco Promotes Informatics, *Media Development*, 4, 40-41.

Dizard, W. (1982). *The Coming Information Age: An Overview of Technology, Economics and Politics*. Longman: New York.

Durrani, S. (1980). Libraries and Rural Development. *University of Nairobi Library Magazine*, 4, 109-128.

Giggey, S. (1988). Rural Community Resource Centres: A Guide for Developing Countries. NY: Macmillian.

Gille, L. (1986). Growth and Telecommunications in *ITU, Information Telecommunications and Development*, Geneva: ITU, 25-62.

Gonzalez-Manet, E. (1988). *The Hidden War of Information*. New Jersey: Ablex Publishing.

Greenberg, A. (1985). Impasse?: The U.S. Stake in Third World Telecommunications Development. *Journal of Communications*, 35(2), 42-49.

Hills, J. (1993). The Telecommunications' Rich and Poor. *Third World Quarterly*, 12(2), 71-90.

Hurtado, E.M. (1987). Computer Hodgepodge Mystifies Buyers. *Media Development*, 4, 15-17.

Hudson, H. (1984). *When Telephones Reach the Village: The Role of Telecommunications in Rural Development*, Norwood NJ: Ablex.

Igbinosa, I.O. (1986). The Public Library Services in Nigeria: A Need for Information and Referral (I&R) Service. *Public Library Quarterly*, 7(1-2), 63-71.

International Documentation and Communication Centre (IDOC) et al. (1982). *International Meeting of Documentation Centres on Third*

World Issues: Documentation for Change, Final Report, W/P8031.

International Telecommunications Union. (1984). *The Missing Link, Report of the Independent Commission for World Wide Telecommunications Development*, Geneva: ITU.

Jacque, S. (1985). Bibliographic Control of Inter-Governmental Publications: User Survey—An Introductory Expose. Draft paper presented *at IFLA General Conference, Chicago*.

Kempson, E. (1986). Information for Self-reliance and Self-determination: The Role of Community Information Services. *IFLA Journal*, 12(3), 182-191.

Kotei, S.I. (1977). Some Variavbles of Comparison Between Developed and Developing Library Systems. *International Library Review*, 9(3), 253.

Mchombu, K.J. (1984). Development of Library and Documentation Services in Tanzania. *Information, Processing, and Management*, 20(4), 559-569.

Menon, L. (1990). *Some comments on communications & networking.* Unpublished paper, IWTC Women's Organization Collection — Documentation & Communication Strategies Files. [Author's Collection]

Neelameghan, A. and Tocatlian, J. (1985). International Cooperation in Information Systems and Services. *Journal of the American Society for Information Science*, 36(3), 153-163.

Raseroka, H.K. (1986). Relevant Library Services in Developing Countries. *IFLA Journal*, 12(4), 288-291.

Roach, C. (1987).The Position of the Reagan Administration on the NWICO. *Media Development*, 34(4), 32-37.

Saunders, J., Warford, J.J. and Wellenius, B. (1983*). Telecommunications and Economic Development*. Baltimore, MD: John Hopkins University Press.

Sayer, J. (1987). Interdoc: A Worldwide Computer Initiative. *Media Development*, 4, 19-20.

Spero, J.E. (1982). Information: The Policy Void. *Foreign Policy*, 48 (Fall), 139-156.

Tocatlian, J. and Abid, A. (1986). The Development of Library and Information Services in Developing Countries: Unesco/PGI's Role and Activities. *IFLA Journal*, 12(4), 280-285.

Tsebe, J.K. (1985). Information Needs of the Black South African

Society: A Conceptual Analysis. *Wits Journal of Librarianship and Information Science, 3.*

Viera-Gallo, J. A. (1981). *Documentation for Change: The Democratization of Data and the New World Information and Communication Order,* Report for the International Documentation and Communication Centre (IDOC) for the Meeting of Documentation Centres on Third World Issues Meeting, Lisbon, Portugal.

Williams, R. V. (1988). The Role of Intergovernmental Organizations in International Information Transfer and Policy. *Special Libraries,* 9(1), 1-8.

Williams, R.V. (1989). Using the Information Resources of the Global Village: The Information Systems of International Inter-Governmental Organizations. *Special Libraries,* 80(11), 1-8.

Chapter XVII

Libraries on the Information Highway: Issues and Lessons Learned

John Carlo Bertot
University at Albany, SUNY, USA

This book presented readers with numerous views, perspectives, and issues regarding the past, present and future of libraries, librarianship and the information profession in the networked environment. By reviewing the various chapters in this book, readers rapidly conclude that the information environment, particularly the digital information environment, requires a reconceptualization of the information creation, dissemination and consumption processes. Information professionals, and those relying on information professionals, are at an exciting and challenging point in their careers — the transition to the networked information resources and services environment. Meeting this challenge necessitates the resolution to numerous issues, several of which this chapter presents below.

SERVICES ENABLER

Clearly, the networked environment provides the opportunity to develop new services and provide access to those services on a global scale. For example, libraries can digitize special, rare or unique collections and make those collections available to the world – not just those individuals who walk into the building housing such collections – via the World Wide Web (Web). Other services include the creation of:

- Regional, statewide or national network-based interlibrary loan systems;

- Virtual tours of collections and facilities;
- Online reference services;
- Online electronic books; and
- Online full-text databases that provide uses with instant access to journal-based literature.

There are other services too numerous to mention here, but the above exemplify the expansion of services that the networked environment provides libraries.

These services, however, come at a price. As identified in ensuing sections, the ability to provide such services *well* has dramatic implications for library technology, physical and human infrastructure.

ACCESS EQUITY

The networked environment, on the one hand, has the capability to augment access to information resources through the vast reach of the Internet. On the other hand, digital access requires the availability of a technology infrastructure for users, libraries and nations. The chapters in this book point to the uneven development and use of networked resources by libraries and nations. Indeed, one could classify the libraries and nations as:

- Bleeding edge, for those on the experimental forefront of technology and application development and use;
- Leading edge, for those that are technologically sophisticated, but approach application and technology development incrementally;
- Grounded edge, for those that rely strictly upon true and tried technologies and applications; and
- Trailing edge, for those that use older technologies and applications.

The technology and application variance of libraries and nations is large and leads to substantial issues when libraries and nations attempt to participate in the global networked environment.

Due to a nation or library's technology sophistication, users can be severely limited or substantially advantaged in their ability to gain access to the vast array of digital information resources. A report published by the United States Department of Commerce, National

Technical and Information Agency detailing such disparity in the United States is available at <http://www.ntia.doc.gov/>. Thus, there is a need to be aware of ensuring digital access equity as increasing amounts of information are created, disseminated and preserved in only digital formats.

Libraries need to develop a vision for creating equity in access. Such a vision might be:

> *Electronic resources of all types and forms would be publicly available for those who cannot connect from the home or workplace. Librarians and educators would serve as electronic intermediaries, navigators, and instructors — being actively involved in assisting people in the best use of the network.*

Libraries, as nonpartisan and often publicly supported institutions, with strong community ties, are well suited to serve in this role. A major role for libraries, however, and the larger education community in the networked society, is to reduce socioeconomic gaps in being able to tap the full potential of the network and provide equal opportunity to networked services and resources that are available to the public.

COLLECTIONS ENHANCEMENT AND DEVELOPMENT

By accessing the Internet in general, and the Web in particular, libraries gain access to digital resources to which they would otherwise not have access. Thus, connecting to the Internet provides libraries, and their patrons, with the ability to:

- Access a seemingly limitless range of resources such as indexes, online collections and databases;
- Organize and create special digital collections such as historical documents and pictorial collections; and
- Redefine their collections development processes and actual holdings.

Together, these capabilities enable libraries to, relatively efficiently, expand their collections without substantial collections development efforts. As discussed later in this chapter, however, providing wide-scale access to Internet-based resources does have other library resource allocation implications.

RESOURCE SHARING

The networked environment offers near limitless opportunities for collaboration in the development of digital resources. It is no longer the case that every library must develop similar core collections. Indeed, by creating various cooperative agreements, libraries can agree to develop various collections (e.g., art, business, historical, rare books) on their own and provide access to those collections to consortia members. Such an approach essentially creates new virtual libraries that enhance access to collections without each member library developing similar collections and resources.

This approach is redefining a "library" in the networked environment, and is akin to the virtual organization promoted in the business literature, and a dramatic departure from existing collaborative, local, regional or statewide resource sharing models for interlibrary loan and networking initiatives to date (e.g., Maryland's Sailor project <http://www.sailor.lib.md.us/>, Ohio's OhioLINK <http://www.ohiolink.edu/>, Victoria, Australia's VICNET <http://www.vicnet.com.au/>). While in its infancy, the potential for collaborative, virtual libraries is substantial.

NEW INFORMATION SUPPLY AND DEMAND MODEL

At the same time that new collaborative models are emerging, the network environment is now fraught with unequal levels of digital effort and development. For example, the Internet Public Library (<http://www.ipl.org/>) provides global access to digital collections and various value-added services with IPL resources. Other examples of such services exist, such as the AskEric service (<http://www.askeric.org/>) which provides educational information services for curriculum content and development to teachers.

This creates a system whereby there are net lenders — those who supply the resources for others to consume — and net borrowers — those who consume the resources provided by others — in the digital environment. This situation can be problematic, as local resources cannot necessarily support global needs.

There is a need for collaborative models, as discussed in the *Resource Sharing* section of this chapter, in which more libraries contribute to the provision of digital resources and services. Perhaps it is time to consider cost-sharing approaches in which libraries that consume the resources of provider libraries make financial or other contributions to the provider library to assist in the development, maintenance and expansion of the digital collections.

ORGANIZATIONAL STRUCTURE IMPACT

New forms of libraries and library services also translate into new library organizational structures. Increasingly, libraries are redesigning their function-based, hierarchical structures (e.g., reference, cataloging) to:

- Team-based/group activities that focus on a particular project (e.g., designing a Web site, digitizing a collection);
- Cross-functional approaches to service development and provision that reflect the reach of network-based services;
- Fluid, matrix-like structures that can quickly form to work on a project and then disband upon project completion; and
- Community-based assistance, where appropriate and necessary, to ensure input from key stakeholder groups.

As such, library organizations are in a process of transition that reflect the rapidly changing networked environment.

REINVENTION

A key theme espoused throughout the chapters in this book is the need for libraries to reassess their roles, services and functions in light of the digital information age. While libraries are and have traditionally been early adopters of automation, the networked environment requires and offers the potential of more than the automation of existing applications and services. Libraries are, therefore, in the process of:

- Assessing their roles as information centers within their communities;
- Redefining the notion of an information intermediary in the networked environment;
- Reviewing the process of electronic resource and information

organization;
- Developing new means of access to and retrieval of digital information; and
- Scanning the technology environment constantly to determine the feasibility of new network-based services.

In essence, libraries are undergoing a reinvention process that is likely to transform and redefine the role and capabilities of libraries in the networked environment. What a "library" will look like in this new environment remains unclear, but the possibilities are staggering.

NEW LIBRARY ROLES

New roles for libraries in the evolving networked environment are still under development. But clearly, the *electronic* library in the global networked environment has the potential to be a community resource center. These roles might be to:

- Introduce new information technologies to the community;
- Demonstrate applications and uses of networking for education, lifelong learning, economic development, telemedicine and a range of other applications;
- Be a local access point to a range of government information resources and services;
- Create, maintain and organize electronic community information;
- Serve as information portals/gateways to digital collections;
- Provide public access to a wide array of interactive digital services such as video conferencing;
- Equalize access such that all members of the local community can realize the benefits from "being connected" to the global networked environment;
- Provide training to community residents on how to use the Internet and interact successfully with a range of service being provided via the Net; and
- Promote collaboration community groups and/or organizations to use the Internet.

As libraries redefine their roles in the networked environment, libraries are in the process of becoming more proactive in defining their community function as an "information place." With increased competition within the information environment for information sources, libraries are looking to make the transition from a *place* people should visit to meet their information needs to that of an information center/hub that actively provides services to the community beyond the walls of the library facility(ies). By creating Web sites, mounting unique collections for global consumption, offering training sessions and organizing segments of cyberspace, libraries are extending their reach and creating a strong community presence.

Whatever the role(s) of libraries in the global networked environment, it is clear that libraries cannot be all things to all people. Thus, as libraries reinvent themselves, engage in new activities and decide on their missions and objectives, they will need to do so in a way that is targeted and makes efficient and effective uses of increasingly limited resources.

MANY NETWORKS, ONE WORLD

As libraries continue to connect to the Internet and increase their use of network-based resources, there is developing a genuine digital information community. The advent of the Internet in libraries, particularly in the last few years, has fostered a global information community the likes of which were not possible, or conceived, in the print environment. The notion of a global library village is no longer an exaggeration, but is developing rapidly — fostering new collaborative models along the way.

The prospect of integrated systems of virtual libraries is exciting for information professionals, libraries and patrons alike. As more partnerships form, there is the potential for:

- More coordinated digital information collections;
- Better organized and designed digital collections;
- Simplified retrieval of digital information; and
- Economies of scale for collections development and maintenance.

With substantial planning and coordination, this can lead to a shrinking of the digital information space through knowledge management and retrieval practices — even though digital information resources will only increase over time.

EVOLVING NEW ACCESS, DISSEMINATION AND RETRIEVAL MODELS

The networked environment clearly facilitates access to and use of a vast amount of information to which libraries would otherwise not have access. This information, however, is multimedia in nature and, thus, complicates the ability of information professionals and individuals to actually access, navigate, retrieve and use the information. The multimedia nature of digital information also challenges information producers to provide access to their information in an efficient and user-friendly manner.

Such key issues as indexing and abstracting images, video clips and other multimedia items; creating meta-data pointers to digital information; standards for *indexing, abstracting* and meta-data tags; and types of information retrieval engines, require substantial collaboration and resolution in the library, information professional and research communities.

ARCHIVING AND HISTORICAL PRESERVATION OF DIGITAL COLLECTIONS

An underlying theme to the book is one of preservation. How does the library community ensure that there is an historical digital record that is preserved for future generations of information professionals, researchers and users? The pace of change in the networked environment is so dramatic, that libraries (and other information-based organizations) are constantly concerned with *today* and *tomorrow*, not necessarily *yesterday*.

As a consequence, substantial portions of the digital record do not exist and will not likely exist unless large efforts are made to ensure adequate preservation of electronic networked collections. Each time a Web site is updated (and this occurs frequently), there is the potential loss of digital content. There is a need to develop a systematic, standardized method of digital preservation.

Related to the issue of preservation is that of archiving. An issue in developing and maintaining digital collections is that of archive availability. Truly digital libraries that provide all services in a virtual, networked environment, will need access to historical data that is not currently available in a digital format. An example is that of online databases — very few provide records (e.g., full-text articles) prior to 1990. Newspaper and magazine, journal or other forms of important information will not be available to digital library users — unless there is a coordinated undertaking to create those digital archives. As such, libraries will need to bridge both the print and networked worlds for the foreseeable future.

ACCURACY AND AUTHORITY OF INTERNET-BASED RESOURCES

As more electronic network information and services become available, there is a strong need to ensure the accuracy and authority of that information or those services. An extreme example would be that of medical information. There are a number of Web sites today that purport to inform users of medical ailments, conditions, cures, etc. However, there is little to no substantiation of the claims reported on those sites. Moreover, there is no guarantee that the information provided on those sites is actually provided by the individuals/ organizations claiming to do so.

Also, without acceptable authentication methodologies (e.g., digital signatures), there is no guarantee that the individual who accesses digital services and/or information is actually the person claiming to do so.

The same situation exists for other types of digital information and/or services. Information professionals, libraries and other information providers will need to develop accepted and standardized authentication and authority mechanisms.

THE NEW LIBRARY PROFESSIONAL

The new library professional is one who is a(n):
- *Information expert*, someone who has a fundamental understanding of information retrieval, knowledge management, information organization and information design and presentation;
- *Communicator*, someone who has the ability to foster and exist within numerous partnerships and collaborative ventures;
- *Manager*, someone who can manage varied and numerous projects, can envision the possibilities of the networked environment, see the "big picture" of a project, and can delegate responsibility to

others (and thereby relinquish direct control);

- *Technologist*, someone who is technology savvy, aware of new and emerging technologies, and can consider the service potential of emerging technologies;
- *Strategist/Planner*, someone who thinks strategically, strives towards a vision, and can develop and implement strategic planning initiatives; and
- *Evaluator*, someone who is willing to benchmark and evaluate various initiatives — both qualitatively and quantitatively — so as to ensure objective/project attainment.

While some of these qualities existed in the library profession, many are new and evolving. The library professional of the future is, increasingly, an information expert with a myriad of technology and management capabilities.

CONTINUAL INVESTMENTS IN PERSONNEL AND EQUIPMENT

Creating the new library professional will require vast retraining of existing library staff and substantial changes to many traditional library education programs. Moreover, the nature of the networked environment is one of rapid change that will necessitate *continual* upgrades and changes to the skills and competencies of librarians. The types of continual education courses and library school training curricula will need to reflect the core competencies mentioned in the previous *The New Library Professional* section. A library degree is a necessary, but no longer sufficient, qualification for a library career.

Libraries must also face the fact that genuine participation in the networked environment — in which a library is an information provider as well as consumer — will require substantial and frequent upgrades to a library's information technology infrastructure. One-shot fixes for information technology in libraries are not a viable strategy. Libraries wishing to provide high quality networked services to their communities will need to develop a rational strategy and budget for the purchase, installation, maintenance and replacement of information technology. Many libraries have yet to recognize adequately the on-going nature of information technology costs and to develop funding strategies to support those costs.

PERFORMANCE MEASURES AND STATISTICS FOR NETWORKED SERVICES

Many libraries are only beginning to consider how to keep statistics related to Internet use and services. Libraries that do provide a range of Web services or other network-based services note that circulation, in-house reference transactions and other traditional statistics of use are stagnant or decreasing. In most cases, electronic services counts are also rising. Thus, in order to have an accurate picture of library use, libraries will need to maintain statistics related to use of Internet services and resources. This is particularly important as libraries increase their use and provision of network-based services and resources.

To a large degree issues related to how best to identify, collect and analyze data to produce statistics of electronic or networked information services are only now being discussed and defined (see <http://www.albany.edu/~imlsstat/> and <http://equinox.dcu.ie/> for large-scale efforts in this area). For example, it is possible to utilize the logs on Web servers to track the number of times users "hit" specific types of networked services. It is also possible to use log server analysis to track patterns and IP addresses that provide a general sense of whom is using what type of services. Libraries that provide electronic reference services will also need to keep statistics of such use or conduct regular surveys to be able to track and document such uses.

In order to develop, collect and compare electronic network statistics within and across libraries, however, will require the resolution of a number of issues such as the:

- Identification of data elements;
- Definition of those elements;
- Methodologies through which to collect the data based on those elements; and
- Ability to compare library-provided data across a broad cross-section of libraries.

Until these issues are resolved, each library will continue to develop its own network statistics and measures.

IMPORTANCE OF THE POLICY ENVIRONMENT

The global networked environment in general, and in the development of digital information collections and services in particular, resides within a complex and often conflicting environment. Substantive policy issues include:

- *Copyright.* Digital copyright issues in a global context in which there are collaborative, value-added services and resources being created remain unresolved. While international digital copyright efforts continue, there are outstanding issues of ownership and what, exactly, is possible to copyright in the digital environment.
- *Transborder Dataflow.* The seamlessness of the networked environment is one of the Internet's major strengths. The transfer of electronic resources across borders, however, raises various data ownership and sovereignty issues.
- *Privacy.* The provision of digital services implies that there will be larger amounts of individual data available across the networked environment. As of yet, there are no global privacy policies — just national or international (e.g., the European Union) agreements that are in conflict with one another.
- *Universal Service.* The United States has embarked on a controversial legislated approach to promoting access to an advanced telecommunications infrastructure throughout the nation (see the American Library Association's Web site at <http://www.ala.org/oitp/univserv.html> for details on the initiative). Other nations have vastly different, if any, approaches to such infrastructure development. There are no global universal service policies in place to promote effective access to the advanced telecommunications infrastructures at reasonable costs required by the electronic networked environment (see Bertot, McClure, and Owens, 1999 for an overview discussion of universal service in a global context).

These issues, minimally, require resolution. But they also point to the importance of understanding the information policy environment by information professionals, librarians, researchers and users. The policy environment can have a tremendous impact on the ability of libraries to provide, access, and use digital information resources and services.

CONCLUDING COMMENTS

This is a time of great excitement and challenge for librarians, information professionals and researchers. The possibilities of the networked environment are endless. The opportunities, however, require the resolution of a number of issues — several of which are identified in this chapter. As the millennium approaches, it is important for librarians and information professionals to focus on the capabilities enabled by the networked environment, rather than the complications brought forth by the complexity of digital information resources and services. Such a focus will evolve the future of libraries — a future that is defined collaboratively and through experimentation.

REFERENCES

Bertot, J.C., McClure, C.R., and Owens, K.A. (1999, forthcoming). Universal service in a global networked environment: Selected issues and possible approaches. *Government Information Quarterly, 16*(4).

About the Authors

Patricia Diamond Fletcher is associate professor at the Department of Information Systems, University of Maryland Baltimore County. She is also Research Associate at the Maryland Institute for Policy Analysis and Research at the University of Maryland Graduate School. She has had a lifelong interest in libraries and takes special interest in their continued prominence in today's information world. Fletcher also studies U.S. government and information policy. She has published numerous books and articles on information technology management in state, county, local and federal government. She is an associate editor of the *Journal for Global Information Management*. She sits on many conference steering committees, the most recent being the CS2000 Committee of the Association for Computers and the Social Sciences and the Technology Working Group for the American Society for Public Administration's Y2K Conference.

***

Monica Adya is an Assistant Professor in the Department of Information Systems at the University of Maryland-Baltimore County. Her research interests are in artificial intelligence, decision support and planning & forecasting. She has published papers on *Information Systems Research* and *Journal of Forecasting* and has given talks at prestigious international conferences. She is on the editorial board for the *International Journal of Forecasting*.

Helen Baigent has worked in public and academic libraries within the United Kingdom. She recently completed a Masters in Librarianship at the University of Sheffield, where she developed a strong interest in plans to transform the UK public library movement. She now works for the EARL Consortium, liaising with more than 150 partners and associated organizations, supporting EARL's avocation to embrace the opportunities to derive from Information and Communication Technologies. Helen would like to play an active role in the development and delivery of new age services within libraries, encourage cross-sectoral collaboration and ensure that the current visibility of public libraries remains at the heart of the political agenda.

John Carlo Bertot is an Associate Professor in the School of Information Science and Policy, University at Albany, State University of New York. He teaches courses in library technology planning and technology applications, telecommunications policy and information policy. He is the co-author, with Charles R. McClure, of *Moving toward More Effective Public Library Access: The 1998 National Survey of Public Library Outlet Internet Connectivity* (U.S. National Commission on Libraries and Information Science, 1999). With Charles R. McClure, Bertot has published several studies of U.S. and Victoria, Australia public library Internet connectivity as well as articles on the use of electronic networked resources by public and state libraries. Bertot and McClure are co-principal investigators for an U.S. Institute of Museum and Library Services National Leadership grant to develop national network statistics and performance measures for public libraries (see <http://www.albany.edu/~imlsstat/> for project-related findings).

José Luis Borbinha is the Director of the Services for Innovation and Development of the National Library of Portugal. He is also an invited researcher at INESC (Institute for Systems and Computers Engineering), and a lecturer of IST (Technical Superior Institute of the Lisbon Technical University). He has a background in Electrical Engineering and Computer Science, and has been deeply involve in national and international projects and activities related with "Digital Libraries." He is a member of the Digital Libraries Working Group of RUBI (Network of Portuguese University Libraries), of the working group DC-International (Dublin Core in Multiple Languages), and of the Digital Libraries Working Group of ERCIM (European Research Consortium for Informatics and Mathematics), which has been promoting the DELOS initiative, the ERCIM/NSF Metadata Task Force and the European Conference on Research and Advanced Technology for Digital Libraries.

Jasmine Cameron is currently the manager of the Serials Section at the National Library of Australia and is the PANDORA Project Manager. She has worked in a variety of positions within the National Library. Most of her experience has been in the area of collection development, description and maintenance. As manager of the PANDORA Project she has been responsible for contributing to policy development relating to the Library's role in collection and management of Australian electronic publications. Jasmine has also been involved in the development of the information paper, which describes the essential functionality of the Library's Digital Services Project (DSP). The DSP is seeking to establish a platform for the provision of integrated access to digital objects over the next five years.

Fernanda Campos is the Deputy Director of the National Library of Portugal since 1992. She has a background in History (Faculty of Humanities, University of Lisbon) and a post-graduate degree in Librarianship, by the Ministry of Education, Direction General of Cultural Affairs, Lisbon. At the National Library, where she started as a librarian in 1978, she was responsible for the Cataloguing Department from 1980 to 1987, head of the Bibliographic Processing Services from 1987 to 1992 and manager of the National Union Catalogue (PORBASE) ever since. Apart from teaching at the Librarianship Course and lecturing in several universities, she is also President of the National Standards Office for Documentation and Information, member of the National Focal Point to the EEC Libraries Programme, member of the Standing Committee of the IFLA Section on National Libraries, member of the Board of Directors of the ECPA (European Commission on Preservation and Access), member of the Forum CoBRA (Concerted Action on Computerised Bibliographic Records Access) and observer of the G7 Task Force in "Bibliotheca Universalis."

Fernando Cardoso has a background in computer engineering. He was an IT manager of BAD (the Portuguese Library Association), and works now at the Division of Informatics of the National Library of Portugal, where he has responsibilities in systems and network administration. He also teaches in the Librarianship Course promoted by BAD, and has been involved in the project NEDLIB (Networked European Deposit Library), as well as in other related national projects in the same field.

Jennifer Croud is the Financial Services and Projects Coordinator at the University of Queensland Library. As well as responsibility for financial services, her role includes coordinating library projects related to benchmarking and best practice; coordinating quality assurance projects, including the development of performance measures; and maintaining a database to facilitate the collection, analysis and reporting of library performance data. Her previous position was as a liaison librarian in the Dorothy Hill Physical Sciences and Engineering Library.

Malabika Das received her B.A. from the University of British Colombia, and her M.L.I.S. from the University of Western Ontario. A few months before coming to Queens, Malabika worked for the National Library of Canada (NLC) as an intern, researching and creating Web documents for NLC's public and intranet Web sites, as well as for IFLA (at that time hosted under NLC's domain name.) She also published two information papers on Community Networks during that time. Malabika has now been with the Queens Borough Public Library for two years and holds the position of Web Administrator/Webmaster. In addition to duties for maintaining the Library's intranet and public Web sites, she also does reference work on weekends. Malabika's pastimes include being a science fiction buff and a computer enthusiast. She presently resides in Queens, New York.

David Dixon is a research assistant at the School of Information and Media. His research interests center around the social and cultural aspects of new information and communication technology. He has a particular interest in the scholarly use of Internet subject gateways.

Lynn M. Fountain is Head of Technology Services at Russell Public Library, Middletown, Connecticut. Previously, she was Director of Technical Services at Heafey Law Library, Santa Clara University located in Santa Clara, California. During her years at SCU, she was heavily involved in technology planning and development within the Law Library and Law School. She holds a B.A. in Anthropology from University of Rochester, and received her M.L.S. from San Jose State University in 1992.

Susan Haigh holds a Master of Library and Information Science from the University of Western Ontario, and has worked in various reference, collection management and standards-related positions since she began her career at the National Library of Canada in 1987. Her current position of library network specialist involves monitoring, evaluating and promoting appropriate use of digital library standards and technologies. She conducted a survey of Canadian libraries' digitization activities that led to the founding of the Canadian Initiative on Digital Libraries in 1997. Her contributions to the National Library's series *Network Notes* [http://www.nlc-bnc.ca/pubs/netnotes/netnotes.htm] have covered such topics as OCR as a digitization technology, technical notes on National Library digitization projects, next-generation networks and measuring Web site usage through log analysis. She was co-author of a paper delivered to the 1998 Kanazawa Institute of Technology International Roundtable for Information and Library Science, Japan, in July 1998.

R. David Lankes, Ph.D., is director of the ERIC Clearinghouse on Information & Technology at Syracuse University. He is co-founder of AskERIC, the award-winning project that provides high-quality information to educators via the Internet, and is founder of the Virtual Reference desk project. He is also a faculty member for Syracuse University's

School of Information Studies and he speaks and consults nationally on Internet issues in education and business. His work focuses on Internet information services and the increasing demands of users in the dynamic Internet environment.

Ook Lee is a Professor of Information Systems in the Department of Business Administration at Hansung University in Seoul, Korea. Previously, he worked as a Project Director at Information Resources, Inc., in Chicago, Illinois, and as a Senior Information Research Scientist at Korea Research Information Center in Seoul, Korea. His main research interests include expert systems, neural networks, software engineering, digital libraries, electronic commerce, critical social theory and the role of IT in Asian economic crisis. He holds a B.S. in Computer Science and Statistics from Seoul National University in Seoul, Korea, and an M.S. in Computer Science from Northwestern University in Evanston, Illinois. He also earned an M.S. and Ph.D. in Management Information Systems from Claremont Graduate University in Claremont, California. He has published in journals such as *Journal of Software Maintenance, International Journal of Electronic Markets,* and *Annals of Cases on Information Technology Applications and Management in Organizations.*

Jay Liebowitz is the Robert W. Deutsch Distinguished Professor of Information Systems at the University of Maryland-Baltimore County. He is the Editor-in-Chief of *Expert Systems With Applications: An International Journal* and *Failure & Lessons Learned In Information Technology Management: An International Journal.* He is a Fulbright Scholar for Summer 1999, and was selected as the sole recipient of the IEEE-USA 1999 FCC Executive Fellowship.

Chris Moore graduated from the University of Loughborough in 1998 with an MSc in Information and Library Studies. His interest in the Web and networking issues led him to take up the post of EARL Information Officer. Chris is largely responsible for maintaining the EARL Web site and mailing lists. As the public library Network rolls-out in the United Kingdom during the next few years, Chris would like to take an active role in delivering electronic services to users alongside traditional ones in a public library setting.

Robert Newton is a Senior Lecturer at the Robert Gordon University School of Information and Media, Aberdeen, Scotland. His main teaching areas are information retrieval and information technology. Current research interests centre around the use and development and classification of Internet subject gateways. Another major research area is in the use of multimedia and Internet resources in delivery of higher education, and this is research which is currently being conducted by building a large multimedia resource for teaching bibliographic classification and assessing the manner in which it is used by students.

Lori Olson received a B.A. in Spanish Education and an M.S. in Education from the University of Wyoming. For the past six years she has been the archivist at the American Heritage Center, a manuscript repository at the University of Wyoming. She has worked with educators in the public schools and with university professors in developing archival teaching units for use in the classroom. She has given papers related to the use of primary sources in schools at the National Conference for Teachers of English and at the National Conference for the American Association of School Librarians.

Margaret E. Phillips has worked in libraries since 1976 and joined the staff of the National Library of Australia in 1987. In 1994 she became the manager of the Acquisitions Section where she increasingly dealt with electronic materials. In 1996, as manager of the newly created Electronic Unit, she began to devote full-time attention to both online and physical format electronic publications. As a member of the PANDORA Project team and the Digital Services Project working group, she has been closely involved with the establishment of policy and procedures for ensuring long-term access to Australian Internet publications and with the development of an archive-management facility.

Andrew Schlein is a native of New York City. He received his A.B. from Middlebury College, M.A. and Ph.D. from Fordham University and M.B.A. from New York University. Although his formal training has been in psychology and finance, he has created a successful career in technology management. Dr. Schlein has been the Director of Information Technology and Systems at Queens Borough Public Library since 1995. Prior to coming to the Queens Library, he was Executive Director of Management Information Systems at the New York City Department of Correction. His professional interests include executive information systems and the integration of mixed platform systems. He is a Certified Beer Judge and enjoys travel, photography, and cooking. Dr. Schlein lives in Manhattan.

Janine Schmidt is University Librarian at the University of Queensland. The University of Queensland Library is the largest library in the state of Queensland and one of the largest in Australia. Janine is responsible for the overall management of 13 branch libraries and their centralized support services. A graduate of the University, she returned to manage the library services in 1993 at a time when changes in information technology, teaching and learning and customer service were altering dramatically the nature and delivery of information services in a tertiary education environment. Prior to this position, she held senior positions at the State Library of New South Wales, the University of New South Wales Library and the Commonwealth Scientific Industrial Research Organisation (CSIRO) Central Library. Janine has also been a member of the teaching staff in the School of Library and Information Studies at the University of Technology, Sydney.

Diljit Singh (Ph.D., Florida State University, Tallahassee) is Coordinator of the Library and Information Science program at the Faculty of Computer Science and Information Technology, University of Malaya, Kuala Lumpur, where he teaches courses on Management, School Libraries, Internet and Digital Libraries. He previously taught in two secondary schools, worked with the Pahang State Education Department and the Aminuddin Baki Institute, Ministry of Education. Currently serving as Director for Asia in the International Association of School Librarianship (IASL), Dr. Singh also serves on the Editorial Boards of *School Libraries Worldwide* and the *Malaysian Journal of Library and Information Science.*

Maria V. Sunio emigrated with her family from the Philippines to the United States, where they settled in Texas and became naturalized U.S. citizens. She received a B.A. in English from Rice University in Houston, Texas, and an M.L.I.S. from the University of Texas in Austin, Texas. Before attending graduate school, she was the managing editor of the refereed science and engineering journal *CORROSION.* Her career as a professional librarian began in 1993 as a reference/serials librarian in the Central Library of the Queens Borough Public Library. There she automated the Central Library's serials check-in and maintenance procedures, converting over 2,000 titles from manual Kardex to electronic format. In her current position as the Queens Library's DRA/Library Applications Coordinator, she pursues her professional interests in information access, library automation and reference services. For amusement, she enjoys the pace and the variety of life in Manhattan.

Deborah Turnbull is the Information Skills Coordinator for the University of Queensland Library. She has held a number of positions in the Library, particularly in the areas of information retrieval and information technology. Deborah has worked extensively in the areas of networking and systems implementation and was jointly responsible for setting up the University of Queensland Library's first Internet Training Courses for staff and students and the Library's first SilverPlatter ERL Servers. Her previous position was Senior Librarian in charge of Online Reference Services and Databases.

Sirje Virkus is Associate Professor, Department Head of the Department of Information Studies and Chair of Information Science at Tallinn Pedagogical University, Estonia. Dr. Virkus serves on numerous scholarly and professional committees and is editor of the electronic journal *INFOFOORUM* (ISSN 1406-9849). Dr. Virkus has published numerous articles and books, particularly related to distance education and open learning. At present, Dr. Virkus is the principal investigator for a grant to study distance learning and teaching in the networked environment for Estonia universities.

Xuemao (Shimo) Wang received his B.A. from Wuhan University, China, an M.L.S from Kutztown University of Pennsylvania, and an M.L.I.S specializing in information systems from the University of South Carolina. Mr. Wang joined the Queens Library as a Systems Analyst in 1994. Since 1995 he served as the WorldLinQ™ project leader and team manager, and he was Supervisor of Web Services until April 1999. Currently, Mr. Wang works for the Metropolitan New York Library Council as Director of Information Technology. Before coming to the U.S., he was an academic librarian in China, where he published articles in several professional journals in the field of library and information science. His professional interests include Web-based distributed systems and Web applications development. He was an invited speaker on multilingual database access at the 1997 American Society of Information Science (ASIS) annual conference. He received the Distinguished Services Award from Queens Library in 1997. He enjoys sports, travel and music. Mr. Wang lives in Syosset, New York.

Paula Wolfe is an Associate Librarian at the University of Arizona Science and Engineering Library. She has a B.A. in Sociology, B.A. in Biology and an M.S. in Marine Science and M.L.S. in Library and Information Science. Her first career was as a marine biologist specializing in marine mammal research. She became a librarian in 1994. Her chapter was developed from a presentation given at the Internet Librarian Conference in 1998 and in collaboration with Lori Olson of the University of Wyoming. Her research interests include information system design for primary resource distribution.

Lucinda R. Zoe is an Assistant Professor and Instructional Services Librarian at Baruch College, City University of New York where she teaches courses in Online Information Retrieval, Information Technology and Internet Access. She holds a Doctorate in Library and Information Service from Columbia University. Research interests include international information systems and services, end-user searching in a multi-cultural environment and the impact of native language on searching in full-text databases and information systems. She previously served as the Information Officer for the International Women's Tribune Center and the United Nations Development Fund for Women (UNIFEM).

Index